c. 4

D1524296

Raw Edges

PHYLLIS BARBER

Raw Edges

A Memoir

UNIVERSITY OF NEVADA PRESS *Reno & Las Vegas*

University of Nevada Press, Reno, Nevada 89557 USA
Copyright © 2009 by Phyllis Barber
All rights reserved
Manufactured in the United States of America
Design by Kathleen Szawiola

LIBRARY OF CONGRESS CATALOGING-IN-PUBLICATION DATA

Barber, Phyllis, 1943-
Raw edges : a memoir / Phyllis Barber.
    p.   cm.
ISBN 978-0-87417-807-4 (hbk. : alk. paper)
    1. Barber, Phyllis, 1943- —Marriage.
    2. Barber, Phyllis, 1943- —Divorce.
3. Divorced women—United States—Biography.
                I. Title.
        CT275.B3675A3 2009
        306.89'3092—dc22
    [B]   2009033725

The paper used in this book is a recycled stock made from 30 percent post-
consumer waste materials, certified by FSC, and meets the requirements
of American National Standard for Information Science—Permanence of
Paper for Printed Library Materials, ANSI/NISO Z39.48-1992 (R2002).
Binding materials were selected for strength and durability.

Portions of this manuscript have appeared in *Dialogue: A Journal of
Mormon Thought* 36, no. 2 (Summer 2003); *Irreantum: A Review of Mormon
Literature and Film* 7, no. 2 (2005); and *upstreet*, no. 5 (2009).

University of Nevada Press Paperback Edition, 2012
21 20 19 18 17 16 15 14 13 12
        5 4 3 2 1

ISBN-13: 978-0-87417-881-4 (pbk. : alk. paper)

Some names and places in this book have been changed to respect
the privacy of certain individuals. With regard to immediate
family members, whose names I couldn't change, I wish to
acknowledge they've been represented by brushstrokes only,
and those from my paintbrush rather than their own.

:: *To David and Geoffrey* ::

::

Cars are all right on occasion,
but they are not moments
of grace as bicycles are.

COLMAN McCARTHY

:: CONTENTS ::

Prologue 1

Blues in the Attic 5

The Two-Wheeled Getaway Car 18

For Time and All Eternity 35

Bidden or Not 54

Homeward to Zion 70

The Unpredictable Body 83

In the Attic with St. Francis 96

The Precarious Edge of Life 102

The Meaning of Goodness 115

The Iron Maiden Cracks 134

The Doves Descending 147

In the Beginning 158

Two Thousand Kisses Deep 168

Filling the Void 184

The Human Head Is a Cube 196

Wedges 215

The Nesting Doll 238

Parting the Waters 251

Afterword 265

Acknowledgments 267

Raw Edges

:: Prologue ::

The folded-tissue ballerinas hang suspended from the mobile tacked to the ceiling above my desk. The dancers twirl, on impulse it seems, but they're being put into action by currents of heat from the fireplace. It's cold outside. They seem to be urging me to action. *Put a word on the computer screen. Two words. Three. You need to finish your book.* They pirouette on strings.

Maybe, I think as I look at the white screen in front of me, most everybody talks of writing the story of their life someday. I suspect this has to do with a secret hope that someone, somewhere, will read their words, be moved, enchanted, or, better yet, assisted on the journey through the minefields of life.

Maybe, I think as the green-tissue dancer twirls counter to the direction she's been turning, writing a book is about leaving a trace. Maybe it's about gathering disparate pieces into a puzzle. Or maybe it's about wanting to be understood. St. Francis of Assisi once said: "Seek not to be understood but to understand." I confess I'd like to be understood, if by no one else but myself.

I have a story to tell about seven lean years of being lost, when life as I'd known it disappeared. 1995 to 2002—those years when I signed two divorce decrees and failed in yet another relationship with a younger man to whom I gave much. There's also the story of riding my bicycle across the Midwest plains (as well as across many other highways and byways) during those years when all I could do was think and try to make sense of my Mormon upbringing, the birth of a son with hemophilia, the end of my thirty-three-year marriage, and the way I had made some odd, impulsive choices that seemed so alien to what I'd been.

The endless thinking on the bicycle was never experienced in well-ordered chronology or form. Rather, it spun out of the vast reservoir of fragments in my head while my legs relentlessly spun the pedals.

It is these bits and pieces I want to finish committing to paper as I sit in front of my computer beneath paper dancers doing pliés and arabesques. I want to capture the essence of who I've been, who I've wanted to be, who I seem to be after all of the trying to be something other than who I am. While this search may be a self-absorbed, even selfish task, I think it's also a dipping into the river of humanity where everyone bathes. It's an examination of what it is to be human, to be sensitive, to be idealistic, to have aspirations, to want to love and be loved, and to make mistakes while engaged in these endeavors. It's also an admission of depression, anger, and self-loathing at times when I'd have given anything to walk on water. It's about what it's like to want to be above the human fray and to realize I'm not.

I am a pianist and sometimes wish I could speak through the keys on my piano in the infinite language of music—less susceptible to being misunderstood or misinterpreted than other forms of communication. But, in truth, I need words to tell my story. I need them to sort out which version of my story is the "real" one. I need words to explore if there's somebody who exists outside this particular narrative I've repeated so many times— the story that can still constrict the narrow passageway of my throat. I need words to find rest, to write "The End" to this part of my life's journey.

If I could, I'd call this book a *novoir,* though there's no such section in the bookstores. That's not because this writing has been fabricated or imagined, but because it's impossible to capture the whole of any person or life on paper. We're all alive—inhaling and exhaling and sloughing off old skin. For every story told, a thousand others are left out, and the past brought to the present is always something new.

My story may be different from yours, with different twists and turns, different conclusions, some self-pity, some self-puffery. But, I still suspect this story is also your story in some way. With that in mind, I dedicate this to those who want to write books about their lives and to the people who've danced, sung, cried, laughed, and forgotten how to laugh. I write for those who've carried guilt, who've sometimes chosen well, who've sometimes erred, who've jumped at both the right and wrong time, who've conquered themselves in one minute and lost to an erratic impulse in the next.

We're all headed for the same shore. We're born. We're human. We laugh, cry, pay taxes, make love, wage war, and then try to figure it all out. And we die. God bless us, every one, every morning, evening, and night, I think, as the dancers on delicate strings turn toward me, waiting.

:: Blues in the Attic ::

Even though the summer of 2002 proved a major turning point of my life, there was that nadir, subzero, bottom-out point: a day, a night, and the next morning. I'll never forget it. I wish I would have remembered about the refiner's fire making gold from dross. Or about the heroine journeying through the labyrinth. But I didn't. In the middle of that fire, I was no philosopher.

Early on the morning of that day, the attic at the top of the three-story house was broiling. Not enough insulation. My second divorce would be final today, kaput, the fastest divorce in the West. On the sixth day of the sixth month, without an invitation being sent, the blues moved in again. Big time this round. They busted in like an unwelcome relative, ready to eat everything in the refrigerator, sleep in my bed next to me, and never stop talking, 24/7.

Perspiring from every pore, it seemed, I stood over the stove in my Emily Dickinson cubicle (my bedroom, living room, writing desk, and kitchen all-in-one). Waiting for the oatmeal to cook, I drank orange juice with calcium. *I would eat good food. I would be healthy. I would take care of myself. I would make a new life, even if I was fifty-nine years old. I would escape this anchor-dragging-on-the-bottom sadness.*

I could be happy, I reminded myself. *Honest I could.* I bent over the stove, as I was too tall for the slanted ceiling. I added raisins to oatmeal and took care not to bump my head. *I could even be light-hearted. I've always been known as a "happy girl." Upbeat. A ready smile for everyone. So why couldn't I saunter down the middle of the road and be cool? Chill? Forget the bad times? And why did I have to be the spoiler at that Memorial Day party last week?*

My mind had been locked into instant replay mode all morning long: push the button; repeat the fumble; listen to the referees; feel lousy all over again.

My ex-husband David said he'd only been trying to cheer me up. He'd invited the family over for a Memorial Day barbecue at the house on Steele Street where he kept his offices and where he'd offered me a place to stay until I got back on my feet. He'd only wanted to bring some good times to the backyard and to me—a refugee from difficult relationships. But then he invited his girlfriend and her family, too. *Sorry, David. That was over the top. You should have known better. You should have warned me.*

I'd lost any composure left in my bag of tools-to-deal-with-the-world when I looked out the third-story window and saw them all converging in the yard, with that woman standing by David as if she belonged next to him, straightening his baseball cap, and patting his cheek. That woman laughing with my son, Brad, as if they'd known each other forever. She'd moved in with David a month earlier, about the same time I'd moved out of Bill's house in Park City. She was taking over at the same time Bill was fading out—the man who was in the process of becoming my second ex-husband after twenty-one months of marriage.

Twenty-one. A gambling game. Had I won or lost was a question I couldn't ask yet as I was so devastated by yet another upheaval in what was beginning to feel like a soap-opera life. I didn't like the script. Or the scriptwriter. There were too many clichés about broken hearts and swooning and dying on the vine.

I'd always thought I could count on David. He hadn't been involved in a long-lasting relationship with anyone since our divorce in 1997. And he'd always been there for me when I called or needed a friend. But now, while those facts were rearranging themselves before my eyes, a territorial dispute raged in my head: *This is mine, this is mine, no it isn't. You said good-*

bye, farewell, it's time for me to go, five years ago, Phyllis. You've been down this road and back. You can't expect anything different.

I hadn't been able to go downstairs to join the fun or eat any of Famous Dave's barbecue. I'd felt like a fifth wheel that didn't belong anywhere, like I wasn't part of my own family anymore even though my three handsome to-die-for sons—Chris, Jeremy, and Brad—and their girlfriends were downstairs spreading mustard on hamburger buns. All I could do was stay in the attic, sit on the futon spread over a bulky wooden frame, and sob. *Memorial Day. The irony of memories.* Didn't David understand that divorce was a wickedly bad spot in the road, a second divorce adding insult to injury? Didn't he understand I was as fragile as stretched chewing gum?

I'd thought a second marriage was a good move, but Bill said I hadn't gotten over my first one and that I should never have agreed to marry him. Whatever the reasons, there were now the bones of two marriages plus the carcass of a five-year in-between obsession with Spinner that proved to be a totally dead-end relationship.

I never thought I'd be divorced. Period. Ever. Or live with someone without being married. After all, I had principles. I was a good person. I tried hard.

On top of that, just a year ago, both of my parents died within three weeks of each other. Mother waited for Dad to go, then insisted she was ready for hospice. She stopped eating. She refused water. She was finished, she said. I couldn't say I blamed her, even though I was now a waif in the world who needed a maternal shoulder to cry on.

Memorial Day: the commemoration of my mother and father; my oldest son, Geoffrey, who would have been thirty-five years of age; my love life.

That day, I'd been a hostage to my regrets. I barely heard Jeremy—my middle son, the concert violinist turned heavy-metal guitarist, his long thick hair fastened into a ponytail—who'd come upstairs to persuade me to join the party. "Come on, Mom. We want you with us. The food's great, and it's not a party without you." When I'd seen him, I'd been reminded of his innate sweetness. I fell apart. He hugged me, tight. He waited for me to stop crying, until I couldn't.

That was ten days ago. Now, I could smell something burning.

I rescued the oatmeal pan with a red-and-white-checkered hot pad I'd purchased from an Amish woman when I lived in Minnesota with Spinner. Homemade. Homespun. All the good things of home and stability in that Amish woman's lean frame and in that hot pad. I turned off the stove and carried the pan to the window to see if, perchance, Sue was outside waiting. I couldn't hear the front doorbell in the attic. No sign of her yet. It was a good thing she'd be arriving any minute to walk with me in City Park. Otherwise, left to my own devices, I might burn down the house. She was one of my only friends in town, someone I'd met at a local art gallery. I'd called her about an hour ago, knowing my own distress signals when I saw them. "I need to take a walk, big-time," I said. "Soon if you can make it."

"Are you okay?" was the first thing she said when I answered the door. "You've got a lot of sadness in your eyes." She gave me a tender hug.

Before I knew what was happening, tears ambushed my eyes and throat and I couldn't answer back. We walked to the corner without saying anything. We crossed Seventeenth Avenue, then walked in more silence as we approached Ferril Lake. Out in the middle, a few pedal boats churned water. "Are you going to be all right?" She wasn't going to let me off the hook.

"I'm in the seven lean years," I finally told her, trying to make a joke that didn't sound like one and didn't divert any tears. "You know. Joseph in Egypt? Fat and lean years? This has been going on for more than seven years, and today my divorce from Bill will be final. When is this nightmare ever going to be over?"

"I know things haven't been easy with your first divorce from David," she responded, "then the whole Spinner saga and now this breakup with Bill."

Sue had been divorced three times herself. She was perfect company.

"Maybe," she said, "you should see someone. Get some help."

"Thanks," I told her. I almost said, *Why can't I just cry?*

Voicing my deepest fear, I asked, "Do you think people can be fixed? Can people change or do they recycle the same stuff over and over?" I fought to hold the water dammed up inside.

She paused, losing eye contact for a few seconds as a gaggle of Canada geese flew overhead. The geese, always magnificent in flight, had almost overtaken the park by leaving their green plugs of droppings everywhere and under every shoe. I felt like commenting on all the goose leavings, even saying the word "sh——" out loud. We watched a group of five birds descending to the water, their wings arching back and high as they skidded into a smooth landing.

"Have you read *Getting the Love You Want*, by Harville Hendrix?" Sue said. She pulled her water bottle out of its carrier, tipped it back, and squirted a long stream into her mouth. "Maybe you should take a look at what he has to say."

Even though I'd asked her to come over, hoping for some kind of comfort, I felt the need to defend my vulnerability. Instead, I let the gates down further. The tears kept coming. I heard myself saying more than I needed to say. "It's about breakups and watching someone I love loving somebody else. It's like being a fraud who can only fool people for a little while. It's like not realizing any of the dreams I've dreamed for myself."

I squeezed the skin of my elbow for a wake-up call. *Don't do this to yourself. Don't do this to Sue again. She's already been through your obsession with Spinner. Stop. Now. Stop stripping in front of everybody. Remember the rule about not taking your burden basket to your neighbor.*

"Forgive me," I said, lifting my chin, taking a deep breath and smiling my stiff-upper-lip smile. "I'm not myself lately. Don't mind me, please." *I could turn the tide. I would turn the tide.* "Are you and Jeff leaving for Wisconsin soon?"

Sue tipped her head. A question she didn't ask crossed her face. "July 2," she said after a pause, squeezing her water bottle back in its carrier. "We're meeting the kids at Baileys Harbor for the Fourth."

"Good," I said, feeling the threat of the ruptured dam in me diminishing. "I'm glad you'll get to be with your girls and their families." I smiled sweetly, unable to say anything else for fear of more leaks. We walked around the lake twice without many words, though I did ask a few questions about her weaving, beautiful basketmaker that she was.

"I guess we better get back," she said when we stopped to decide on a third circling or not. "Jeff's waiting for me."

We left the path, crossed Seventeenth again, and walked back on the old sidewalk on Steele Street ruptured by tree roots. Down the block I could see David's house where he no longer lived. No one waited for me there. No family. Dust on the plants in the atrium. *Where did I belong anyway?* Another solitary tear slipped out of the corner of my eye and slid warm over my already warm cheek.

"Thanks, Sue. You've been a good friend through all these ups and downs."

"No problem," she said. She crossed the strip of grass next to the curb while clicking the unlock button on her car key. "Give me a call if you need anything." She dropped into the driver's seat and drove away.

I groped for the key in my shorts pocket. I felt like a balloon at the Macy's Thanksgiving Day Parade, a gigantic, bloated Inner Child leering down on my entire neighborhood, scaring everyone, taking up too much sky. I jiggled the key, pushed open the antique door, and closed it behind me. All I could think about was me, me, me. My pain, my pain, my pain. *But wait a minute,* I suddenly said to myself as I unlaced my walking shoes. *Why are you mocking your pain? Who's taking care of who around here anyway?*

But still, when I climbed the three flights of stairs, untied my shoes, and then scrubbed the burnt oatmeal from the bottom of the pan, I knew I was falling into a deep hole again, the thousands-of-feet-deep one. The place that was dark, dank, and oozy. I'd never seen any handholds, footholds, or ladders out of that hole. No exits. I felt armless, legless. My bones were cottage cheese when I fell into that negative space. I wanted to escape before I fell into that place again, maybe even cash in my chips, Nevada girl that I was.

I sat in my swivel chair. I put my elbows on the desktop that was also my dining table, then drew a circle with my finger on the wood surface. I could hear some birds singing, Denver birds, whatever they were. I wanted to strangle their cheerful noise. What did they know about the blues shouting, "Here I am?" What did they know about a 350-pound dog-day butt sitting on the cushion of my soul, pressing and squeezing the air out?

I touched my hand. My long-fingered, piano-playing hand. It was still there. I touched my other hand. It was there too, even though the skin seemed thinner than it used to be. My Old Faithful body was reminding me it was still there and that I could pick me and my trouble up, out of that deep hole. But I was tired. Those deep holes weren't easy. They bruised my insides. Still, my eyes kept staring at the hands that could soothe me— the hands that had played exquisite music on the piano, that had calmed babies and lovers, that had written many stories. I still had hands.

You also have the blues, Phyllis. Face it. You've got blues as big as the ocean, sweetheart. There are blues pirates swashbuckling through your body demanding the booty. Nothing less than your soul. What's with these pirates, anyway, and this falling into holes? *Do they want your life? Do they want to take it or give it? What do they want? What do you want?*

When that long afternoon of June 6 turned into night, I read the newspaper to delay the prospects of going to bed. The last thing I did, before turning out the lights to do battle with sleep again, was to read an ad in the newspaper: "Volunteers needed for a study concerning depression. . . . Results are confidential." I crumpled the paper, irritated at the thought of someone waiting by the telephone to hear from a depressed person. I threw it in the wastebasket.

But in the middle of the night, a particular bad-dream dragon appeared from the shadows to chase me. I should have groped my way down the three flights of stairs and followed the back walkway out to the garage where I kept my bicycle. I could have unlocked the door, squeezed past the mound of my worldly possessions, backed my beloved Cannondale out into the yard, and opened the gate into the alley, hoping it wouldn't squeak too loudly. I could have ridden past Denver dumpsters and recycling bins and outdistanced the dragon. I could have escaped. Maybe. After all, my bicycle had always been my two-wheeled getaway car. Instead, I woke with the swirling sense of "Where am I?" and stayed put.

I hated waking to empty space, nobody next to me, my mind racing, twisting and turning. A tear traced the curve of my cheek bone. Then another.

Not this "poor me" business again. Not this business of the sunrise never coming, my sorrow being deeper than five oceans, this "I don't matter" stuff. I should shout at the night and get angry. But being pissed off was a foreign country to me. Feeling sad was my home turf. Getting depressed. That's what I did.

I looked up at the ceiling, my near-sighted eyes without eyeglasses imagining vague shadows of a dragon switching its tail and swiveling with wicked joy. I turned onto my stomach and squeezed my arms tight against my body, totally uncomfortable.

I'm not a tidy package, am I now?

As if they were riding into that dragon's lair on a misbegotten conveyor belt, I saw my parents' faces slowly moving through my mind. Around and back again. Herman. Thora. Worried faces. Laughing faces. Loving faces. Suspicious faces turning into rubbery faces stretched out of proportion. Anger in the tip of my father's pointed finger that seemed to grow longer as he passed by. There was that old glint off the wetness of his crooked bottom teeth shaped like a fan.

Herman and Thora were alive, in frightening ways, that night.

Mother at her Singer sewing machine making thick-seamed clothes that I didn't like to wear. *Yes, I was ashamed to wear the dresses you made for me, Mother. Forgive me. You worked hard.* Mother sitting at a quilt frame with her church friends, poking her needle in and out of layers of fabric and cotton batting with tiny-stitch finesse, me as a young girl beneath the quilt fiddling with the C-clamps that held the frames together, wondering what would happen if I unscrewed one. Thumbtacks. Thimbles. Thumb cots. Thread. Needles poking in. Poking through. I could see those menacing needles that seemed to stretch toward me as I looked up at the bottom of the quilt stretched tightly across the frames.

Mother, singing excerpts from *Aida* in her rich voice while I accompanied her on the piano (she'd once sung in *Aida*'s opera chorus in Idaho Falls), longing to come into the voice she knew she possessed if only she had more confidence. As she sang to me on the night of the dragon, her mouth opened wider and wider until she seemed like a lioness roaring. And then her mane turned to flames as I imagined her reaching into that old gas oven again with a wooden kitchen match, just as she'd done when I was a child, reaching into that dark space where there was too much gas trapped inside. There was an instant combustion, the flames rising until she grabbed a kitchen towel to smother them. My mother on fire. My mother roaring. And then I gasped at the short, fuzzy, singed hair on her arms, the bright redness of her flesh, until she opened the kitchen door and walked outside to the wide blue sky and sand of the desert to find the calm after the storm. When she could breathe normally again, she patrolled her dusty, desert homestead: two fruit trees, a sandy yard, a succulent named Hens and Chicks, and a patch of sweet peas growing up the coarse string she'd strung at the edge of the house. My determined-to-have-noble-children mother who gave me life and wanted it to be shaped in strict accordance with the rules of the Church of Jesus Christ of Latter-day Saints, the Mormons. And then I heard her roaring again, a lioness bound and determined to have her child "Choose the Right."

Then my father appeared in the dim light in his no-rim eyeglasses, Bishop Herman Evans Nelson, standing in front of the congregation at a sacrament meeting in the Boulder City, Nevada, LDS ward house—the small, yellow, wooden church brought in on a flatbed from Las Vegas—conducting the service, making announcements, offering tidbits of wisdom, bearing his testimony of modern-day prophets and the gospel of Jesus Christ. My father chopping the head from a rattlesnake in our yard at the back of our red-shuttered, white-washed house, taking us on the Hoover Dam tour where we wandered through the old diversion tunnels that seeped water and smelled like barbarian caves, driving us before dawn to the top of a hill in a stiff wind to watch an atomic bomb explode with smoke rising like a phantom mushroom against a paintboard sky—fire in the middle. Yellow into red into gray into black dusty smoke and billows of sand and more sand. My father, a charming, bright, lovable man who loved to dance polkas in our living room; a man who could explode into fire-flashes of temper, but who would have given anyone his last dime; a man with contradictory faces.

Then, because the dragon whispered more fire in my ear, I remembered the time when he'd stood at a pulpit in front of a large church meeting in

Las Vegas. He'd been called to serve on the stake high council. The chapel and the overflow vestibule were brimful of Latter-day Saints. I sat on the piano bench, accompanying a ladies' quartet that warbled a song called "I Have a Testimony." I played faster than I should have because I was proud of my father and wanted him to have time for his twenty-minute speech. He wanted to do a good job to demonstrate his worthiness for his new calling since our family had just moved into the Las Vegas Stake boundaries. He'd worked and worried over his talk all week long. But the first speaker, perhaps enchanted by the sound of his own voice, had left only six minutes for my father.

After the quartet and I returned to our seats, my father stood at the pulpit in his shark gray suit, new from J. C. Penney for the occasion. A few people in the back row were standing up and walking out—escapees from a too-long meeting. Something about this caused my father to snap. Some gap opened up in time and space. My father slipped through the cracks. In a moment of pure rawness, he said, "Well, you can leave if you want to. Don't worry about me up here who's been left with six minutes to give a talk I've prepared for all week. Go ahead. Leave."

Even now as I perspired beneath the rumpled sheets, I remembered sitting in the middle of what felt like the largest silence ever known to humankind. Ripples of astonishment. People caught off guard. Me, a tall, skinny, pimply, awkward pubescent with braces and glasses who needed all the help she could get, sitting on those green-cushioned seats with her mouth and eyes wide open.

This was my father. The one who was my anchor, my guide, my stay. This was the man who was supposed to make my life safe, who was supposed to be strong, powerful, on top of things. He was telling people exactly what he felt and not keeping this embarrassing information to himself. His chest was wide open—his wiring exposed, the broken glass inside glittering. I wanted to run away and hide. My father wasn't doing what fathers were supposed to do. He wasn't living up to my image of the patriarchy. How could I possibly survive this?

He delivered his speech at high speed, hurrying to keep inside the allotted time, as if his words were bare branches and twigs from a windstorm blocking streets and needing to be cleaned up posthaste. I faced the audience, which, to my fearful self, looked like a pack of wolves. I swelled with unreleased air, ready to burst with shame. My father had done what I'd always suspected he was capable of doing, the Big No: *Do not make a fool of yourself. Be contained. Stay inside the line. Don't lay out your insides for everyone to see.*

But he wasn't always like that, I reminded myself as I turned onto my right side for the umpteenth time, closing my eyes to any glimpse of the dragon. Why was I concentrating on this picture of the man I usually called Daddy when there were other, better things to remember?

I couldn't help myself. I was leaky too. The skin on my body was too thin, not thick enough to resist the pressure from inside me to let everything out and let it be seen. My father and I were glass-window people who couldn't keep anything hidden, not then, not now. Why did we need to tell the world that we were these paper people required to speak the whole truth and nothing but the truth about our insubstantiality?

I turned and tangled with the sheets. The sheets seemed to be on fire now.

I was permeable, gas, a penetrable membrane that could be subsumed by more substantive substances. I was immaterial in a material world, my physical body made of layers of papier-mâché—*wastepaper pulped with wheat paste and slathered over my vaporous self. Me and my father. Me and my lineage.*

I undid the twisted sheets and kicked them to the side. What was I doing awake at this ungodly hour? The walls too close. The room too stuffy. There was no one's cold or ear infection to worry about. No unruly sons to bust for breaking curfew, so why couldn't I go back to sleep? Why was I asking stupid questions like, "Do I matter or not?"

Go to sleep, I tried to calm myself. *Seal off the brain. Take your foot off the accelerator. Accept the good things—the friends, the small gifts nature gives you every day. Stop moaning. Stop wallowing. Stop being tempted by self-pity. Accept life's terms, even if they are not what you would have chosen for yourself. Stop waiting for the chariots with all the answers to roll through golden gates to the sound of long trumpets blaring. Listen to the whispers:*

"Be patient. Stand your ground. Don't run away. And do something about this insanity when you wake up in the morning."

If I had only known that Spirit was cleansing me of my greatest fears, scouring my weaknesses with a Brillo pad, purifying the impurities. When I finally opened my eyes, it was morning in the attic. I had slept after all.

Thrusting my feet out from under the warm comforter, I put them flat on the floor, turned on the bedside light, and dug the newspaper out of the wastebasket. After searching through sections A and B, I found the notice on page C-7. There it was. "Volunteers needed for a study concerning depression. Call 303-BI-POLAR. Results are confidential." I picked up the paper and looked at the clock to decide whether or not I should call. It was still too early.

After a bowl of Kashi and a soy protein drink mixed with bananas and strawberries in a blender, I decided, Why not? What can it hurt? I sat in a comfortable chair, put both hands on the arms, took ten deep breaths, then dialed the number. When a voice answered, I wasn't sure how to say what I needed to say. I took the most direct approach. "I'm interested in your study."

"Do you suffer from depression?"

"Yes, I do, especially right now."

"Do you generally suffer from depression?"

"Off and on."

"Would you call it a chronic condition or situational?"

"Right now, it feels chronic."

"All right. We'll transfer you to one of our screeners and let her determine if you're qualified."

She put me on hold. I waited about one minute with the word "qualified" ringing in my ears. Was this some kind of competition? A woman with a crisp voice came onto the line.

"Hello. Do you mind if I ask a few questions?"

"No." I sat back in the chair and briefly assessed my body. Tension between my shoulders. Pressure at the base of my neck, the same pressure I'd felt in the past before the onset of a migraine.

"Are you depressed all the time?"

"No." Why was she asking the same questions. I'd already answered them.

"Are you more likely to experience depression in tough situations?"

"Yes."

"Have you had some upsetting situations lately?"

"Yes. Two divorces. A bad relationship. Moving away from my family. Yes, these things have been upsetting."

"How extreme are your moods?"

"Mostly extreme on the sad end of the spectrum. Melancholia, maybe. My grandmother was diagnosed with melancholia, but that was a long time ago. In the thirties, I think."

After a few more questions, the woman with the slightly impatient crisp voice said, "I don't think you're the right candidate for this study. We need people who have more marked reactions in general. People who suffer chronically. You seem to have situational depression. We're looking for more extreme cases. Sorry. Thank you for your interest."

I heard the click of the phone and a new dial tone.

For a minute, I stared at the receiver in my hand and wanted her to come back on the line so I could tell her she'd hung up too quickly. I needed some help. I couldn't get out of deep water with a snap of her fingers. *Weren't there people at this number who could help me?*

I held the phone against my chest, feeling rejected. It was like standing in line and not being chosen for the field hockey team. Or like standing on the sidelines at a high school sock hop and not being asked to dance.

Why wasn't I good enough to be on somebody's team?

:: The Two-Wheeled Getaway Car ::

A bicycle had been my getaway car ever since I was a five-year-old in southern Nevada. I'll never forget the morning my father said to come outside, he had a surprise for me. His eyes and the glass on his rimless eyeglasses sparkled as if they were party lights. He opened the front door, took my hand, and walked with me down the front concrete stairs painted red.

There it was, leaning against the palm tree my father had planted a few weeks before. The low bar in the middle meant it was a girl's bike to make straddling easy. It was painted black in a futile but tender attempt to disguise its age and infirmities. Its two battered fenders capped two large balloon tires. Whatever its condition, however, it shimmered with sheer beauty in my eyes.

"Oh, Daddy!" I couldn't stop dancing around his legs.

Out in the street, he lifted me onto the pedals.

"Let go," I told him. "I can do this."

"Are you sure?" he asked. He still held on to make sure I wouldn't fall.

Freeze-frame: the bulky black bicycle, my handsome, lovable father holding the handlebars, me ready to ride away on the wide pavement of Fifth Street in front of our red-shuttered house—that moment like a commemorative stamp in the story of my life. He steadied me on the first few rounds of pedaling, then I burst out of his arms. I took off—thin, shy me, pumping pedals down Fifth Street in Boulder City, off into the sunshine, into the possibility of turning wheels forever until I reached infinity—something that fascinated me even then. (I doodled the figure eight symbol on the margins of our phone book and on the back of Mother's recipe cards.)

While my feet turned those wheels on my new/old black and dented bicycle, I sensed I could ride down the street into something much more

 exciting than ordinary life. The pedals would spin around and around until they became something more than pedals with a chain. My bike was Pegasus headed for the summit of Olympus, though Daddy had read to me about Zeus getting angry at Bellerophon for trying to ride Pegasus to such great heights. I knew better than to go too far. Still, on my new bike I wasn't human anymore. I wanted to be bigger than everything around me. I wanted to be everywhere I wasn't. Something in me had thought I could arrive at infinity.

It was only natural, therefore, that forty-eight years later in 1996, I succumbed to the temptation of Pegasus again and riding off to salvation.

A student of mine in the Vermont College low-residency creative writing program where I taught, a young woman I'll call C. J., had bet another student five dollars that I'd say yes if she asked me to ride bicycles with her from Colorado to Vermont. "We'd start early enough," she assured me, "to arrive in time for the summer residency." When I answered, "Why not?" she seemed genuinely surprised. Her friend who proposed the wager was surprised. Even I was surprised, knowing I was so casually turning a deaf ear to a more prudent internal voice: *What in heaven's name have you just said you'd do? Are you an idiot?*

All internal and external warnings ignored, C. J. and I decided to ride our bikes from Fort Collins, Colorado, to Montpelier, Vermont, starting on the last day of April in 1996. Why not believe we could ride across the United States of America to feel alive again and find clarity in the smoke-gets-in-your-eyes of love?

I was definitely disenchanted with infinity at this point. Thirty years of marriage had been burned to a crisp despite David's and my nonblinking vow of "forever." We'd promised in the Mormon temple that our marriage would last for time and all eternity, not just "til death do we part." But we'd removed our wedding bands inscribed, "United We Stand," and left our broken promises flat in the road where a semi could finish them off. On top of that, separation from both David and my boys—me leaving them in the mountains of Colorado while I moved to Denver to be close but yet far enough away from David—sucked. Sucked! Over those years, I'd developed into a highly tuned Mother motor. I didn't know what to do with myself when there was no one to look after. I was used to having boys to organize, hug, and even harass when necessary, despite the fact that my three sons had minds of their own and were irreverent, rambunctious, raucous, and bursting with testosterone. And then there was the hopeless romance with a much younger man whom I'll call Spinner.

I knew C. J. only through her innovative writing when she'd been my student for a semester and from a few encounters at a couple of two-week residencies. Some of my colleagues had asked me why I'd make such a difficult trip with someone I didn't know well, with someone who seemed so temperamentally different from me. But I'd lost my ability to judge anything. All I saw was a chance to get out of the quicksand of abandoned love. Both C. J. and I needed to save ourselves. We were the perfect match to do something indescribably insane—a 2,300-mile transcontinental bike ride from the Front Range of the Continental Divide to Montpelier. We agreed to ride fifty-five miles a day with no time scheduled for days off. We carried forty pounds of gear in our panniers and had no support vehicles. We'd camp out every night. And all of this during tornado season in the Midwest.

I still thought of myself as being bigger than life. (Hadn't Albert Einstein thought of the theory of relativity on his bike?) It didn't matter that

I hadn't ridden seriously for years (if ever), that I had only three months to train and didn't have a clue how best to do it, that no one would describe me as a jock, and that I hated hills. It didn't matter that C. J. was sixteen years younger, much more fit, more

savvy, a more likely candidate to complete such a trip. It only mattered that both of us wanted to get out of Dodge and fast. Escape our lives. Escape everything, even with a half-baked plan.

I waited to tell my mother about the trip. When I finally decided to break the news and drop a few details in her lap during a short telephone conversation, she said she was in the middle of something. Could she call me right back? Which she did in less than two minutes.

"Is this some kind of midlife or predivorce crisis?" The hiatal hernia somewhere in her larynx infused every sentence with an involuntary vibrato. Her voice wavered as if it were an indistinct radio signal from Mesa, Arizona. I could picture her sitting in her La-Z-Boy chair, her dowager's shoulders sloping too much, and her head too high off her neck. I could envision her signature elegance as she said, "I gather you and David are still getting your divorce?"

"We're filing papers as soon as I get back from teaching in Vermont, Mom."

I imagined her expression, the one mothers reserve for their hopeless offspring who are about to set off on yet another wildhair adventure.

"You're strong, but not that strong," she said. "You're fifty-three years old. And aren't you supposed to train on a bicycle for months and months to be in shape for this kind of thing? You have four weeks before you're leaving on this trip and you say you haven't tried any big hills yet?" She sipped something, definitely water or fruit juice, between words. "That's pretty ambitious, I'd say. Why do you have to do this?"

"Mom, skip the drugstore psychology." I was alternately sitting, standing, and pacing in my kitchen, my body choreographing its own dance under the glaring light fixture while night blackened the windows and cooled the tiles on the floor.

"You don't have to be snippy. Remember what your dad said about pride."

Of course, of course: the story about Prince Bellerophon riding to Mount Olympus on Pegasus. He thought he could become Zeus. *Hubris ate nemesis.* "I've heard it all before, Mother, and you're barking up the wrong tree. This isn't about pride." I kicked off my loafer and then inattentively wriggled my foot back inside.

"But everybody can see you're hurting. What's so bad about that? Just accept the fact of hurting for a while and then come back and live with the rest of the human race. That's how it works." Her voice had power over me. The voice of authority. The voice of right. *Mama mia.*

"I need to do something I've never done before, Okay? It's crazy. It doesn't make sense, but I'm going to do it. Period."

"You always were impulsive."

I could picture that subtle pout, that subtle disdain in her brown eyes, a little like a camel looking down its nose, annoyed with petty humans. "That information is useless, Mother."

"Are you taking a cell phone?"

"No."

"What about anything for self-defense?"

"I'm taking a self-defense class. That should be sufficient." Though her voice quavered, I could hear mine losing ground.

"I just heard about a man on a long bicycle trip who got kidney stones from being on his bike so much."

"Mother!"

"You always were the strongheaded one, weren't you?"

"Nothing matters. Can you understand that nothing matters to me right now?" I choked the phone cord in my hand. Strangled it. I hated this gray place where nothing mattered.

"But there are better options than riding a puny little bicycle across the country. What about your joints? You're not a spring chicken, you know. You could seriously damage your body. Did you ever think to compute just how many spins of the pedals it will take to get you from Colorado to Vermont? Think about it. And what about your boys?"

Pow. The Achilles' heel. My unpredictable, wild-card, free-spirit sons. My broken family. A failed marriage. The maxim drilled into my head from doll-dressing days, both from my mother and the teachers at church, went something like, "No success can compensate for failure in the home." It had made its Big Foot imprint on me.

"They don't need me anymore. You know that. They're almost finished with college except for Brad, who's decided to build golf courses instead.

They're big boys." I struggled to draw a complete breath. "They need to be taking care of themselves now, anyway."

"So they might say. Why don't you make an appointment with a therapist?"

"I just need to do something reckless. I want to take care of things myself. Can you understand?"

My mother took a huge sigh drawn from the eons of her experience. "Where's your sense of humor? You've gone dry as a bone. Can't you laugh at yourself anymore?"

"You're right, always right, Mother, but I don't feel like laughing, period."

"Just laugh, Phyllis. Start now."

"Yeah, yeah, like Daddy used to say: 'A merry heart doeth good like unto medicine.' Don't you know yet that I've had it with scriptures, Norman Vincent Peales, and drugstore analysts?"

I emptied the dishwasher single-handedly. Spoons clanked into the utensil tray. Plate bruised plate. I didn't want to talk any more. "Anything else before I'm off? Any other words of encouragement?"

"No, Miss Temperamental. Why are you in such a hurry? You're always in a hurry."

"Trust me, Mom. I'll call you from somewhere in the Midwest."

"You and Dorothy and her red shoes. You always thought you should be wearing red-sequined shoes, didn't you? The people who care about you are more real than any of your fantasies or glittery shoes, believe me."

"Dorothy and I are showgirls. What can I say? Gotta get to Kansas, Mother, except," I almost laughed but wouldn't let myself, "I'll have to do my number in Nebraska instead."

"You don't need to run away, but if that's what you want to do, then good luck. God will help if you'll humble yourself, but I know you don't like me to talk about God or the Church."

"Mother."

I slammed the phone into its cradle. Be still my heart.

A List of Ways to Matter:
　　Do something nobody's ever done before.
　　Be beautiful, sexy, and irresistible.

Write a book, be a good mother, or be a concert pianist (a superstar
of some kind).
Get in shape, climb Mount Everest, or at least get to the top
of a Colorado fourteener.
Make lots of money or be for a good cause.
Be spiritual, have no desire for worldly things.
Be kind, caring, and sensitive and listen to everything people have
to say.
Be a beauty queen or a CEO or run for
office.
Adopt a life-saving profession.
Be perfect, or at least maintain the
perfect body.
Be happy and be a light for all the world to see.
Save someone else if you can't save yourself.
When none of this works, ride your bicycle across the United States.
Believe that everything matters, or that nothing matters.

And so, the training continued. There wasn't much to do on the long
stretches of bike path that ran along the Platte River to the south of Little-
ton except to guide my bike over the occasional bridges and around the
curves in the trail. After I'd trained for two months, gradually building up
the distances, I took the first thirty-five-mile test run in preparation for
the big ride. On the last day of March, I biked out to Chatfield Reservoir,
made a U-turn, then pedaled toward home.

Brittle plains grasses from the previous year, crushed by clumps of lin-
gering snow, splayed every which way at the sides of the path. The asphalt
was lumpier and less dependable than usual—a victim of freezing and
thawing. With the overcast day being gloomy and confusing as it made its
transition into late afternoon, the last few miles were feeling like eternity
stretched out in front of me.

I've committed to go on this trip. But should I?

You're going. Stop equivocating.

But this is stupid, just sitting on a bicycle all day and pedaling. Where are your brains? This is boring.

Stop making excuses. You can do this. You've said you'd go. End of argument.

Suddenly, some muscle to the side and just below my left knee exploded like a bolt of electricity. It seized up. Faster than Jack be nimble, I skidded to a stop and leapt off the bike, barely able to stand, hobbling, doing a half shuffle-ball-change to ease the pain. "Ow, ow. Ouch," I yelped, trying to dance out of the muscle seizure. Finally it eased, but only slightly.

I knew that pedaling would only exacerbate the pain, but I was still two miles from home. Against my better judgment I tried the bicycle again for about thirty seconds before the leg seized up once more. I jumped off, then proceeded at an invalid's gait past the trees and bushes I'd flown by earlier in the afternoon. Chris, my twenty-eight-year-old son, was due for dinner. I had to get home soon. Stopping to rest every few minutes, I finally turned into my alley and limped to my back door.

When I called the doctor, he said the problem sounded like an inflammation at the stress point where the ligament attached to the tibia. "You're trying to do too much too fast. Rest a couple of days, then you should be okay. But don't forget to stretch. And get off your bike from time to time when you're riding. Stretch even then. All right?"

"Do you think I should go ahead with the bike trip?"

"Sure. Just don't go overboard. Take it easy when you can. You're in good shape. You should be good to go."

"Okay," I said with no enthusiasm. I'd been secretly hoping he'd lay down the law and say absolutely no way should I go on the trip. But he hadn't.

I hung up feeling out of sorts and crabby. With Chris due anytime now, I didn't want to fix dinner. I wanted to escape and chill out under my goose down comforter. But he'd called that morning to say he was coming down from the mountains to buy an amplifier for a big gig at the Church of Rock and Roll, soon to be in session at the gravel pit warehouse at the edge of the Blue River near Silverthorne. David had bought the property and was letting Chris and Jeremy use the office for a temporary home. When Chris called to say he'd like to drop by, I'd invited him for dinner. Of course. I loved seeing any of my sons, anytime. I just wouldn't bother telling this one what had happened today.

I need to train more gradually. I'll be all right. I have four weeks left. All the time in the world. Right?

After I dished up our plates with spaghetti, garlic bread, and green salad, a no-brainer meal, I sat across from Chris at the dining table and watched him twirl spaghetti on his fork.

"So, where's Spinner?" he said after his first bite.

"He doesn't stay here all the time," I answered, not telling anyone in the family that Spinner had moved back in with me. He'd been painting my house to repay me for some "borrowed" items. He'd been staying over to save on travel time. That was the excuse.

"I can see why you like him," Chris said.

"And why's that?" Beneath the table, I rubbed the painful spot beneath my left knee.

"He's cool. Handsome. He has a great laugh. A pretty nice guy all in all even if he has his drug habits."

I rolled my eyes. "It's nice you think so," I said, keeping a flatness in my voice, no emotions revealed. I'd been trying to get over my obsession with Spinner. He'd left the day before with a few more of my belongings. I hadn't heard from him and figured he was on another crack run. But sad thing was, I didn't get upset anymore. I knew he'd be back with some tall tale and his "I'm sorrys." I knew he'd make it up to me. *But what's with this numbness? This acceptance of the unacceptable?*

"Is the gig Friday or Saturday?" I asked, always a fan of my musician sons, always in the audience when humanly possible.

"Saturday. You'll be there won't you?"

"Wild horses couldn't keep me away."

We both chewed our food. I poured another glass of milk. For strong bones. I offered Chris a second glass.

"I had a terrible nightmare about you and me," he said.

"When you're finished eating, why don't you tell more me about it?"

I watched him sink his teeth into the garlic bread. I stood up to get some napkins and suddenly felt self-conscious. I was still dressed in my show-all-the-lumps bike pants—a "Bike America" poster for a midlife crisis in my thigh-popping stretch shorts and neon purple shirt. *Even if my children are supposedly grown up, I'm still a mother, not some diehard training to ride cross-country. Isn't that still my job? If it isn't, what is?*

I sat back down, still hurting and in a piss-poor mood. I knew I'd never be ready for the bike trip—not in this lifetime. While I waited for him to finish, I broke a piece of garlic bread and used the side of my hand to sweep up the crumbs that fell on the table.

Christopher, Christopher, I thought. I looked across the table at my son who was now six foot three, this baby of mine who grew in my body before I'd known he was growing there. *Baby unplanned. Bundle of surprise for those mortals, David and Phyllis. Baby, baby. There had been too much blood, baby, baby, and I didn't know how to put it back inside Geoffrey's body where it was supposed to flow just right and make him a healthy boy. That's something I didn't know how to do. And your blood might have run away from you, too, Christopher, and I was too tired to stay vigilant, little one. Too tired to watch and protect you, too, baby, baby. I might have been a Madonna who smiled so sweetly, yes, I could do that. I learned how to smile, but I never could have fought for my country when I understood how it bled. The thought and the sight of blood made me too weak for you, you beautiful boy who smiled like the sun. My arms were frail when they held you, like they couldn't do the job of holding another baby, baby when the first could bleed so easily.*

"The dream was awful, Mom," Chris said. He sopped the last of the spaghetti sauce with his bread. "I was no bigger than Tom Thumb. I was sitting in a corner, huddled in a ball. You were shouting. Exploding. You were so big and like fire shooting off everywhere. I can't believe how vivid nightmares can be sometimes."

"Maybe it wasn't a nightmare, Chris," I said, spearing a piece of spaghetti lengthwise with all four tines of my fork, ready to break into tears.

"What?" He stopped in the middle of wrapping some noodles around his spoon. "I said maybe it wasn't a nightmare." I wasn't in a mood to make light of anything.

"What are you saying? That I was having sweet dreams or something?"

"Maybe there were times when I acted like that, times when all I could see or feel or believe was my own frustration. I failed you sometimes, Christopher Jon."

Clouds blocked the sun outside the window behind his head. The light on his face changed. Darkened. His chestnut hair hung long at the sides of his face and rested on his shoulders.

"Failed me? What's that supposed to mean? You failed me? That sounds so grand and sweeping and martyred. Like you think you're Phyllis of Arc or something. Are you really listening to me or are you too wrapped up in your own failure?"

"Only you . . ." I said, "the Master of shooting arrows into Achilles' heels . . ."

I tried to curb the sudden burst of anger swelling inside me and in the process dropped my spoonful of spaghetti onto my purple shirt where the red sauce didn't complement the purple. I dipped my napkin in my glass of water and swiped at the remains. "Only you could say things like that to your mother. Who do you think you are?"

"Only you were so wrapped up with Dad and your arguments about other women. I was in the house. You forgot I was there. You forgot all of us had ears. Always your problems. I only wanted a mother to call off the drama and be happy to have me. To have all of us." A tear appeared on the rim of his eye.

"Is this a contest between drama potentates to see who's the most hurt?" I was leaning on my forearms, heedless of knives and forks and sauce on my plate. "You or me? Is this the way we hurt each other?"

"We're two peas, Mother. That's why children have to leave their mothers. I have to know who I am without you under my skin all the time. We know each other too well. From the time you thought you were going to miscarry me, the time they put you in the hospital and waited for me to slip away. But somebody needed to stay on the scene to keep you in check."

"I'll always be under your skin, so get used to it." I sat back against the spindled chair and folded my arms. "But why do you want to twist the blade of the knife when I'm only saying I'm sorry for whatever I did. It doesn't make sense. I just need you to know that *I know* I'm not perfect. I've made mistakes. I still make mistakes. Lots of them."

The final rays of the setting sun that had escaped the clouds backlit his head. A stark halo. His face softened. The last burst of light gentled the corners of the table and chair backs.

"You're in love with the struggle, *Mamacita,* with how hard everything is. You're attached to the victim act. Why can't you just love me? Laugh with me. I'm your son."

"Who's calling who a victim? I wish things could have been different. With you. Geoffrey. Everything." I stood to put my plate in the sink, then returned to twist Chris's black hair into a loose knot in my hand. "Maybe you'd be better off with a different mother, but here I am." Standing behind him, I wrapped my arms around his shoulders and hugged my ear to the back of his head.

"Things are how they are, Mom. You are my mother. Whether or not you think you were a good mother is beside the point. Now you're taking off on a bicycle for who the hell knows where, just so you can find yourself or something like that. I don't know why you're doing this, but I'm here. Jer's here and Brad's not far away in Arizona. This is life, Mom. You don't have to get on your bicycle in your purple shirt to escape it. I'm your son. Just be my mother."

He carried his plate to the sink. I followed him. I'd taught him something after all. "I'm your mother, so just be my son, why don't you? I'm doing the best I can."

He bent over and gave me a half-hearted hug. I was tall but he was taller. I loved that moment of feeling small, even delicate inside the tentativeness of his arms. My son. My second-born. I followed him down the hall and helped him put his long arms through the sleeves of the blue plastic coat he'd found at the thrift store, plastic coats from thrift stores being the rage.

"Someday, when you're a parent," I said as he turned the doorknob, "you'll understand your parents are only frail humans who can't figure out everything. But," I said, catching hold of the back of his coat, "you know I love you, don't you?"

"Sure, Mom," he said. Turning back, he wrapped his arms around my shoulders in a much more genuine article of a hug, suddenly my little boy again. "I love you no matter what you do. In fact, you know better than to listen to me. I rant sometimes. You're a great mom. Go for it. Tear up the highways. Do whatever you need to do, but just don't hurt yourself."

He descended my front porch stairs, stepped into the street, and wrestled open the faulty-hinged door of his Stevie Ray van.

::

A few weeks later, the day before May Day in 1996, two weeks shy of age fifty-three, I straddled my three-month-old black cherry Cannondale with twenty-one gears—a far cry from the dented black-fendered workhorse my father had repaired for me back in the day.

"America, here we come," C. J. shouted, grinning at me as she put her feet to the pedals of her spring-green bicycle, a strand of hair blowing across her face.

"Yes, yes, and yes," we shouted in unison. We laughed at our brashness, at our sheer chutzpah on this brisk, windy, clouds-rolling-like-featherweight-bowling-balls day.

Leaving Fort Collins on that morning of April 30, we planned to arrive in Montpelier by June 15. We headed out of town on Highway 14—me on my touring bike with Blackburn racks, a North Face two-person tent tucked away in Jandd panniers, Pearl Izumi long bike pants, Shimano clip-in shoes, a Giro bike helmet, Patagonia vest, and a long-sleeved shirt. C. J. rode a custom-designed bicycle, a gift from her soon to be ex-husband (before they'd ever talked about divorce he'd special ordered it for her), who knew state-of-the-art equipment. We'd outfitted ourselves for wind, rain, cold, heat, and every emergency we could fathom. All of this, weighing about eighty pounds, was stuffed and rolled into plastic bags and fitted into front and back panniers on both of our bikes. Gear queens, we were ready to burn up the long, straight, two-lane road into the farmlands of eastern Colorado, those acres and acres of newly planted crops barely showing tips of green, and acres and acres barely seeded in this late spring.

As we climbed to the top of the overpass across I-25, commuters passed beneath us, their expressions hurried and worried behind the windshields of their cars. They couldn't feel spring. They couldn't smell it. They couldn't feel the sun and the way it touched our shoulders. They were locked inside metal and glass, fenced off, corralled like cattle and speeding down a chute into the feedlots of the big cities: Fort Collins. Boulder. Denver. Lucky us on the open road in the great outdoors, C. J. singing a Broadway tune, "There's a bright, golden haze on the meadow," me humming along.

After the original thrill had worn off, however, maybe after ten miles, I felt like a piston keeping a flywheel in motion. The scenery started to repeat itself. The newly planted fields ticked by until they were rarely planted fields and then grazing pastures of no special account, a few complacent cows standing alone, masticating. But they were all fenced off, one fence like the next one. The birds dotting the telephone wires like Braille no longer drew an emotive response from my insides. The broken yellow strips in the middle of the road were not only losing their charm, but taking on a menacing aspect.

Ready for a diversion, I looked at what people had tossed out their car windows to the side of the road, and lo and behold, just like magic, there was an empty pack of Marlboros lying on the gravelly shoulder. So soon a reminder of Spinner: red, white, the image of a crown between two mythical, gold-colored lions facing off on this flip-top box of "20 Class A Cigarettes." Out of force of habit, I squeezed both brakes. Spinner was always on the lookout for empty Marlboro packs because of the free gifts he could get from smokersignup.com if he saved enough bar codes. I wanted to jump off and grab this squashed, deserted package, put it in my panniers, collect it so Spinner would be happy. I wasn't even on the road for one hour yet, and here I was, a puppy ready to carry the ball back to its master. *Shape up.* I let go of the brakes. *Forget Spinner.* But then something else, another red and white piece of roadside trash caught my eye—a smashed Coke cup tossed by sudden wind. Waste. Detritus. A wind rising. A storm coming. *Red and white. Me and men. I am stuck.*

I'd been separated from David for two and a half years, waiting for tax implications to settle before the final step to divorce. After being Ms. Lonely Heart Supreme, I'd found a primal man: uncomplicated, uneducated, a house painter whom I saw with my movie camera eyes as a hunter stepping into the light from the dense leaves of the north woods. He seemed the perfect antidote to my cerebral husband and his complicated psychological rationalizations. Spinner's main goal in life was to make enough money to support his daughter who lived with his ex-wife in Montana and to drive a Pontiac Trans Am. Red. He and I were more different than night and day.

Maybe because my nest was not only empty but obliterated, I'd needed someone to fill the void. Maybe, because I'd been well-schooled in the Christian way—believing all are equal in God's eyes—I thought I could be involved with anyone who was a child of God. I could see into his soul, after all. There was a good man in there somewhere. Or maybe I wanted to break all the rules because the ones I'd followed so scrupulously had failed. There were times I felt like riding a Harley in a snowstorm in a leather jacket with nothing else on, wind blowing my hair every which way, me not caring how fast I drove or whether I crashed.

"I need help," Spinner had said when he came to my house one night. We'd known each other for just over a year. "I was," his voice broke, "so stupid." A tall, rugged man with strong arms and back and legs, he was also a boy standing in front of my gas fireplace with his hands covering his face, crying. "She's staying with me for the summer. She trusts me, and I left her alone in my bedroom last night. My eight-year-old daughter, Maggie. All by herself while I smoked crack in the living room. My crack dealer knows my number." He was sobbing now. "Maggie's the only thing that matters to me. She was scared. She was so scared."

"Sit down," I told him. He wiped his nose with his hand, oblivious to anything but anguish. "I'll get some tissue."

"I can't go on hurting her like this." He followed me into the bathroom.

The words came out of my mouth like automatic lightning. "Why don't you move over here with me? That place where you're living is a pit. I could watch Maggie while you paint during the days. Then you'd both have a safe place at night."

Things were earnest and pure until the next moment.

"I'm going to quit. I am," he said, his tears suddenly dry.

Something in me jerked to attention. It was almost as if, relieved to have wriggled free once again, Spinner felt he could afford quick promises. "If you can help me out of this, I'll quit. I can't do this to my daughter anymore."

Something about his tone of voice rang a bell in the deep recesses of my bullshit detector mind. But because I wanted to believe in repentance and wanted to be the kind of person who could help him accept responsibility and find his strength, I didn't listen. I was seduced by the possibility of righting a sinking ship.

And now, on my bicycle with a breeze at my back, I vowed not to think of Spinner anymore. Period. Or David. I would look at the same scenery until I became blue in the face. *I will not think of Spinner anymore. It's over.*

I sat glibly on the seat made for a woman's butt wearing brand-new fingerless bike gloves, black bike pants with a chamois insert, and clip-on shoes with which I hadn't practiced the unclipping except once or twice. I proceeded confidently, even if I'd only practiced with three of the twenty-one gears on the flatland trails where I'd trained. My philosophy: who needs twenty-one gears anyway? After all, I'd learned to ride my balloon-tire bike in a flash with only one gear. I was old-school tough. If a person believed strongly enough, a person could do anything. And I was a woman who could do anything. Right?

The next morning, however, on the outskirts of Sterling, we faced the first truly major hill of the trip. C. J. got a head start. I watched her with some envy becoming a speck in the distance. I followed with determination, but all of a sudden, the grade being much steeper than I'd anticipated, I found myself at an abrupt standstill and unable to clip out of the pedals fast enough. Everything tilted and forty pounds of equipment plus the bike smashed on top of my right leg. My shoulder crushed into the asphalt. *A downed, wounded warrior, and the war hasn't even started.* My leg throbbed with unbelievable intensity.

Turning onto my back, I bit my lip hard to wait for the seething pain to subside. I focused on everything I could besides this assault: the clouds, the scarce bits of blue, the surrounding hills that looked as if they were triangles on a dinosaur's back, the fact that I was a mother riding away from her children even though they were grown children who shouldn't need a mother anymore.

When I picked up my bicycle and dusted off my pants, I noticed a tear on the right knee on the pants that were supposed to last forever. *Battle scars already. Too soon.* I pushed the bike and the weighty panniers up the hill, leaning forward, pushing everything ahead of me until I was almost parallel to the road. The hill was a long one. My leg ached with the deepest, purplest pain. Up and up and still too steep to start pedaling again. A tumbleweed flew across the two-lane highway, which was suddenly a lonely place with no cars or trucks or even C. J. She must have reached the top already.

As if it were happening right then and there, I could hear the squeaking hinges on Chris's van door. I could hear him saying, "Just be my mother"— echoes off the walls of the cave of my mind.

:: For Time and All Eternity ::

In the spring of 1963 when I was a sophomore at Brigham Young University, something happened in a chemistry classroom built like a pit. The real chemistry happened when I walked through the door and down the stairs, swinging my purse on its long strap. I was only half aware I'd outgrown my gawky high school body and that I could register an effect when I ran my fingers through my long, silken hair, and slid my long, smooth legs under a desk. Unbeknownst to me, David sat in the fifteenth row, watching. Later, when safe to admit it, he said that when he saw me that day his heart skipped a few beats. He intuitively knew I was a woman with whom he could have children and someone who'd be gentle enough to understand him. Girls my age fantasized about love at first sight. The Knight. The Prince who was speechless with awe—that, of course, being my rendition of our beginnings.

It was spring, when sap ran high and colts ran frisky. We'd gone to the chemistry pit to take a required constitution test—BYU's constitution. I was a candidate for Vice President of Culture (the office managing weekly student assemblies and serving as a liaison with faculty regarding visiting artists and performers); David was another hopeful for student body office—Vice President of Student Relations (the office managing pep rallies, songleaders, cheerleaders, flag twirlers, in other words, the campus hotties). He, a returned missionary enrolled as a junior, I a sophomore, conducted hectic campaigns and emerged victorious. At the executive council meetings, we bantered and flirted, and yes, there was chemistry. During summer vacation, David pursued me with carefully calculated, beautifully written letters sent from his home in California.

Attending an executive council training in September at Aspen Grove in the canyon where Robert Redford would play a role as Jeremiah Johnson and where he'd soon buy a ski resort, name it Sundance, then bankroll a film festival of the same name, David asked me to be his wife. Beneath the autumn leaves drifting to the ground, he quoted Marx, something about striding through the fields of the world with our love to conquer all. I was impressed, political science major that I was. I said yes. And because we were introduced to sensitivity training that same weekend, a method encouraging us to speak our feelings truthfully, and receive each other's truth, it became the basis for our communication.

During that year, we met with the executive council weekly, sometimes with the university president and administrators, attended social functions as school dignitaries, and after being nominated by the Tribe of Many Feathers as their candidate for homecoming queen, I was selected as one of five finalists out of a field of fifty-five. Who knows why the president of this club for Lamanites—one of the four groups described in the Book of Mormon, seen as the ancestors of Native Americans—asked me to be their hope, but I was pleased. With my black hair and olive complexion, I could have passed. I was flattered, that is until the school newspaper's photographer snapped my photo at the bottom of a dim stairwell near the student-body offices and said he was afraid it was difficult to capture beauty on film. The campaign photo appearing in the *Daily Universe* was abysmal, as semi-prophesied. I didn't receive enough votes to make the royal trio.

Traveling with David at Christmastime to meet his family, I was shocked after walking into his not-so-gregarious Mormon home. Even though my family had troubles of its own, it was alive with a rough-and-tumble sense of affection and loyalty. There was sterility permeating David's small home—a starvation and an uneasy truce between his parents. I felt secrets in the walls, though no one mentioned the sister being kept at the

Veteran's Hospital in Palo Alto. His father rarely joined our conversations, retired to his bedroom at 6:00 p.m., and disappeared onto the morning streets at 6:00 a.m. His mother seldom arrived at a period in her sentences and seemed full of a deep hunger to be heard.

As our car crept back to Utah through a soupy fog near Sacramento, I had serious doubts about our engagement. Several times, I bit back the words, *I don't think this will work.* For the fourteen-hour drive, I vacillated, sometimes repeating the mantra to myself, *I can do this, I can do this,* then thinking, *No, I can't.* But David seemed to me an anagram, a complex puzzle. He fascinated me. While sensing the road would be rough, I believed in the prospects of love and that I should consider myself lucky that someone so outstanding had asked me to be his wife. My parents had sent me to BYU ("Bring 'em young," some people joked) with hopes that I'd find a good husband, their concern about the best education or a degree reserved for my only brother.

For all we knew about love (neither of us had dated much—David shy with women, me plagued by feelings of awkwardness from growing too tall too soon), we were free-falling into love with no parachutes. Love could conquer all. We were also free-falling into the ritual ways of our culture: Young men, go on a mission, then find a wife. Young women, find a good husband and settle down. Don't wait to have a family. "What's best for me" was not a question either of us had been taught to ask. We followed the footsteps of many who'd come before us, those who believed this to be the best way "to do" life.

On Friday, May 29, 1964, in the company of our parents (his father had quit smoking for a few months so he could be worthy of a temple recommend), David, age twenty-four, and I, barely twenty-one, were married in the white, nineteenth-century St. George temple set against red rock cliffs and a sailor's blue sky in southern Utah. David beamed and I averted my eyes shyly as we knelt on either side of the altar repeating our promises of loyalty for time and eternity. When David took my hand in his, I allowed myself to feel as if I were the maiden granting her hand to the knight ready to carry her off to an estate of forever happiness. Already suspicious of fairy tales, I still wanted to be in one.

After a few snapshots with our parents' box cameras in front of the temple, we sped in David's brown, boaty Plymouth back to the local Travelodge to lose our virginity. An industrial orange and brown bedspread turned back, there were innocent fumblings and then a rapid, naive con-summation of our marriage. Me squeezing next to my true love's shoulder, we drove to Las Vegas for a traditional Mormon wedding reception—punch, nut cups, and wedding cake served on glass plates on card tables set up in my parents' backyard. Beneath an arching trellis woven with blue net and twinkling white lights and standing between two columns covered with white corrugated paper to resemble Roman columns, we stood in a reception line to greet friends surprised at the good weather at the back of my parents' small, yellow, two-story tract home with its cinderblock fence. "The wind's blowing like crazy, and it's raining everywhere," they said. "But it's perfect here in your yard." My mother said God had answered her prayers. I didn't doubt her. She had a good thing going with her faith in outcomes.

Back in Provo, we hit the ground running—David to finish summer school and me to work in the telegraph office at Geneva Steel. Ready to live the charmed life, I encountered both honeymoon cystitis and Ruby in the first two weeks. One of the two regular telegraph operators on the job, Ruby seemed repelled by the idea of a bright-eyed BYU student working in the same small room with her and her best friend, Carol. Every day was a strain, though Ruby had to bite her tongue. I'd been hired to cover her summer vacation. Not helping matters, the executive who'd hired me asked me to play the role of secretary to a steel executive in a promotional movie for U.S. Steel. Things worsened with Ruby. Whenever she had a chance, she made it all too clear I was distasteful to her time on the job. Thus, the fingers of the real world started thrumming on the consciousness of what I liked to think of as my wide-eyed innocence.

As I proved my good Mormon wifeliness by canning cherries in a hot, steaming kitchen, all the time sick with cystitis, I thought of Ruby. Beneath her tightly curled red hair and behind her narrow eyes, a resentment simmered. I couldn't understand why. Only later did I begin to comprehend how some people begrudged BYU students their golden glow, their BYUness, their goodness, their mission in life. I brashly thought everyone loved a good, wholesome BYU student with bounce to every ounce. Little did I know how offensive I must have been to her—my enthusiasm, my cockiness, my arrogance, even though I wouldn't have called it such a thing at the time. Everyone had to love me and my love of life and God. How could they resist?

::

Marrying David and moving to the Bay Area in 1964 was, for me, like the disturbing of a tightly composed seashell. As the larger ocean washed my small shell onto a beach and forced an opening, I was impacted as snails, clams, and mussels are impacted. I felt the pull of the moon, the wind, the rain, and the unceasing rhythm of water moving me through hot sand.

David had received scholarship offers from the University of California's Boldt Hall in Berkeley as well as from Harvard, but we decided to stay on the West Coast because of his aging parents. We chose Stanford over Cal. While visiting the Berkeley campus earlier in the year, we'd both felt a turmoil, even a violent rumbling beneath the surface of students ambling from class to class. By the time we arrived in Palo Alto in September, the Free Speech Movement was well under way and sending shock waves through the nation.

The missile crisis. Bay of Pigs. Malcolm X. Selma, Alabama. Meridian, Mississippi. "We Shall Overcome." And, of course, Vietnam. Sexual freedom rallies in Berkeley. The burning of bras. Volunteer psychological drug tests at the VA Hospital in Palo Alto where David's sister had been kept for twenty years, where we visited her on Sundays and where Ken Kesey, the Merry Prankster and future author of *One Flew Over the Cuckoo's Nest*, had been employed as a janitor. A qualified Stanford student could be paid

$140 for four weeks of testing: LSD the first week, psilocybin the second, mescaline the third, and a mixture of all three on the fourth.

Even though I strolled the quiet downtown streets of Palo Alto and inhabited such normal establishments as Liddicoat's groceries to buy asparagus and strawberries, and even though I attended the Stanford LDS Student Ward and taught "cultural refinement" lessons in Relief Society, I sensed something tidal happening outside my safe shell, the cotton gauze wrapping of what I'd known.

There were the lost flower children drugged out on stoops in Haight-Ashbury while television reporters spoke to anxious parents who couldn't find them. There was free love tangling around societal consciousness like tendrils on a vine. Bread trucks and step vans painted in psychedelic flowers sported mattresses in the back. Everything was clad in tie-dye shirts and dresses and scarves—bursts of yellow like bursts of acid, luminous greens, blues, and reds. Long, flowing hippie hair. Jesus types. Birkenstocks. No makeup. Mother Earth women with pendulous breasts hanging behind a veil of Mexican cotton.

Palo Alto, where hibiscus and calla lilies grew like weeds. Palo Alto, with the Bijou where we saw our first Bergman film, where David and I discovered Kepler's Books on El Camino Real and spent Saturday afternoons searching the shelves and reading posters about North Beach happenings in San Francisco—readings by Kerouac/Snyder/Ginsberg, performances by Carol Doda, the topless dancer.

I was a shellfish being asked to step out of myself and swim into the bigger world even though I was still a hometown girl from Las Vegas, which was, in 1964, a small town. I'd had cosmopolitan beginnings at a classical dance studio in Las Vegas, playing piano for ballerinas and showgirls from the Strip. I'd watched Sally Rand, the famous fan dancer, warm up at the barre. I'd had high school friends whose parents were pit bosses, casino managers, dealers, even a president of one of the hotels. But none of this could compare to the Bay Area, where I was caught by the forces of tides and sunspots and occasional meteors.

Employed at the Stanford Development Office, I composed letters to corporate donors from President J. Wallace Sterling and helped prepare the annual corporate donor list. Everything seemed so calm in the sandstone halls of Stanford, and yet, outside, I wasn't sure I could trust the serene rows of eucalyptus trees lining the main boulevard.

One Saturday afternoon, looking for something to fill my alone time because David's first priority was law school, I wandered into a Menlo Park music store on El Camino Real, your average-looking music store with cymbals, guitars, and banjos hanging from the ceiling. A sign behind the counter read, "Banjo Lessons Available." I'd always been involved in one kind of music or another, so why not learn the banjo and sing like Peter, Paul, and Mary?

"How much does it cost to rent a banjo?" I asked the clerk wearing a T-shirt that read "I Want to Take You Higher," cut-off jeans, sandy-colored Birkenstocks, and small rounded granny glasses.

"Fifteen dollars per month, which we'll write off if you take lessons."

"Sign me up," I said, always good for an impulsive act. Three days later, rental instrument in tow, the clerk accompanied me to a small cubicle at the back of the store.

"You look like Joan Baez," he said, grinning in a cool, hip way. "A buttoned-down version, but yeah, there's a resemblance."

"I love her voice," I said, as if I knew a lot about her, though I'd only heard her once or twice on the radio. I'd heard about her husband, Dave Harris, a student at Stanford getting press for antiwar speeches. I'd heard she had a shack in Big Sur.

"You're taller, but it's uncanny. You have that dark hair and olive skin and same kind of eyes. Even the full lips." He looked my twenty-one-year-old self over, smiled again, and held back the curtain of the practice room.

"I hope to hear her sing in person sometime." I carried the five-string banjo awkwardly to take a seat on a folding chair.

"Jerry," he said. "Your new banjo student. Phyllis."

Jerry doodled with his banjo, barely looking up. He played a quick scale, then stood and extended a hand. He had dark intense eyes peering over the dark granny glasses, a head full of blue-black shoulder-length hair, and a turquoise tie-dye shirt over cotton pants and sandals. I felt overdressed, even alien, in my uptown bell-bottoms from Macy's and brown turtleneck sweater, and I didn't like that buttoned-down feeling in this store with these people. I wished I had some free and wild gypsy clothes and outrageously long hair down to my waist.

"So you want to learn the banjo?" He pushed the glasses back up his nose and sat down.

"I've been a pianist since I was seven. It's time to learn something new."

"Sounds good."

"I haven't been in Palo Alto long," I said. "My husband's a law student at Stanford."

"My wife takes film classes there."

"Cool," I said, though I wasn't feeling cool. The underarms of my turtleneck sweater were turning a moist, dark brown. This wasn't a world I knew. Something was different here.

After he showed me a few chords that he told me to practice, he broke into a banjo riff. "Little Birdie," he said, as he planted his left-hand fingers on the frets with lightning speed. He was good. More than good. Even amazing, and then I noticed. He was missing a finger.

"How can you play like that with a missing finger?" I blurted out.

He didn't answer. He was off in another world, playing for a larger audience, standing in front of big crowds, off like a wild horse in the desert.

I sat quietly, enjoying the music but hoping he'd show me the chords one more time so I could remember them. "Could you help me with those chords?" I finally asked.

"Sure," he said, not happy to be corralled, and I began to suspect he was bored with basic chords and these lessons he probably taught to keep the wolf from the door. Nevertheless, I left the music store thinking I might be good on the banjo because, after all, I was a pianist who'd gotten lots of strokes through the years.

After three lessons, however, I found the chords harder to manage and wondered if this was a good idea. When I arrived at the store, a few hippie girls with pale blue, starred irises, rippling hair, and the heavy scent of incense hung out by the guitars. Jerry was talking with the clerk, who raised his hand to greet me but kept talking. I heard new language: "Strobe lights, Merry Pranksters in the warehouse, a batch of electric Kool-Aid, and Bob Weir's coming in tomorrow." When the clerk finally said to Jerry, "Your 3:30's here," then to me, "Enjoy your lesson with Captain Trips Garcia," they both laughed and kibitzed for at least five more minutes. I felt like a square-shelled creature with tight hinges, not privy to this language or this scene that felt way out of my league.

He wore dark glasses, as always, and as we walked back to the practice room, I wondered about his name. "Garcia," I said. "An ancestor of mine wrote an essay called 'Message to Garcia.'"

"Lots of Garcias." He sat down with his banjo and picked at the strings as if he were a perpetual music box, always riffing, while I waited to learn a few elementary chords. Who was this mysterious man called Garcia, I wondered, and suddenly I knew I was a stranger in a strange land where something foreign, something I didn't understand, was happening. Garcia of the dark hair, the dark eyes that seldom surfaced from the realm behind his dark glasses. When they did, I thought I saw a trickster in them, something mocking my conventionality and limited perception.

Suddenly, the cubicle felt especially small and insufficient. The tide was running too high here, and even though I felt a strange pull toward the edge of something, I knew I had to stay away from edges. While I played my c, g, and f chords with awkward fingers and akimbo elbows, Jerry stared off into space as if something waited for him. He didn't belong in this small room behind a curtain at the back of a music store in Menlo Park. He was a man consumed by this instrument, by its speed and possibility, even though we played the game of teacher and student.

"Wait a minute," he said, adjusting my inward-bending fingers that wouldn't perform like his could. My lobster-pincer hand, wrapped around the neck of the banjo, cramped.

"Maybe I should spend my extra time with my piano," I said in a moment of truth, thinking that dabbling wouldn't do and suspecting that the world beginning to intrigue me here was a place into which I shouldn't tread. "I need time with the piano."

"Whatever works," he said, though he'd answered too quickly. Admittedly, I was hoping he'd coax me to change my mind, tell me I had talent, and that I shouldn't give up so easily. Everyone always told me I had talent.

Instead, he scurried his fingers over the strings absentmindedly. Maybe he was waiting for me to have more moxie and to say how could I pass up a chance to work with the Master, but maybe he was just sitting there—in the room but not in the room. I was too naive to realize that the dark glasses probably hid a pair of dilated, spacey eyes, that he could have been tripped out on acid and off to another country, that his disinterest had nothing to do with me sitting there.

"Thanks." I rubbed my thumbprints off the banjo's frets with my sleeve so I could return it to the clerk. I wasn't sure what to say in this awkward moment. "You're great on the banjo," I tried.

Jerry lifted his banjo off his lap and climbed out of the strap. He sighed. "Yeah, yeah. Take care of yourself."

I, without a clue as to who this man would become and how he'd soon be a legend, felt hurt by his distance, and wondered why there was a part of me that wanted to know more about him and his world but who also suspected I should run away without hesitation. I was a Mormon girl through and through, with no intention of deviating from my principles. But I sat there for a minute, my feet crossed at the ankles, wanting to say something that would bridge gaps, wanting to make some connection.

I looked at his granny glasses that had slipped halfway down his nose. I looked at his face that had seen hard times, unsmooth, pits in the crevices. But I couldn't find the words I needed. I felt too much like the Buttoned-Down One with the Prim and Proper Lip. My be-in-the-world-but-not-of-the-world sensibilities ruled the day. I stood up and left in an awkward rush, leaving him sitting there alone, fleeing from his remoteness. But after I returned my banjo to the front desk and saw the extra-thin hippie girls sitting on stools behind the counter, I wondered what I'd left behind. A cardboard cutout of the Other? A wooden Indian with no feelings?

As I drove home in our brown-finned Plymouth that was getting more and more unreliable, this unsettled me. Of course I'd heard the Haight-Ashbury stories about the lost people, their parents gnashing their teeth, and combing the world for their children. I reminded myself how lucky I was to have the Gospel according to the Latter-day Saints to help keep me found. I would keep myself pure and unsullied, and that was that.

As I turned into the driveway of our apartment on Waverley Street, however, I wondered about something my father had quoted more than once: "My strength is as the strength of ten because my heart is pure," a line from the writings of Alfred Lord Tennyson. When I and my siblings were young, my father loved to read to us from *One Hundred and One Famous Poems*. He'd inscribed the date of April 6, 1944, on the flyleaf and recorded the fact that he'd purchased his copy at the U.S. Naval Reserve Training Station in Farragut, Idaho, just before being shipped overseas. His father had read another copy of the same book to him, and had, in fact, memorized most of the poems, and recited them after supper to his children. The fact that my grandfather loved these poems was my father's best memory of him. I can still remember the squat but somehow majestic grandfather who stood before us children filled with awe on the one or two Christmases he dropped by, reciting these same lines in his Royal Shakespearean voice, becoming larger than life before our eyes even though he never graduated from high school or walked the boards of a stage. But what did it mean to have clean hands and a pure heart and not lift one's soul up to vanity? What did it mean to treat all men as equals? That God loves everything under the sun, good and bad and indifferent?

I couldn't draw lines in the sand that day. It wasn't that easy. And I regretted my inability to reach across chasms and the way I'd turned my back on Jerry Garcia and rushed away from worldliness and the fear of what his life was adding up to and left him sitting there on that chair by himself, me full of anxiety that something might corrupt me, the pure one.

::

I sat on the hard piano bench waiting for David to come home. He and I now lived in a gardener's cottage on a large estate in Los Altos Hills, surrounded by ancient oaks, tall eucalyptus, horse pastures, and old money. I was a piano major at San Jose State, David a second-year student at Stanford Law School. Into our second year of marriage, I sat at the piano waiting. He'd been gone for almost a day and a half.

The estate belonged to John and Eleanor Fowle, Eleanor the sister of Senator Alan Cranston. I performed secretarial duties and odds-and-ends tasks for Mrs. Fowle to cover the rent, and we paid twenty dollars per month for utilities. Head of the California Democratic Women, which included Dianne Feinstein, the soon-to-be mayor of San Francisco, the senator in training, and other up and coming Democratic distaff notables, Mrs. Fowle asked me to write letters, do calligraphy for invitations to her parties and events, run errands, and help tend the rose garden. On weekends, David and I bought tickets in the nosebleed section of the San Francisco Opera. At the San Francisco Symphony, we watched Stravinsky's protégé, Robert Kraft, conducting *The Rites of Spring,* and Seiji Ozawa guest conducting Ravel's *Daphnis and Chloé.* At Stanford we watched Ray Charles playing a concert grand and getting so muscular in his enthusiasm that the pedal column fell off. We were being exposed to a larger world. I was growing up fast, so fast.

The bulky, massive upright piano had a good tone. We found it for $125 in the want ads. The rack for holding the sheet music was elaborately carved with arches, and a long mirror above it stretched across the top where I could see my eyes and forehead while I practiced. This was my place of refuge while David studied twenty hours a day for law school. I played scales. Brahms's exercises. Poulenc and Haydn sonatas.

After David's first year of law school, we moved from our apartment in Palo Alto and I stopped working at the Development Office. We decided our finances would be tight, but that I should finish school. "You only majored in poly sci to be close to the interesting men on campus," he said. "You're too talented in music. Why not change your major?"

I was rusty, having ignored my piano for four years, and not confident enough to try for a scholarship to Stanford. I applied to San Jose State instead and sometimes sang, "Do You Know the Way to San Jose?" when I drove south to classes in our "new" '57 Chevy.

That day, I'd been practicing a Haydn sonata, lots of catching up to do. The walls of the cottage were thin, not well insulated, and the air was chilly as it usually was, even though we'd bought a secondhand, stand-alone heater. In the mirror's reflection, I could see our kitchen. I could also see the empty space behind the front door where I hoped David would appear any time now. But I didn't want to keep thinking about him.

Most of the time, when David came home at night, tired and frayed, he laid his books on his desk, then spent an hour trying to relax. When we found snippets of time to talk and honor our commitment to share feelings and tell each other the truth, he told me he was cracking, that there was a psychological warfare going on inside him. He told me he was tired of being a doer and an achiever to compensate for some lack in himself. After all, in the space of four years, he'd been a missionary, a vice president of student relations, a founder of the Cougar Club for athletic boosters, a straight A student at the same time he was a guard for the varsity basketball team, and now he was a law student who'd just turned down a position on the law review because the pressure to perform was so great.

He also admitted—though it wasn't easy to tell me, his young Mormon bride—that he was troubled by Mormonism, tired of the conflict of trying to please his mother, and, as a consequence, displeasing his father, who wasn't a faithful member. David, beloved of God, was in pain. He wanted out of something. He wanted to breathe easier.

We still attended church at the Stanford Ward, though he often begged off, much to my dismay and hurt. Mormonism had always been like my shoes and socks, my hat and my gloves, the warp and weft of my being— basically the essence of who I'd become. Though I may not have earned my dedication and/or testimony through a deep study of scripture and doctrine, I had never considered any other way of life, even if I had my rebellious moments. How could I possibly separate from something woven so tightly into my being, the threads inseparable? How could David even think he could pull these threads apart?

But I busied myself. I taught piano lessons in Palo Alto and Menlo Park, including to the family of Gene England—a cofounder of *Dialogue: A Journal of Mormon Thought,* a future epicenter of intellectual Mormon scholarship. David attended meetings with Gene and Wes Johnson—discussing how they could best promote the journal—but he thought they were fighting a losing battle. To him there seemed to be little place for dialogue and discussion in the mainstream Mormon culture, maybe because he was fighting his own battle when it came to expressing the divergent feelings exploding inside him. He spent hours at the makeshift desk we'd put together with cinder blocks and an old door, brooding for hours and reading book after book about how to escape this tension.

Two nights before, we'd sat together in our old-fashioned bathtub with sloping sides at both ends. That was our personal conversation parlor embellished with the bright pink polka-dot curtains I'd sewn to cover the window.

"You tell me you want to understand me," he said, soaping up a washcloth, "but if you don't understand this about me, you can't understand me at all."

"I'll do my best." I leaned onto the long sloping back of the tub while he leaned against the rim to the side of the faucets at the other end.

"I've got this tension in my body that won't quit, no matter what I do."

I didn't understand the male psyche, I knew that much. Or testosterone. Or penises that reacted of their own free will. I retrieved a fresh-out-of-the-water washcloth and laid it over my breasts.

"I was humiliated when I was about to go into the temple for the first time—just before leaving on my mission. One of the Church authorities gave a stem-winding speech on sexual purity the night before, saying if any of the missionaries had ever had sexual intercourse or were masturbating, he'd have trouble as a missionary unless he repented and sought forgiveness for his sins. You can imagine I laid awake all night thinking about that one."

I nodded my head, trying to stay with him through this story that seemed to be forever haunting him. He didn't remember he'd told parts of it before.

"I'd been interviewed by my bishop and stake president, both of whom asked me if I'd masturbated. How could I disappoint my mother by telling them I had? But in the mission home in Salt Lake, after I heard that speech, I knew I had to say something. I hadn't set out to do something bad. Masturbation started innocently in the bathtub when I was twelve, though I did feel guilty about it when older friends made jokes."

"You never knew you were in deep water," I attempted my own joke. Even though I'd never thought much about masturbation and knew next to nothing about my own genitalia at the time, in truth, it didn't seem like such a big deal to me. But it was a big deal to David.

"I thought they'd probably send me home and prevent me from being a missionary," he said without skipping a beat, re-wetting the washcloth and running the bar of soap over his forearm, "where I'd have to face my mother and her friends besides being disgraced in front of other missionaries.

"The morning after that speech, when all the missionaries stood in line to go into the Temple, I asked if I could talk to someone. I had to wait at the side of the line while all the other missionaries filed past me, all of them probably knowing I'd done something wrong or else why would I be standing out of line? I was taken into a room where I waited alone for over a half hour, until a general authority finally came in. 'What's the problem?' he asked me curtly, obviously sandwiching me in between a thousand other things. I summoned my courage and prepared for the fact that the world might swallow me up. 'I've had a problem with masturbation,' I told him. He didn't look at me or into my eyes. It was like he didn't have time for this kind of problem. 'Don't ever do it again,' he said abruptly, then left the room without another word or the slightest hint of compassion. I was devastated. I felt like wringing his neck."

The water cooled as he spoke. I was tempted to ask for fresh hot water, but David's words were tumbling out too fast. I could see he was in pain, but I didn't think a general authority would be that inhumane. They were men called by God to their positions. I thought that maybe David was being extra-sensitive because these men were supposed to understand Christ and his compassion. Maybe he was too harsh in his interpretation of the incident.

"I made it through Hong Kong and most of the Northwestern States Mission where I was transferred. I almost made it to the very end by shutting my body down like a clenched fist and reining myself in. But one day when I was riding horses with a group of missionaries . . ." His voice faded. "What could I have done with that one?"

"Horses do bounce," I said in a half-whisper, a half-baked attempt to show my sensitivity.

"It made me feel like I'd broken my promise. After that, I was assigned a companion who wouldn't do any missionary work. I finally gave way one day and let myself fantasize about a girl I'd just met. I tried to stop, but before I knew it . . ." He paused for the second time, then looked up at the white paper Japanese lantern that covered our overhead light, not able to look at me.

"I felt like a total failure." He made cups of his hands and splashed water on his face. "I was depressed for weeks. Ashamed. Worthless. It was like I locked up any kind of spontaneity I ever had. There was no way I could advance in the leadership of my mission anymore." His voice was building in volume, sounding almost hostile. "From that point on, I couldn't allow myself to feel sexual feelings of any kind."

He reached around for the tap, turned it on to piping hot, and let it pour into the cooling water. My bare shoulders suddenly felt exposed.

"It's getting cold in here," I said, crossing my arms over my breasts and grabbing my upper arms. "Time to get out."

"But one thing you should know, Phyllis. This tension is driving me crazy. My sexual feelings keep trying to emerge, but I unconsciously keep shutting them down. This is interfering with our sex life."

"David," I said, getting impatient with the cold and the words I didn't want to comprehend. "It's hard for me to imagine what you're talking about. I don't have the same bodily equipment you do or the same kind of experience with Church authorities, but maybe you should pray about it." I tried to couch my thoughts in the spiritual terms of the earnest believer I thought I was, not knowing what else to say. Our sex life was something I'd accepted for what it was, something I didn't know enough about to know it was troubled.

He pulled on small sections of hair on his chest. "I'm tired of people thinking they can control other people's genitals. Mormonism's too tight and bureaucratized these days, nothing compared to Joseph Smith who started it all. Most members don't understand what he was all about. Wash my back before you get out, will you please?"

It hurt my ears to hear his talk about people's genitalia being controlled and about the problems with Mormonism. "You don't need to make things so complex," I said, scrubbing his back in large circles, dunking the washcloth, rinsing off the soap. "You can't figure it out all by yourself, anyway, can you? You need to trust more and not be so ready to take offense."

"When I hear you talk, it's like my mother has her hands around my neck. I did everything she wanted."

"But I'm not your mother. I'm me." I rested my hands on the rim of the tub in preparation for lifting out of the water. I was a person who liked to fix things, but this was beyond my scope.

"That's what you think." He laughed and patted me on the head as he stood up in the tub, water dripping from his thighs. "Remember *The Manchurian Candidate,* the brainwashing?" He laughed again. We both laughed, but I was only covering my hurt. How could he talk about brainwashing like that? He just didn't understand what the Gospel was all about or he wouldn't be talking, or even suffering, like this.

"Thanks a lot," I said, as we dripped onto the bath mat and patted ourselves dry with thick white wedding gift towels.

Still at the piano, I found myself sight-reading the Poulenc without being aware of the notes. My fingers felt stiff today. I couldn't keep my mind on the piece. I could only think about how David still wasn't home, my  David who graduated magna cum laude from BYU, first in a class of four thousand, a prestigious Hinckley Scholar. He was the bright hope (for different reasons) of his devoted Mormon mother and his anti-Mormon high school teacher father. David being an excellent student and star basketball player in high school, his father wanted his last son to go to Cal/Berkeley, but his mother prevailed: BYU the Mormon-owned school, salvation for her son. He'd played ball for two years— first-string freshman and first-string varsity basketball—before being called on a mission. In those days, the coach didn't allow players to return to the team if they chose to leave. The catch-22 was Please Mother and God, OR, Please the Coach. It didn't hurt that he wasn't happy with his coach's approach to the game.

His mission assignment was Hong Kong, and because there were no language-training schools at the time, he struggled with Cantonese as well as the prospect of teaching Mormonism when he wasn't sure of it himself. He gave it all he had, but then he was assigned a new companion—the same Daniel who took David off to the coast yesterday and the same one who had no problem ignoring mission rules when they stood in adventure's path. One night, at Daniel's instigation, they put a two-pillow decoy under their separate bedcovers and escaped to the gambling dens of Macao in the Xi delta west of Hong Kong. Against all mathematical odds, however, they ran into Daniel's aunt from Vernal, Utah, playing the wheel of fortune in one of the casinos. "What a surprise seeing *you* here," she said.

Auntie reported the infraction, even though no one questioned why she was gambling in Macao. Soon after that accidental meeting, David and Daniel were transferred to separate missions. Elder Gordon B. Hinckley, who'd been sent by the Church to straighten out the Hong Kong Mission (because, according to David, the mission president had lost control of his elders), accompanied David on his flight to Oregon to serve his remaining time in the Northwestern States Mission. Whether he did that to make sure David made it to Portland without a hitch or whether Elder Hinckley (later to become President Hinckley) needed to stop there before returning to Salt Lake City, David never knew. He was too distressed—starting all over again in the Northwest, with Daniel doing the same in Texas. But their friendship remained intact. David accepted Stanford's scholarship offer, partly because Daniel would be there attending law school.

Ah yes, Daniel. Yesterday, they drove off on an adventure to Big Sur to check out Esalen, where I heard there were clothing-optional, mixed-gender hot tubs, and people and philosophers espousing free love. They were also visiting an LSD-inspired visionary painter and hippie who let goats wander through his house. Daniel was a moon-faced, dreamy-eyed eccentric who lived on a page I hadn't yet come to, but, on the other hand, he'd been a bright light for David, a friend who'd understood his struggles when no one else, especially me and David's mother, had been able to do so. I felt left out—disbarred from some secret fraternity—but understood that people needed their own friends.

I took a break from the piano and wandered out the front door to gaze at the water tower, the bright yellow fields of mustard, and the massive branches on the oak trees. I wondered if David would be coming home tonight. A dark pink camellia bloomed on the front porch of our cottage, a small, plank porch four inches above the ground and four feet square. The plant was a gift from Daniel, who'd been dropped from the law school after his first year. He was bright enough, but much more interested in the vast world outside the classroom. He stayed on another year to study philosophy, but never attended classes in that department either. He was constantly in rapture over the beauty everywhere: Carmel, Stinson Beach, Point Reyes. Yesterday, he phoned David and said he needed to celebrate nature. Wouldn't David come along and drive down Highway 1 to visit Etienne Pelletier, who, according to Daniel, was the most sublime of artists, no matter how he was inspired?

I wished I hadn't suspected Daniel of moving into my emotional territory and hoping David might change his affections. Open-minded, after all was said and done, I still worried when he and David drove off for the day and said they didn't know when they'd be back. There were so many adjustments to be made. So many new things to decipher.

My mind spun with everything I was supposed to tolerate in this bigger, more sophisticated world of Stanford and the Bay Area, this mosaic of mind-blowing ideas. And so I returned to the piano and practiced and practiced to celebrate my life in my own way. I wanted to rise above my humble beginnings and be somebody. I had natural talent. I had energy. And I was hungry for stars. But maybe I'd made a fundamental mistake and hitched my wagon to the wrong star, who should have been home by now.

:: Bidden or Not ::

God, Goddess, Yahweh, Jesus Christ, Allah, Krishna, the Sun, the Moon,
the Virgin of Guadalupe. And God's messengers: Joseph Smith, Buddha, the
Pope, Mohammed, Confucius, Lao-Tse, St. Francis and his birds, Mother
Teresa, Mary Baker Eddy, the Mystics . . . Somebody. Something. Help me.

Bidden or not, God, by whatever name, was on the heels of each of my footsteps, even if I didn't look behind me to take notice. I believed in the Divine, whatever it is, whoever it was. I knew I did. But all I could do the first two months in that Denver attic in 2002 was to wake in the middle of the night crying, surprised my bed hadn't floated away or that the seams of the house hadn't dissolved. In the dark of night, I slid off the bed onto my knees and prayed for help. Sometimes I begged. I didn't know if I was praying to God, Goddess, Nature, the Mountains, the Ocean, the Sky, Imagination, Angels, my Loved Ones who'd passed, or what. Maybe God was a noun for all deity, people, and things, and maybe no one needed to know or could ever know the real name. I didn't know who had the right answers about God. But maybe there was no choice to be made. Maybe life was the only true church, the only true religion.

That summer in Denver was a repeat of the six-week crying jag I had when David's and my marriage was coming apart, and also of the three months after Spinner and I broke up and he left our home in Minnesota. I couldn't deal with breakups. Now there was a third. Why couldn't I let go as everyone told me to do? Why did I cling to everything I'd thought belonged to me in love and relationships? Was it the middle child syndrome (me being the middle of five) where everything got taken away by either the oldest or the youngest? Where was the braided metal cord I could use to pull my spine straight and fix my head on right? *Damn these tears. Damn them.*

Last April, a month before Bill and I split, we both knew our marriage was in trouble. A chasm had been widening between us—maybe because we'd both been down the road and back too many times, maybe because we'd married too soon before we knew each other well enough and hadn't taken the time to sort out our substantial differences, maybe because neither of us was in any shape to say "I do" in the first place. In a last-ditch effort to see if we could make things work, we planned a trip to South Carolina. But the tears were starting to fall again, even in the airplane and at the hotel. The sadness was creeping back, slowly inching up on me.

I told him that the two things I most wanted to do on our trip were to find (1) a good blues club in Charleston and (2) a small, out-of-the-way African-American church where I could find some descendants of the Gullah people, the ones who made sweetgrass baskets and had dreams about catching the moon with a fish net. I had a passion for gospel music and for the spirit of people who worshiped in small churches: Second Baptist churches, charismatic Christian, wherever I could find simple worship. I wanted to experience worship totally different from what I'd known. I suspected the Africans were my true spiritual fathers and mothers.

We'd been driving around Port Royal on a Sunday morning for about fifteen minutes, looking for a church to fit my specifications, when Bill spotted a tiny white clapboard building. He braked. A dark blue van was parked in front of a simply constructed church that needed a paint job. A man sat in the driver's seat behind a steering wheel. Another man sat on the passenger side. And there were others in the shadows of the back seat behind the window glass.

"Is this what you're looking for?" Bill asked, the motor of our rented car idling.

"Sure," I said hesitantly.

"You don't sound too sure."

"No. This looks good." I swallowed, the swallow sounding in my ears.

"If you'd like me to, I'll talk to the people in that van and see what's going on."

"That would be nice."

What's with this obsession, I wondered as he walked to the van and the driver leaned out the window and they exchanged words.

In my passenger-side mirror, I caught sight of a bent, dark gray woman walking toward the church, leaning on her cane that stabbed the dust with each step. She looked like Mother Time getting an eight-month start on the new year. She made her way slowly to the steps of the church with its bare-spotted siding.

Bill smiled as he slid back under the steering wheel. "You're in luck. He says you're welcome to join them when the service starts in fifteen minutes." He put the transmission in drive. "We'll drive around before it starts. Okay with you?"

"What do you mean?" I said suddenly, the impact of his words sinking in. "*I'm* welcome to join them? I thought you'd agreed to do this with me."

"I've been thinking about it. You have respect for this kind of thing and at least you're a Christian. I'd only be an observer. Some kind of sociologist. That's not fair to these people."

"But . . ."

"Think about it."

As I considered his words, I decided he was right. Even though I'd have liked his company, I didn't mind being alone. Not really. I'd been haunting African-American churches since I stopped going to the Mormon church, starting back in Salt Lake City at Calvary Baptist with my son, Chris.

This morning, the inside of that church seemed smaller than the outside. Two slightly dusty windows allowed a share of morning light. A congregation of eighteen people, including five children, sat in sparsely populated rows. I sat by an older woman with a green pillbox hat and greeted her with a handshake—the way Mormons greet each other in church. "I'm happy to be with you today," I said. Her hand shrank back from mine. She didn't seem eager for more conversation.

A young boy sat across the aisle staring at me—this tall, long-nosed, long-boned, olive-white woman with graying hair. I smiled at him. He smiled back, then ducked his head. I got the impression I was a strange creature sitting on the pew of his Sunday experience.

I hoped a choir would appear soon, dressed in their long robes, swaying from side to side as they rocked down the aisle, but nothing seemed likely to appear from behind the speaker's stand. This appeared to be a one-room church with maybe a small cloakroom attached at the side.

Just then, the minister appeared from a side door in his dark blue robes, the man who'd been in the driver's seat of the dark blue van, a man whose skin reminded me of the backdrop of the starry heavens, planets, and moon. As I sat in a small sea of dark blue, the sun shone through the four-paned windows and slant rays rested on the backs of the mostly empty pews.

"Welcome," he said, shyly at first, glancing my way. I sensed I was an unusual intrusion on the regular doings of his Sunday mornings. "And we welcome our visitor. Let's all of us make her feel part of our worship today."

All heads turned in my direction. There were small recognitions and unspoken greetings, some distrust and definite curiosity.

"We're low in numbers today, which means we won't have a choir, sorry to say. Next week, Easter vacation being over, we'll be back in full swing. Mama will now pray over us." He stood back and folded his arms. The same aging woman I'd seen working her way toward the church outside rose slowly, her hand resting on the back of the pew, her eyes closed, and her head bent back to beseech the heavens. The room was absolutely quiet. The April sun warmed the panes of glass, and thus the room. I saw a spot of sunlight across the knees of myself and the woman next to me. I saw a piece of reflected sunlight on Mama's eyeglasses. Prisms of light.

"I thank you for the lying down at night," she began, ever so slowly in a soft, low moan of a voice. Her hands were clasped in front of her. I could see the long muscles extended at the sides of her neck, the tired ones that had been with her for a long time. Her voice sounded like the sea that carried her ancestors here on those slave ships. It had a slow, mournful sound of a language I didn't know, a language with its own music, possibly something from West Africa, possibly a deep melody from the Ancient

Mother, the old whisper of wisdom rising up from the earth, saying, "Here I am, my children. Been through hard times. I'm weary. But, children of my loins, I'm standing solid." The mournful yet grateful sound worked its way through the layers of my skin, through my ears and mind. She was a lullaby I could listen to all day. The Mother caressed each of us with her voice. As we listened, we were carried beyond time.

"I thank you for the rising up in the morning," she continued. The word "rising" sounded like a word stretched into flight. I felt myself rising with the upward thrust of her voice before it fell again, slow, steady, more like the mellow waves that feathered a shallow beach.

Tears slipped through my closed eyes as she said, "I thank you for the blood that runs through my veins and gives me life." She sounded as if she were a preacher herself, each word of her prayer an invocation and a blessing at the same time. I'd never thought to be grateful for the blood that ran through my veins, or for the rising up and the lying down—those too-simple things for which I never thought to be thankful. Her powerful gratitude was woven into every syllable of every spoken word, even every space between the words.

My hand was all I had for a handkerchief. I couldn't hear the rest of what she said, her voice being so soft like the way we used to sing "Swing low, sweet chariot" when I was a child. The hauntingly beautiful words touched me even without the full hearing.

Slaves. We are all slaves. Slaves to our fears, hurts, anger, jealousy, greed, and envy. Except those people were no metaphor. They were the embodiment. Their fathers and mothers had worn the visible chains. They had felt the scorn of words and hearts much darker than their skin. And here they were, giving thanks while I was crying—a child among those who had suffered greatly and who knew the inside-out of crying until their tears had calcified.

At the end of the sermon, the minister called the congregation to gather in a circle. He told us to hold each others' hands. I stood next to Mama and felt the delicate bones of her hand, a hand that had done much, that had been witness to much. Delicate, yet firm. Strong. Resolute. Unafraid. This was the hand of a redeemer, a healer, one who had seen it all and could still forgive, one who could open her arms and receive the least of her sisters. I felt her power through my fingertips. I felt electricity coursing through my hands and arms to the woman on my right. A circle. An unbroken circle.

"God bless this sister who visits with us today," the minister said. "Bless her to know that God lives, that Jesus will comfort her."

When I shook hands with the minister, I couldn't hide the river on my face or pretend it was dry. "Thank you for your sermon," I told him, trying to collect my tears with my fingers. "And thank you for allowing me to be with you today."

I walked out onto the small porch. Bill waited by the car. My face was a mess.

"I knew you'd be crying," he said, patting my shoulder, trying to be a friend, yet not sure how to be. "These things really get to you, don't they?"

"Thanks for finding this place," I told him. "It was perfect. Just what I'd hoped for, if I could just stop crying."

But I was in Denver now on another Sunday morning. I'd promised myself I'd get up, get dressed, and join my friends, Gil and Laney, at the Heritage Christian Church, which had a sign out front, "Sinners Welcome Here." It had the best gospel music in Denver, or so I'd been told. And I'd probably cry during the services.

::

After C. J. fixed two flat tires within five minutes of each other and after we packed up the cookstove and extra clothes we'd brought and sent them off from the tiny eight-by-eight post office in Paoli, Colorado, we followed Highway 6 through Holyoke and over the state line into Nebraska.

The first billboard at the edge of the road made a significant announcement: "Nebraska . . . The Good Life." The skies over Colorado had been gloomy and overcast and drizzly, but crossing the border felt as though we were penetrating a curtain some member of the Junior Chamber of Commerce had hung from the sky to the earth to hide the real truth of Nebraska. Thick herds of black-elephant clouds suddenly filled the sky. The temperature plummeted. Thunder rumbled ominously and created big questions about Nebraska's "good life."

"Ditch your bike at the first sight of lightning," C. J. yelled back at me. "This looks bad."

The raindrops slapped hard, then progressively harder, against our helmets and the pavement. Then the storm amped its rpms until heavy-duty raindrops feeling like tiny fists of hail punched our helmets and our shoulders and arms.

"One one thousand, two one thousand, three one thousand, four one thousand," C. J. counted loudly so I could hear, measuring the time between thunder and the lightning strike. In a matter of seconds, serious rain sheeted out of the sky, and we were both pedaling furiously. While I pushed hard to catch up to her, she jumped off her bike and ran to a small building just off the road and rattled its door and checked its windows covered with nailed boards and graffiti. But the door was padlocked, the windows impossible. Running back to the insta-river that Highway 6 had become, she shouted, "Follow me." I pedaled wildly after her single track wake, the sky opening up and all the cold water of the world falling on top of us and Nebraska.

"We've got to find shelter," she shouted. "Ride as fast as you can."

No time to think, I suddenly felt Christopher's presence with me, dressed in his blue plastic coat, squeezing my shoulders with affection, saying "Tear up the highways, Mother."

As C. J. and I head-butted the storm, our wheels cutting through at least three inches of water, suddenly, out of nowhere it seemed, a man in an ankle-length, hooded slicker appeared like a genie at the edge of the road, motioning with propeller arms, shouting at us. Directing us, the only oncoming traffic, he gestured toward a split-pea-colored garage we could barely see in the torrential downpour. We raced under the sign that read "Lamar Fertilizer Company" and into an industrial garage where a violent smell greeted us. The rain on the metal roof sounded like top-volume bad static on an old TV as we parked our bikes and the man pushed a red button to shut the door. Our shoes squished. Our hands shook as we unbuckled our helmets and hung them over the handlebars.

Struggling with our sopped jackets, we saw for the first time bags of fertilizer and chemicals stacked high against the wall. A spray truck idled noiselessly against one of the walls, the sound of its engine drowned out by the rain.

"You better get out of this garage," the man said, walking up three wooden stairs and opening the well-insulated door into a well-lighted office. "The trucks that come in here leave chemicals everywhere. My name's Pete Dillan, by the way," he said, holding the door for us. "The guy over there in the red hat passed you two on the road. Said to watch out for you. That's my wife and bookkeeper over there, Paulette."

"There's coffee and hot chocolate in the other room," Paulette said, calm in the middle of the storm. "You might as well be here as out there in that storm." A group of nervous farmers in seed caps and rain slickers stood gawking at green blobs on the TV weather map glowing like a fluorescent jungle.

"That storm's everywhere," the red-cheeked farmer in the red hat said. "All of southwest Nebraska. I couldn't believe my eyes when I saw you two out on the highway. What are you doing out here during tornado season anyway?"

"Thanks for watching out for us," C. J. said, pulling a cloth cap out of her pocket and snugging it over her wet helmet hair. "We're biking across America."

"Really?" Paulette said, pausing from her numbers, her pen poised in the air. "This storm's not going to let up anytime soon out there. If you two have sleeping bags, you're welcome to roll them out in the back office where no one tromps around with their boots covered with everything. Help yourself to anything you need. Just know the guys'll be back at about 4:30 in the morning."

After the farmers clomped in with their infamous boots the next morning to check out the green blobs on TV that had thinned somewhat since yesterday afternoon, we washed our faces, brushed our teeth, and made

ourselves hot chocolate and coffee from Lamar Fertilizer Company's stash for "the guys." We rode off in the light of weak sunshine, the clouds on hold for a few hours.

Imperial. Wauneta. Hamlet. Into Hayes and Hitchcock County where we made a pit stop at a crossroads. While C. J. made adjustments to her bike computer, I spread-eagled in a damp patch of grass to watch the leafing branches of the cottonwood trees overhead and their swirling specks of cotton. I felt happy to be next to Mother, to feel her pulse somewhere inside this huge earth. But then, Spinner showed up in my thoughts.

I'd promised myself I wouldn't call him for at least two weeks. I'd made sure my worldly possessions were safe by locking off the basement and asking a young woman to live in the upstairs and take care of my dog, Ivan. But I could feel him pawning something, that ESP thing we had with each other, taking something out of the basement and loading it onto his truck. Had I left something in the basement? Even though my mind and spirit were supposed to be free out here on the Great Plains, I could still see his face—his dark hair, the circles under his eyes, his deeply tanned skin. I could feel the "please take care of me" look in his eyes burning into my brain.

Out of nowhere, an official white Dodge with two lawmen braked next to C. J., who was bent over her bicycle with an assortment of Allen wrenches in hand. "Hey, you girls," the sheriff shouted as he climbed out of the cruiser, all two hundred plus pounds of him, and lit a small, thin cigar. I sat up. Stood up. Dusted off my bike pants.

"We're here to handle a funeral procession," he said, his arms folded across his barrel chest, his cigar suspended between two fingers. "Gotta get at least a hundred cars across the highway. My name's Hoss, by the way. You girls need any help?"

"Nice to meet you," C. J. said, holding her hand out for a handshake. "We're from Colorado. We're biking across America. Is there anywhere to camp in Palisade that's safe from rain?"

"Whatever you need. There's a bandstand in the city park that's covered. But be careful. Tonight's graduation at the high school, so watch out for kids with pranks on their minds. They could be celebrating all night."

A hearse boiled up out of the horizon, followed by a long line of cars and trucks about to intersect the highway.

"Gotta go," he said. "Safe travels."

After an hour of pedaling and after Hoss, his partner, and the Dodge whizzed by us at 100 mph as if to demonstrate their sovereignty, we reached Palisade, population 375. We stopped to talk to Hoss, now sitting in his idling car at the local gas station and shooting the breeze with some local boys, who, when we paused, asked us what we did in real life. After we followed directions to the park, I carried my bike inside the bandstand, locked the wheels, dove on top of my sleeping bag, pulled off my long bike pants to get more comfortable, closed my sandbag eyes, and became one with my down-filled bag.

"Wow," C. J. said, peering down at me from above. "Did you know your thigh looks like a massive green and purple grapefruit? What have you been doing to yourself?"

"It's something old." I hadn't told her about my fall when I hadn't been able to clip out on the second day. I didn't tell her about the sharp pains I felt at night. "Not to worry."

After a ride into town for a quick dinner, we zipped ourselves into our sleeping bags by 8:30. Rain padded like soft animal feet on the park's grass. It dripped from the gazebo's eaves. The sound lulled us toward sleep until sometime in the middle of the night when we heard a car rolling down the dirt road that wound through the park, tires crackling on gravel, brakes squeaking to a stop, our hearts triple flipping. Hoss had warned us about all-nighters. He'd said to be watchful. Dragging our sleeping bags across

the wood floor like snails in a shell, we huddled next to the gazebo walls listening to the idling car, waiting for the sound of a door opening, for some feet to swing out of the car, and walk to where we were crouched, holding our breaths.

After a painful minute of both of us holding stiller than still, the car finally rolled away, slowly, but not before I found a knot in the wood slat through which I saw the unlit bar of lights across the top and a government-issue license plate lit by taillights.

Hoss and his cruiser. Hoss, the Protector, a Guardian Angel of the Great Plains, keeping watch. It seemed as if God had hitched a ride on the back of our bicycles.

::

Reasons for celebration:

The first, David graduated from law school in June of 1967 (though, unbeknownst to me, he'd learned there were exceptions to every rule, including "Thou shalt not kill," and was beginning to suspect that sexual morality could be likened to rules of law). He accepted a job with the First National City Bank of New York and requested their South American or Hong Kong division. The previous summer, he'd interned with Millbank, Tweed, Hadley, and McCoy, a Manhattan law firm, and had received a permanent offer from them, but we opted for something we thought more adventurous. We made plans to leave for New York for his training with the bank as soon as our expected baby was old enough to travel.

The second cause célèbre was that I'd finished my final course in counterpoint, earned a BA degree in music, and realized I'd grown considerably as a keyboard performer.

Last but not least, the third and best reason for celebration was the birth of our first child in mid-July.

As planned, my mother arrived the day after the baby's birth—July 22. And yet, on the morning of July 24, all of us were at home except the baby. Mother busied herself in the kitchen, soaking cracked wheat to provide a substantial breakfast to help us through the day. David studied for the imminent bar exam under bedcovers. I played Poulenc at my mother's request to hear what I'd been learning in music school. All of us were waiting for 9:00 a.m., when we'd drive to the hospital and see if our newborn baby,

Geoffrey, could come home. The night before, the doctors had advised us to please go home and get some sleep.

At Stanford Hospital, Geoffrey rested inside an incubator, half of his straight, black, full head of hair shaved clean and an IV attached to a bump in his skull. I'd been nursing him after his circumcision when a huge red spot spread before my adoring eyes. Beneath the baby. The white sheets and cotton bedspread. Red spreading slowly, a sickening scarlet plume. I frantically pressed the nurse's call button and then frantically handed the baby to the nurse, who ran out the door. Then a string of doctors came in with questions, including the exasperated doctor who'd performed the circumcision. They'd checked for vitamin K deficiency. They were waiting for the results. Any hemophilia in our families? No. We'd never heard of it on either side. They shook their heads. Their expressions were grave.

Today, Geoffrey could probably come home, because our pediatrician said he needed his mother. We still didn't know why he didn't stop bleeding when he should have, the doctors still at a loss for a diagnosis. I played Poulenc even more wistfully under the light of the piano lamp so early in the morning, ate breakfast with David and my mother, and then we drove to Geoffrey's side to wait for the doctors to release him and for the nurses to put him in our arms again.

He was bundled tightly in a receiving blanket as we turned toward our cottage in Los Altos Hills. However, when I changed his diapers for the first time, the blood drained from my face because I saw his blood. Again. Spreading. My mother panicked for a brief second, then recovered her composure. She'd probably been swept away by déjà vu, thinking of the son who'd died in her arms on the way to the hospital that day so long ago. But she hid her fear where it couldn't be seen. She took charge. She told me to lie down.

Geoffrey bled off and on for two weeks. The scab that formed briefly kept being chafed away by the wet cotton diaper. Finally one night, Mother, David, Daniel, and I devised a plan. We'd keep vigil. We'd hold his diaper away from his body to allow the blood to form its crust. In teams of two, we took two-hour watches, rotating our services with catnaps. All through the night we caught whatever urine streamed from his tiny penis. By morning, we were exhausted, but the bleeding had stopped. The wound had healed sufficiently. When we told her the news, our pediatrician seemed surprised at our primitive methods. But we were proud of our ingenuity. We thought we'd won a major battle—that is until six weeks after his birth when the doctor informed us that Geoffrey, indeed, had hemophilia. Definitely hemophilia. Classic factor VIII deficiency.

Suddenly, our plans exploded. Instead of leaving for New York to join the First National City Bank, David scrambled to find work with a law firm in the Bay Area. We needed to stay near the best doctors possible. David was hired by Petty, Andrews, Olson, and Tufts in San Francisco, and we stayed on in the gardener's cottage, too stunned to do anything else. I walked Geoffrey up and down Old Trace Road in his buggy, cooing to him about the blue sky and the oak trees, sometimes taking joy in this beautiful baby, sometimes crying. If I were the carrier, as they said I must be, why couldn't anyone find a trace of any such thing in my bloodline? What had I done wrong to earn this punishment, to bring this affliction down on my son's head?

David, however, didn't see this as punishment.

One night, as I slept next to him, he woke me. "This room's too warm." He threw off the covers. "Does it seem warm to you?"

"Yes," I said sleepily, throwing off my covers as well. The cottage wasn't well insulated. The room was usually cold except in high summer.

"Before you woke up, the room was filled with light," he said, excitement in his voice. "The Spirit came to me, and believe me, this is the first time I've personally experienced a spiritual force in the universe. I feel this deep peace. I feel totally transformed."

Unable to comprehend this sudden revelation in my groggy state, I listened for sounds of the baby stirring in the next room and fought the urge to ask David to whisper. I'd already been up once. I didn't always know what to do with his words and his intense engagement with the life of his mind.

"I felt like God was telling me He loved me, that He forgave me, that I was on the right track. He said to do what I had to do, but to do it in a loving way. I've never felt peace like this before, Phyllis. And, I feel Geoffrey has come here for a brief time to give me this message."

"A brief time?" I snapped to attention.

"Well, maybe not that exactly. But I get it that he doesn't need to stay here long. He's already perfected. He was born with hemophilia to keep us from going abroad. I need to take care of my parents."

"That's amazing," I said, not knowing what else to say and feeling a bit hollow not to have come up with a better response. *Our baby. A brief time?*

"I was also told the Mormon church isn't the only source of contact with Spirit. God has given me a blessing, don't you see? I won't be condemned for what I've done. And I feel peaceful. Maybe for the first time ever."

"Oh," I said, pulling the sheet back over my shoulder to cover it from the torrent of words I wasn't sure I understood. Why did David have to have this continual battle with the Mormon church? Why couldn't he understand it was established as a vehicle to help people get to God and that the Church itself understood it had been formed as a temporal organization? He didn't need to carry on this battle indefinitely. "They" weren't out to get him. But to hear David say he felt peaceful was something rare. I wanted him to feel peaceful. And yet, I believed he could find even more peace if he'd give himself over to God's understanding on a daily basis.

His euphoria lasted for six weeks before old patterns of stress resurfaced. Even so, he seemed more confident that his beliefs were taking him in the right direction to rebuild what felt to him like a shattered self.

::

I pounded the octaves of Hungarian Rhapsody no. 6 on the bulwark of our piano, my battleship, my long fingers like an octopus over the eight-key intervals. Geoffrey was asleep in the back room, surrounded by mobiles and educational toys. He would, he would, he would be a very smart baby to compensate for his blood. My fingers cramped, not sufficiently warmed up, but there was something powerful about thundering over the keys in loud octaves heading for the climax of this showboat piece. My hands could create powerful magic, cramps or no cramps.

But Geoffrey's only ten months old, and I'm three months pregnant. "Three months," the gynecologist said this morning. David and I don't know how to deal with the baby we already have. And we never thought I'd get pregnant like this. I've been nursing, for heaven's sake. Isn't that supposed to be a protection? If it's a boy, will he have hemophilia? A girl could be a carrier? How will we ever manage?

It was as though I'd committed a crime when I'd come home that morning and opened the door to David's study to blurt the news. His blanched white face reflected my trembling insides. We were scared. I was scared.

I stopped pounding octaves and got up to check on Geoffrey, who was still asleep, beautiful in his womblike scrunch beneath his blue flannel blanket. *How could we have gotten pregnant again? How could we have been so careless?*

Then the phone rang. Mrs. Fowle on the other end, probably talking on the red phone in her bedroom. "I heard your music over here in the big house. It's wonderful." She'd never said much about my playing before. "In two weeks there's a $100 per plate dinner for my brother, a fund-raiser for his senate race. "Would you please, please play that piece for us?"

"Yes, of course," I said, too flattered to tell her I was scared of everything right then and that the public was the last place I wanted to be. But the keys on the piano. I could control them. I could do this.

For the next two weeks, while Geoffrey slept and the new baby slept inside me, I practiced and practiced to do a good job for Senator Cranston, Mrs. Fowle, and the state's prestigious Democrats. I imagined myself in front of those people dressed in black tie, glorying in the octaves that would curl their toes. I practiced for hours, determined, that is, until the day of the dinner.

That morning I felt peculiarly nauseous, and suddenly while I practiced, my stomach cramped violently. Then blood trickled onto the piano bench and spread to the size of a saucer. David at work in San Francisco, I called out the window to Tony, the gardener who was feeding roses in the formal garden. "Can you drive me to the hospital, please, oh please?" He ran for the big house to bring Maitland, the Fowle's full-time maid, to the cottage to watch Geoffrey.

"You won't miss the performance tonight, will you?" Mrs. Fowle said when I phoned her from the hospital that afternoon.

"The doctor said I'm miscarrying. That I need to lie still and wait for it to happen. I'm sorry, I really am. About everything."

"I'm sorry, too, dear. Good luck."

They left me in a darkened room for a day and a night. But this baby was determined to stay. It wanted its life. I waited for it to slip away, and yet something in me held on as tightly as I could. The baby stayed steady in my steady body with the unsteady mind that wasn't sure what to do with a second baby so soon, so soon. Thank God, he stayed steady.

The next day, David drove me and the unborn baby back home, both of us still intact. When I sat at the piano again, I didn't want to play the Hungarian Rhapsody anymore. Debussy this time: images, impressions, "The Engulfed Cathedral," Mont-Saint-Michel barricaded by the sea at high tide. No octaves for a while. Rather the early morning fog on the north coast of France, mist opening and closing, hiding unchartable fields of quicksand until the tide rolled out.

:: Homeward to Zion ::

With a new baby on the way, we couldn't stay in the gardener's cottage any longer. We drove away with our belongings. We left behind the estate on Old Trace Road, with its tall oak trees and rows of eucalyptus that dropped silver leaves and brown seed pods everywhere, the quaint rose garden surrounded by a picket fence and crisscrossed with brick paths, the secretarial duties in the big house where Mrs. Fowle conducted phone conversations on her red phone.

Peculiarly enough, our new Los Altos home on Parma Way, about two miles from the cottage, had been owned by the daughter of Reed Smoot, the senator from Utah who'd been the subject of a bitter four-year battle in the U.S. Senate. The Smoot hearings, begun in 1904, centered on whether or not he was eligible to be seated in Congress. He'd been called to be a Mormon apostle, *and,* the outraged said, Mormons were *all* polygamists. Even though the LDS church had discontinued the practice of plural marriage in 1890, after Utah was threatened with refusal of statehood if it didn't, congressmen still suspected that Smoot, never a polygamist, was nonetheless involved. If Smoot wasn't personally involved, they insisted, he was still an integral player in the hierarchy of the LDSchurch, some of whom were rumored to be keeping their plural wives hidden from public view. Complicity. No doubt. Some even claimed that temple-attending members had taken an "oath of vengeance" against America for past grievances. Eventually, Smoot was given his seat in Congress and remained in the Senate until 1933.

David and I were both descended from this polygamous bucket of worms. It was part of our heritage, even a notion skirting the edges of our modern-day sensibility. We'd heard the stories of great-great-grandfathers—our own and others—with three or more wives. We were acquainted with the vast scope of Joseph Smith's efforts to restore the pure religion, and, like it or not, Abraham and other Old Testament notables had more than one wife.

If asked what I thought, I would have said that polygamy had some strong attributes as well as problems: women had more time to pursue their professions, their independence, and self-reliance; child care was shared; single women and widows could be included in a family where they might not be otherwise; and ideally, everyone could work together to build the Kingdom of God here on earth. When I thought about it in any depth, the concept seemed at least more responsible than serial mono-gamy, affairs, mistresses, or a ménage à trois (though the literal meaning of that phrase is "a household for three").

Not a simple matter of lusting after young women in their first bloom, as many of its current-day critics were insisting it had to be, polygamy, in its early incarnation among the Mormons, was supposed to be a matter of everyone involved wearing bigger shoes and filling them well. Yet living idyllic lives of loveliness without envy or jealousy proved to be a next-to-impossible challenge. The tendency to compare who received more or less attention was too insidious. When practiced in pioneer days, polygamy, for the most part, worked better in theory. Even though undertaken with eternal significance in mind, it had been a less-than-desirable situation for many of the wives: the first wife having to share what she thought was her given right, the second or third (or more) wives only allowed into the fam-ily with the first wife's permission. This led to a complicated pecking order. And, when a woman's salvation depended on marriage to a righteous hus-band, as Church leaders preached at the time, there weren't many avail-able: "Many are called but few are chosen"—the scriptures echoed the sentiment. If a man was considered righteous, did this mean he knew how to treat his wives equally as the ideal suggested? Because of these complex factors, divorce in Utah in the late 1800s was easy to come by and the numbers were astonishingly high.

When we still attended the Stanford Ward, while we were students and I'd helped my Relief Society sisters sew items for the Christmas Bazaar, we'd discussed what it would be like to live the practice if it were sanctioned by law. All of us rolled our eyes at the thought. While we stuffed cotton socks with brown heels to make sock monkeys, we talked about whether or not we could be comfortable if our husbands loved someone else as much or more than he loved us, whether we were strong enough to be able to love each other as sister wives and learn to live in harmony. Could we rise to the idealistic place in ourselves where community was more important than the individual, we asked each other, much like religious philosophers discussing how many angels could fit on the head of a pin?

Maybe polygamy was a higher form of love, a higher law, we concluded as we sewed buttons for eyes on the loose-limbed monkeys, but none of us were interested in sharing our husbands. We would have been poor candidates for the practice. We laughed when one of us pricked her finger with her needle—an apt metaphor. We concluded that the business of marriage and raising a family was a tough enough challenge without running any kind of interference.

In our new home, Senator Smoot's daughter, Chloe Cardon, had left behind a beautifully carved mahogany cabinet when she and her husband moved into a nursing home. As I filled the well-made shelves with our wedding crystal and china, which had been packed away in boxes, I wondered if this antique had been passed down from Reed Smoot or even from her grandfather, Abraham Smoot, who'd been a mayor of Salt Lake City. Maybe it had been pushed against a wall in the senator's home in Washington DC. Maybe his wife had taken her best bone china from those shelves to serve him sympathy dinners while he battled with Congress. But other than this infrequent musing, polygamy was a subject that didn't interest me except as quaint history that could possibly be restored in the hereafter. To my way of thinking, anybody who practiced it in our day and age was a fringe oddball going against everything the Church preached.

After bed rest for two months in our new home, I gave birth to our second son on November 14, 1968: Christopher Jon, a bundle of smiles, and a sweet-natured child, forgetting that David and I were both wary about how we'd deal with two children after being introduced to parenthood with a hemophiliac child. Because of some problem with his tiny veins, we waited nervously for three months to find out whether or not Christopher had the disease. Meantime, two babies proved more work than I'd ever imagined, especially when one of them bled on a whim and needed to be watched with hawk eyes. On many mornings, I wanted to stay asleep and mumble to someone else to take over while I rolled over and buried my nose in my pillow.

It wasn't just the work that had doubled. It had more to do with being responsible for something happening to Geoffrey. Secretly, I begged in my prayers for this nightmare to pass, for the blood to right itself, cooperate and do what it was supposed to do. Christ had healed the woman with an "issue of blood," after all. But no miracles dropped into our laps. In fact, the answers I received seemed to be God telling me that I couldn't run; I needed to face the facts; I needed to learn how to deal with adversity.

One morning, after tests had finally pronounced him free from hemophilia, Chris was taking his morning nap. I sat cross-legged on an overstuffed sofa watching Geoffrey explore bookcases and cupboard doors. Every unanticipated move he made changed the rhythm of my breathing. His blood was unpredictable, even arbitrary about the times it would and would not clot. Sometimes his disease seemed as if it had gone on vacation. Sometimes Geoffrey could escape it, but there was no telling when that might be.

Keeping an eye on him, I daydreamed about last night in David's arms when he stroked my back and caressed me and I felt full to the point of bursting, full of the exquisite loveliness of love. Maybe, with the magic powers of my mind, I could build a cushion of air around our son so he'd never have to bump into anything. No falls. No crashes. Maybe the loveliness of love and an absolutely still mind could stop everything else.

Geoffrey was reaching up higher and higher toward something he'd been told not to touch, things out of his normal reach, things that could fall on his head. I held my breath. I could stop time if I stayed still enough. Me, playing the part of Master of the Universe, sitting on the sofa controlling a time bomb about to explode.

He reached up for our eighteen-inch television set and pulled a corner of it toward the edge of the cabinet. I said "No" and lifted my arms that could stretch across the room to save him because I was the Master who could freeze things. I was also Rubber Band Woman whose elastic fingers could reach as far as I needed them to without the rest of me moving. Nothing could happen if I sat still enough to make time stop.

Get up, get up now. Don't sit here. Run. Save the baby.

No. I can't move because if I do, the playing field will change. I need to stay still.

Get up. Now. Save your son.

The TV tilted and stayed at a freeze-frame angle. The television wasn't falling. It was tilting as if it might fall, but it wouldn't because I'd frozen time. And yet Geoffrey's hands pulled at the thing he wanted to have, pulled insistently. I could see how his desire was greater than my powers to stay things. The television tilted further and tipped.

I ran for the fly ball. I caught the television set like the best of left fielders. I intercepted, but then Geoffrey was crying, the television having grazed his head as it crashed onto the floor by his side, a crazy angle, a crack in the screen. He was still standing. I held him and rocked him and comforted him with the power of my magical arms.

"Mustn't do that," I scolded. "Mustn't. Mustn't. Mustn't," and all the time I was scared out of my mind that a big bruise would swell on the side of his head as it had before. A big puffy blue bruise that took days to unpuff. My power to stop all things bad or dangerous, however, had protected him and made the television glance off the air around him. He was safe. He wasn't crying anymore. His head wasn't swelling anywhere that I could see.

Good boy, Geoffrey. You and me, boy.

::

My touchstone with God, my connection to my church that had nurtured me since birth, seemed to be shifting from rock to sand, not unlike everything else. As David begged off more and more meetings, I felt like a scrappy fighter at the local gym trying to get into the inner circle of the ward body. Twenty-five years old with aspirations, I wanted to serve God, yet couldn't do it alone.

To this still newly married woman, in the Los Altos Ward, there sometimes seemed to be a golden ring, a place where concentrated light shone down on the golden people—the members called by those in authority (prompted by God's wisdom) to serve in the lay ministry. A call to a high position seemed as if it were the Victory, especially when I was in my twenties. After all, being married to a righteous man with his heart set on building the Kingdom of God on earth was not only a mark of distinction, but essential if your family wanted to take the necessary steps toward the Celestial Kingdom, the highest realm of heavenly glory where you and your family would live in eternal harmony. That meant following a path of good works, service to others, compassion, nonjudgment, and obedience to the laws of God mediated through a modern-day prophet.

David's restlessness seemed an obstacle, however. I wanted my family to be in the inner circle, yet slowly I felt that while I'd once been inside a Mormon glass globe, the kind where snow fell over happy figurines when you shook it up and let it settle, I was moving toward the outside looking in. Because of David's need to make his own tracks, I found myself unsure of my once sure place. He was my husband, all said and done. I'd chosen to be with him. *You've made your bed, now lie in it. That's what mother would have said.*

We stayed in the Los Altos house with the tall summertime dahlias and a white picket fence for two years. David, stimulated by the bustling, savvy, sophisticated San Francisco, started looking for ways to make deals. Having come from a family with a high school teacher father and very few assets, and being the father of a hemophiliac child, he saw the acquisition of money as absolute necessity. Determined to change the status quo, he worked long hours and looked at every venture capital deal he could find. Meanwhile, he was always stressed.

As much as two beginners in the school of love could, I loved David and he loved me. We were too young and too new at the game to really understand what love was all about, but we had the large canvas of life in front of us. We believed in bold strokes and bright colors. We were cavalier. Energetic. We could keep the vows we'd made to each other.

We were supposedly grown-ups now: a young family firmly grounded in a conviction in all things Mormon, or so I liked to think. Despite his discomfort in Sunday meetings where he heard rules, shoulds, and oughts being prescribed, David's hero was still Joseph Smith.

"His mind," David insisted in one of our 4:00 a.m. discussions during a period when he was reading obscure literature from early church days, "is a fascinating labyrinth. His vision of men becoming gods—'As man is, God once was'—and his introduction of polygamy as a means to achieve godhood might have had more to it than he himself understood. He was martyred at thirty-eight, after all. And remember that famous statement of his: 'No man knows my history.' Who knows what might have happened had he lived longer. There might have been a church one and a church two."

When David was asked to teach the teenagers in Sunday school in the Los Altos Ward, what other modus operandi would a frisky and newly graduated Stanford lawyer have than departing from the requisite lesson manual and teaching his emerging worldview: sensitivity training, how to communicate with each other, how to be alive outside clichés, and how to make decisions for themselves out of their own circumstances and needs? His approach caused a stir, but the teenagers and some of their parents thought he was a godsend.

"My daughter just loves your husband's class," one woman told me. "She hasn't wanted to come out to church, but his class has made a huge difference. It's so refreshing for her to ask difficult questions and not be dismissed." Other parents wondered: "My daughter enjoys your husband's class. What do they do in there anyway?" Others bided their time and kept their questions to themselves.

Believing that God had a plan for each of us and that our salvation hung in the balance according to our good works, I was a hundred percent active church member called to serve in the Primary Presidency for the children of the ward. While I was still trying to navigate church waters and hold onto my pair of oars because of my strong sense of God's interaction with our live-the-Mormon-way lives, David was seeking out a more varied circle of friends, putting together a couples' sensitivity group composed of people from the Stanford psychology department, some living-off-the-land hippies, and one couple from our ward whose marriage was in trouble. Even though I hesitated, I'd give that game a try. But I felt nervous in that increasingly foreign country. It wasn't how things were supposed to happen. A prescribed way back to God had been given. We were veering off the path.

Truth be told, underlying battle lines were being drawn. If I believed that the life after this one was the goal and found myself longing for a better home where God lived, didn't that create a disconnectedness with my body and my flesh, with the people in my home? Didn't it create an inability to live in the present moment?

Gradually, it seemed, David and I were eroding, the stone of ourselves being worn away by pounding waves of contradiction. As hard as I tried to pretend that everything was on schedule according to the plan outlined by LDS doctrine, to the plan I firmly believed would bring us the greatest happiness, I felt the ground giving way.

When the partners in David's law firm found out he'd been meeting with other young associates to talk about starting another firm, they called him in and asked for a long-term commitment. David couldn't give one. He left the firm, and, after a year as legal counsel for a small computer company in Palo Alto, a friend asked him to consult with him on how to take over an insurance company in Utah. After the board of directors bought the plan, his friend, now the new president of Surety Life Insurance Company, asked David to come with him to Salt Lake. This meant he'd be leaving the practice of law. Not knowing if he could come back to the profession, he felt tentative and unsure about the offer.

In the end, we moved to a place to which we said we'd never move. "The Utah Mormons don't understand Mormonism," was something we said from time to time and something we believed. Utah had its own brand of cultural Mormonism. A parochial brand, we said with our worldly Bay Area arrogance as we drove our children and our belongings back to Zion. And thus, the shoes got tighter on David, and therefore on me. My job was to keep my family together however I could.

::

Southwest Nebraska: Culbertson. McCook. Indianola. Bartley. Cambridge.

The headwinds blew strong in the open prairies with nothing to slow them down. Rain fell off and on. Temperatures in the high thirties were dropping. We hunched over our handlebars, our heads into the wind. We pedaled steadily, only looking up for signs of a prairie lighthouse—a grain elevator co-op with tubular ladders, and catwalks on the sides, and long arms of metal pipe suspended midair.

Riding strong, I'd found my second wind, so when a truck with a country song blaring out the window slowed next to us and the driver asked if we wanted a lift and C. J. said, "Yes," I was shocked.

"No thanks," I told the driver, overruling C. J.'s answer, this departure from our plan. I pushed my bike pedals forward willfully, leading the charge for a change.

"Why did you do that?" she said, following reluctantly.

"I thought you wanted to stay on the bicycles."

"I did, but I'm having a lousy day. It's bitter cold, and I can't get warm. This wind's the worst."

"I thought you were kidding," I said, though the truck had disappeared.

By the time we stopped in McCook for lunch, my surge had evaporated, rain had returned, and we both had frozen toes, frozen fingers, icicle noses. We shivered uncontrollably. Our waitress, Alison, came to the rescue. "If you don't mind me saying so," she said after we told her our plight, "you both look like you could use a little help. I'm off in ten minutes. How about if I take you as far as Indianola? My Buick's got a trunk as big as a barn." This time, with the trees outside the rain-specked windows, bowing and scraping to the wind, there was no debate.

The comfort of a big Buick. A toasty heater. Indianola coming too soon.

Back on the bikes in the wind and rain. Bartley. Holbrook. Arapahoe. Holdredge, where we rented a room at the Plains Motel from Mr. Metric, who quizzed us about metric distances to Toronto, San Francisco, to the north, east, and south edges of Nebraska before giving us our key.

C. J. took a hot bath to defrost. I made a phone call to check on my rock 'n' roll sons back in the Colorado mountains. I caught Jeremy at "home." I could picture him in the makeshift kitchen built in the defunct office of the former gravel operation. Maybe he was watching the sun set on the sparkling man-made lake outside the window, the deep lake where gravel had been excavated for many years. "Hey, Mom. How's it going?"

"Don't ask, and I won't tell. Mother Nature's doing a number. How's the band?"

"We found a new drummer since Brad moved to Phoenix. We're rocking Summit County tomorrow night over in Breckenridge. And, by the way," he said excitedly, "we have a gig in Vail this weekend. We'll be warming the room for Jorma Kaukonen, you know, the guitar player for Hot Tuna? Jefferson Airplane, too? We'll be at Jackalope's in Vail." His voice infused me with new energy—my son, my blood and bone, my baby, still and forever.

"Wish I could hop on a Jefferson airplane and be there to hear you. That's great!"

"Gotta go, Mom. I love you."

"Glad I caught you."

"Me too, you."

I put the phone back in its cradle, enjoying the afterglow until I got that ESP feeling that Spinner, the Magnet, wanted me to call. As I hung my only pair of long riding pants, thoroughly soaked and dripping, on a jerry-rigged clothesline across the tiled entryway, I felt his will tugging at me. I wrote in my journal, put clean underwear next to my bed, reorganized my panniers, and did everything I could to avoid punching numbers into the phone. But then I picked it up and dialed, glad C. J. was behind the door in a world of steam and out of hearing range.

"Why haven't you called?" he blurted without saying hello. "I'm going crazy here."

"I said I wouldn't be calling often." I spoke softly, covering the side of my mouth as if I were a teenager and C. J. were my mother who shouldn't hear. "It's hard to find telephones when you're camping out and sleeping gratis at fertilizer companies. We actually slept in a fertilizer company last night. How's that for big-time news? How's painting, by the way?"

"I lost a job this morning. The guy gave me the wrong fucking address, and by the time I got there, he was pissed and told me he'd found somebody else." I knew what this translated to: I've been out on a coke binge for two days and couldn't get out of bed on time for work.

"So, do you have anything else lined up?" I commanded suspicion out of my voice.

"You know I can always find a job. That's one of the two things I'm good at: painting and finding work."

"I can think of something else." I couldn't help but smile, thinking of Spinner's long, strong back and how good that back looked sans clothes.

"Sure," he sounded agitated. "A lot of good that does with you gone for two months. How can you just take off like this and leave me here by myself?"

"It's something I had to do. You know that."

"This is hurting our relationship."

"What relationship? You always tell me you need to take care of yourself and find someone your own age. You know we're dragging a lame horse here."

Silence on his end of the line.

"Sorry, I've gotta go. Take care of yourself. And," I added, wishing I could close the book instead of opening it for another chapter, "I still love you."

I heard him taking a draw on his cigarette, the pull, the drawn-out exhalation. "I love you, too," he said. "Call sooner next time. I hope you're doing okay. Are you?"

"As good as can be. Good luck finding another job, pal. Bye."

Click. I held my hand over my heart racing with passion, worry, and frustration. I bit my lip and gathered my wits. Ah, yes, pay attention to your 120-percent-saturated bike shoes.

The next morning everything was still wet. Rain all night. Rain falling now. We asked Mr. Metric if we could use his dryer before venturing out into the misty, moisty, windswept plains again. We needed dry socks at least.

Thirty-five degrees. On the road again.

Funk. A stop for photos in Funk, of all places. Axtell. Minden. Biking had become a sentence a vindictive Greek god might mete out; our bikes were machines on which we were condemned to pedal for the rest of time, water falling on our heads as if we were stones at the bottom of a waterfall. Shoes filled with water. Soaked riding pants. Rain gear. Water dripping off the bill of the hood of my Red Riding Hood raincoat.

Frequent billboards advertised the Pioneer Museum in Minden: antique cars, turn-of-the-century gadgets. We decided to stop and do something besides turn the wheels on our bicycles. But after standing in the museum's entrance, realizing we weren't in the mood to gander at obscure paraphernalia, we decided Pizza Hut might be a better idea.

As soon as we slid into the booth, my meltdown began—one of those crybaby, I-don't-care-about-my-pride-anymore moments. "I can't do this," I said from behind the sunglasses I still wore. "It was stupid of me to take this on. You were right when you said I didn't think about it hard enough. You were right."

"I'm not unaware of your feelings," C. J. said, her eyes flat and tired but not uncaring, as the waitress set the pizza in the middle of the table.

"I know this trip means a lot to you, but I don't have the same investment in it you do. I'm not this kind of strong."

"What kind of strong are you?" she asked simply, taking a big breath, exhaling.

"Maybe I used to be strong. But maybe I'm kidding myself about that, too."

"I can't carry you. I can barely carry myself."

"I'm not asking you to carry me, honest I'm not."

"Then what are you asking?" she said, stirring her Diet Coke with the straw.

"Maybe I just need to stop pushing myself. I'm falling to pieces."

"When all's said and done, you're the only one who can deal with those pieces. I'm the only one who can deal with mine."

"Sometimes I hate being an adult."

She finished the last bite of her pizza, wiped the corners of her mouth with her napkin, and motioned to the waitress for our bill. "Right now, I'm worried. Don't think I don't care about what you're saying, but we've got to make the next thirty miles to Hastings before dark. We've got to give it our all, no dawdling, or we won't make it before sundown."

It would have been easier to hitch a lift for those next thirty miles. Half an hour. A short distance in a car. But we unlocked our bikes knowing we needed to ride hard. And I needed to stay on my bike, no excuses. By the time we passed the sign that said "Hastings," the last daylight remained only in a deep purple swath across the sky. The rain had stopped.

After dismounting, C. J. held her sunglasses at a jaunty angle. "I knew we could do it," she said, putting her hand on my shoulder. "That you could do it. By the way, that's the best I've seen you ride."

"Thanks," I said, catching hold of her elbow. "You weren't so bad yourself."

We pitched our tent in the grass next to a pasture's fence, behind the shield of two defunct and rusted vans.

:: The Unpredictable Body ::

A snapping turtle. A snake's tongue. Something that acts with speed and withdraws in a flash. Stinging, biting. A whip that strikes hard and fast, just like the leather belt unbuckled and yanked out of the loops on my father's slacks on the very few occasions that he was exceedingly angry. As soon as it hit the mark, it was gone. But my flesh remembered.

What else was fast like that—something that snapped hard and snapped right back? Lightning struck fast and stunned whatever it hit. The back of the hand, too. Wrist action, I've heard it called. The fingers making a quick getaway. An insult, sometimes leaving a red mark or a stinging sensation if the surface was flesh. And a stinger was another fast thing—the way some insects pierced and poisoned and made a quick getaway, leaving a person smarting with a big red welt in no time at all.

My father's hand also knew the fast getaway. His wrist was something like a rubber band—tension in the stretch pulled back and back and snapping hard when released—though the back-of-the-hand wrist action didn't hurt as much as if it had been a rubber band. My father's hand had its own peculiar schedule: when the temperature got high, when harsh light refracted off his eyeglasses, and redness flushed his face, his reptilian brain took charge and his wrist snapped. A snapping turtle. High heat, tantrums, tempers brought the hand out of the turtle shell. His hand. Then my hand.

THE AGE OF REPTILES

Irritability. Irritated. Iridescen Irreverent. Iridology. Erie Canal. Iroquois. But I couldn't play word games. I needed to face this. Maybe agitated was mostly what I was. Agitated with feeling all alone. No friends. A workaholic husband who left at 6:45 in the morning and returned home exhausted, drawn, worn out at 6:45 p.m. No connections. No ties to anything yet. New in Salt Lake City. Missing California, the Bay Area, and Los Altos.

The morning sunlight was backward in that house. Full sun in the afternoon, but dark in the morning as if there were a cold shadow over the roof when I needed the glowing generous sun so I could sing "Good morning, merry sunshine, why did you wake so soon? You woke up all the little birds and scared away the moon." I'd always been a sunshine girl according to my parents. A sunshine girl.

Spilled milk on the floor. Soggy cereal. Disintegrating Cheerios turning to mush under my slippers as I reached for a dishcloth and knew I shouldn't because I should keep the dishcloth sanitary. For dishes only. But I was tired. All my cells weren't awake yet. I smeared a big round circle of milk on the floor with the loosely woven cloth. I wouldn't cry over spilled milk.

The phone rang. My mother. "How are things going, dear?" but I couldn't hear her because the baby was whimpering and Geoffrey was tugging at Christopher's favorite Gumby toy. Geoffrey wanted it right then. I smelled urine in both their diapers. I couldn't have a decent conversation with my mother. "Things are too crazy today. Geoffrey's nose is running and he coughed all night and . . . Geoffrey . . . stop it. That's Chrissy's toy. Go get your own."

Two little boys were startled by the sound of my yelling voice, and my mother said I'd better go take care of things though I still wanted to talk, to laugh with her and play sunshine with my mother who loved her Sunshine Girl. And Geoffrey was tipping Christopher's cereal bowl with a long wooden spoon, lifting it up at the edge—and tipping it—a lever against a bowl of cereal and there went more Cheerios onto the floor. O O O, I wanted to say, making a joke, but as I stretched the phone cord tighter, I shouted, "Oh, oh, you bad boy, stop it," and felt my arm raising and lowering and the wrist snapping, the back of my fingers snapping like a rubber band against Geoffrey's forehead. One snap of the fingers against his head. But then my head began to swim as if I had snapped my own forehead. I looked at my hand and wondered if my arm had really gone up and back down at all and made my hand do what it had done. The moment streaked and blurred and I couldn't put two and two together and wondered if I were trying to burn myself at the stake again. After all, I, bad person that I was today, caused all the grief in the world.

"Good-bye, Mom," I said, slamming down the phone, and I felt like opening all the doors of this cage and letting the babies outside to be wild in the Great Outdoors, and I'd be wild with them and scream and tear off my clothes and fall into the grass that was still cold in the mornings in May in Salt Lake City and I'd beat on the earth and tell Mother Nature it was a bad idea to make babies who taunted and mothers who were irritable, irritated, not well enough irrigated yet at this time of the morning. I couldn't do this. I couldn't. I couldn't. How could my fingers snap at Geoffrey? He was too fragile. He could break. He could bleed.

And suddenly, I was sitting cross-legged on the floor, who cared if there were Cheerios on the butt of my purple bathrobe, and I took Geoffrey into my arms and held him so close against the lapels of my robe and my breasts and squeezed him and said, "Baby mine" and "Honey doll," and he looked up at me with wet eyelashes and accusation like "Bad Mama."

I wanted to make him smile. "Hey, Pie," I said. "Punkin Pie," and his eyes changed from dark to partly cloudy skies and a little smile softened the pout on his lips.

"Why do you pick on the baby, Geoffrey? He needs to eat his cereal. Not a good idea."

I squeezed Punkin again and brushed hair from his big blue eyes and kissed his cheek, and, even as I think back on that kiss, I wonder if my arm lifted up and back down and if my fingers really did snap, as if they were a belt or a turtle and make contact with Geoffrey, a quick encounter with his head.

::

The next morning was quiet. David had gone off to work. It was early. Around eight.

I considered pulling myself out of the covers, but I snuggled deeper under the blankets. It was May in Salt Lake City, and although the house should have been warm by this time of year, it wasn't. Winter clung to the walls, not ready to leave until summer baked it out, maybe. I heard no stirring from the babies—an unusual thing, this absence of sound, no noise from Chris in his crib and Geoffrey in his bed. No signs of their waking, but then again, I'd been up in the night with Geoffrey, giving him cough syrup the doctor prescribed yesterday for a congested cough. Everyone was sleeping late.

The house sat in the shadow of Mount Olympus, which kept the morning sun away from this pocket of the valley. The walls had felt like ice cave walls since we moved to this temporary house—a stopgap measure until we could find our own home. March. April. May. Three months in the Arctic in the Cottonwoods. Despite the chill in the house, the stream in our backyard usually managed to find a way to run, ice or no ice, but even that seemed subdued this morning.

The amount of morning light straining through the drawn curtains told me it was way past time for everyone to be awake. But this quiet morning was such a luxury. I hugged my pillow to my cheek and tucked the blankets around my shoulder, even though it was time to rise. I needed to pull back the covers, find those warm slippers for my feet, and a robe for my shoulders and legs instead of waiting for the sun to warm the white bricks and walls of this chilly house.

I'd peek in on the babies as soon as I emptied my bladder, but then I rinsed my mouth with water, even brushed my teeth with what was left in the nearly spent tube of toothpaste: white paste, a small spurt, enough to clean my mouth and teeth. Then I let the water run to warm, soaked the washcloth, lifted the soap to my nose to sniff before turning it over and over inside the wet cloth. I ran a hairbrush through my hair. Tied it back with a clip. The babies. Check on the babies. I found my red-framed eyeglasses. I'd put in my contacts later.

The door to Chris's room. I opened it slightly to see that he was barely awake, barely stirring. A few more minutes of quiet. One of those rare mornings. The door to Geoffrey's room was slightly ajar as I'd left it last night when I'd given him his dose of cough syrup. Maybe his cough was so bad because of the cold weather still trapped in the walls of this house, no summer to warm it yet. Bad coughs. Where do children get these things, these colds? Geoffrey was so still under his covers. That cough syrup must have had a sleep component to it.

"Geoffrey," I said, padding further into the darkened room and closer to his bed, my slippers schussing the dark blue carpet. "Punkin Pie."

I sat down beside him. I touched his light brown hair and thought of how the doctors shaved a swath through his newborn head full of wild black hair to find a vein for a transfusion. So beautiful and silky. This now brown hair. My angel, so sweet in this shadowed light. Babies so sweet when they're sleeping.

I shook his shoulder. "Punkin," I said, "wake up." And then I wondered if it had been wise to give him that extra dose of syrup in the middle of the night. The directions said every six hours and I'd waited for five only. I hoped that was all right, but he'd been coughing so hard.

"Geoffy." I leaned over and whispered in his ear, and then I knew something I didn't want to know. Maybe I knew this something when I was clinging to the covers of my bed and trying to avoid this moment.

He was quiet. Unresponsive. Then suddenly I was cradling him in my arms.

"Geoffrey," I spoke loudly. I didn't know what this was in my arms, but it wasn't my baby. This was a strange limp thing, except when I put my ear close to his mouth, I thought I felt the softest of breaths against my cheek. When I held his wrist with my thumb and forefinger, I thought I felt a bead of something, a small chain of heartbeats, however soft and filmy and muted they might be.

I held my Punkin Pie as if I were the mother in the *Pietà* and ran into the kitchen and dialed a phone number. Three rings. Four. Receptionist. I asked for David, please, oh please let me speak to David. And I heard his voice, and I tried to tell him what was in my arms and that Geoffrey was the thing in my arms except it wasn't Geoffrey anymore, and he said he'd be home as fast as he could. He said he'd call the police and when I hung up the phone, I stood there with our first son in my arms, our baby we waited nine months for, our little boy, and I felt as though he and I were spinning like a slow propeller, that we were lifting off together, except I was holding him back in my arms to keep him from flying and wondering if I should change his diaper and yes, I decided I should. I smelled that heavy smell of early morning diapers, and I loved to have sweet smelling babies, that sweetness of talcum powder, a clean diaper, a clean pinkish bottom.

He was dressed in his blue woolies—the blanket sleepers with feet that had little hard-rubber bumps on the bottom so the babies wouldn't slip when they walked or ran. I laid him carefully on the floor, pulled each leg out, unpinned the blue-duck safety pins, took the sopping diaper, dropped it in the diaper pail, and powdered his wet bottom dry. I slipped his foot back inside his woolies, then held my sweet child next to my heart. I wandered through the house, not knowing where I was or where time was going and suddenly there was a siren coming down our lane, two policemen at the door, David behind them, a neighbor behind him who said she'd watch Chris for us, and the policeman took our child out of my arms and put him on the floor and gave him mouth-to-mouth resuscitation, and then they were rushing out the door, our son in a stranger's arms.

"We've got to get this baby to the hospital," they said as they ran. David and I followed the police in our maroon Pontiac with a white top. Following. Following. Fast driving. No stoplights. Following to Cottonwood Hospital. Respirators. Doctors. Nurses. Huddles. Finally a private room where we watched our Geoffrey fill up and then deflate with each pump of the respirator. A lone nurse kept constant watch over him. "This baby's in a bad way," she said.

After ten hours of sitting, watching, saying silent prayers, and staring vacuously as the nurse performed her duties at the monitors, we heard her telling us to get something to eat. "You need to have strength," she said. David went out for one hamburger. We ate half of a half of it. I went to the bathroom after we wiped our mouths with napkins and threw the leftovers into a white plastic bag lining the wastebasket. I didn't look in the mirror or check my hair when I washed my hands.

David, the nurse, and I kept watch all day and into the evening, and about seven in the evening he and I decided to make a final plea. We found an alcove outside the room where no one watched. We put our hands and heads together.

"Bless this child to live if he can have a full life," David prayed. "If not, thy will be done. But if he can live a normal life, God . . ." And we stumbled in our words, in our prayer, in our beseeching, knowing there was not a normal life for this son. "Whatever is best," David concluded.

We said this prayer outside Geoffrey's room, as if we didn't want him to hear our bargaining with God. We held each other's hand and kissed each other's cheek and held tightly to each other before we walked back into that room where our son had been inflated and deflated all day. The nurse stood over him, disconnecting tubes, coiling tubes over a hook.

"He made his own choice," she said. "You don't have to make decisions now." Then she looked at us with sorrowful eyes that said, It is finished. It is done. And when David and I reached for each other's hand, it was with a calm resignation that we commended our son unto the Father.

::

He died when I was twenty-seven and he was not quite three. Our first child. Our young son. After his death I wanted to talk about this baby I loved with all my heart and feared with all my fear and what happened to him, but that would have made most people I knew uncomfortable. Nobody wanted death coming down their street. Most people shifted their eyes when the subject slipped out. It was unsocial. Gauche. Their alarms went off when the Nice Talk Rules were broken. I wish I'd had innocent, uncomplicated sorrow to share with them. I wish we could have cried together for this death with pure, unsullied grief.

David and I stood in a hushed room of a Mormon chapel with sage green carpet. May 1970. Friends and relatives were loosely assorted around an open casket made of tucked-and-gathered blue satin while we shook hands with a flow of blurred people. I wanted to apologize for what they saw: the size of the casket, the small shape inside that said, I knew, that I'd failed as a mother who was supposed to protect her child.

"I know just how you feel," a woman with a tightly curved nose said. "I lost a son, too." She patted my hand delicately and curled her bony hands around my cold fingers. "God needs your child now. It's his time to go." Sister Hansen seemed so sure of God's ways. The wax of my friendly-face smile felt tight. "Nice of you to drop by," I said.

The line wound like the Great Wall of China as people dressed in silk and suits waited to express regret in the dim light fanning from the wall sconces. Curious people who'd taken time from their daily routine to pause and honor the dead, so many who hadn't known, who said they had no idea.

We hadn't advertised Geoffrey's hemophilia when we moved to Salt Lake City. Everyone seemed to back away at the mention of the word. The royal disease. The rare blood disease. We'd learned to be selective about whom we told. We knew that superstitious fear bred unconscious cruelty.

Even I was afraid of his unpredictable body that had come through mine—something so out of the ordinary that no one in the family had ever had it before. And on that day, in that sage-colored room, I was a *publick* example, standing before the mourners in a moss green dress with a striped top (I hadn't wanted to wear black because it was such a cliché), a woman needing comfort, but also a woman who'd played a part in passing on a thing called hemophilia. I was a link in something to which I didn't know I was linked. The carrier. I thought maybe someone had dropped a drop of mad-scientist potion into my amniotic fluid. Or maybe that I'd done something wrong before I conceived—something I hadn't owned up to, even to myself.

"God will watch over your child now." Sister Hansen was speaking to David, whose gray-crescent smudges beneath his eyes seemed darker because of his navy blue suit and tie. "It's better this way. God's plan is bigger than we can know."

Was I really standing in a reception line at my son's funeral in a Latter-day Saint ward in the Salt Lake Cottonwoods that day—my shiny black hair limp and disinterested in holding a curl; a tall, olive-skinned actress in a tragic play, shaking these hands, shifting my weight from foot to foot, and having a hard time finding a place to put my arms in between handshakes? The day and the people coming through the line seemed diffuse, separated into particles.

"Thank you, Sister Hansen. Thank you for coming today." David seemed a cipher to me in his simple acceptance of her sympathy. He wept openly as she squeezed his hand. I was feeling hostile as I heard her platitudes and felt her fingers curling around mine. He was a simpler man than I was a simple woman. He still held her hand.

The interminable line needed to move. The next mouth needed to offer condolences. In that in-between space I overheard a gathering of relatives talking to each other—the in-laws to the out-laws, depending where one fit into the hybrid family tree David and I had joined together by marriage—a group of people bunched tightly and unaware of anyone else around them.

"This didn't come from our side of the family," someone said from the cluster of all-my-relations. Battle lines were being drawn. "We've never had anything like this ever. Hemophilia is not in our bloodline."

"Well, it didn't come from our family either," another definitive voice said as the soft light of the hushed room failed to soften the words. "Never heard of it before now, except in books."

David and Phyllis, xy and xx, husband and wife, two young parents standing in a room full of people shaking their heads and the responsibility from themselves. Looking uncomfortably at the casket. We had failed genetic engineering. Mis-manufactured the blood. Marred the family myth of perfection. But why should blood have misbehaved for any family? Why had the blood turned on us and our child lying in a nest of blue-satin pleats with powdered, rouged cheeks, and a faint touch of lipstick on his lips?

Everything was turning, it seemed. Turning strange. My body had secrets it had kept from me, things such as physical changes in chromosome relations, biochemical changes in the codons that made up the genes. Mutations. Changes in the lineal order of the ordered. Accidents. Surprises. And, my emotional body was more complex than I'd imagined—pride and wounded pride, shame, anger, motherly love for the flesh issuing forth from my body, and frustration at being asked to carry this burden. All this behind the face I thought it my duty to compose.

Is this what two people got when they made love, when they had sex, when they obeyed nature's imperative? Hot to trot and what have you got? A little boy whose blood won't clot. Now we stood like two Jobs in the middle of the desert. Why us, God? Why Geoffrey?

"Be grateful you have other children," Sister Hansen said in parting. "Life does go on, so be grateful for everything it gives you, even the difficult things. Only you can lay your suffering at the feet of God."

Her words made me more tired than I already was. I wanted my own grief. And why was she so sure of herself? Why was David still holding her hand as if she were his mother, and why didn't his tears stop rolling down his face?

::

After we buried Geoffrey at Wasatch Lawn Memorial Park on a slanting hill beneath a sycamore tree, we returned home for a post-funeral dinner prepared by the Relief Society of our ward. Because none of my siblings ever missed each other's birthday, my sister Elaine led a chorus of "Happy Birthday" for me after dinner. I was touched that she remembered, but it wasn't easy listening to four lines of happy birthday. The song sounded strange. Everyone seemed far away. Off in the distance and out of reach.

For four days I couldn't get out of bed, except to care for Christopher. My dear friend Sandy Ellsworth came to the house, washed the heap of clothes in the laundry room, and labored over the ironing board for hours. The neighbors brought food, people were kind, cards came in the mail. The days passed while David and I drifted, numb and imprisoned in a vapid space that surrounded us until one night when summer crickets began to sing under the eaves of the house.

The backyard stream ran high after rain, the night breathed hot, the brick walls were not arctic anymore. We slept beneath a single sheet, rumpled and skewed between us. David reached over and shook my shoulder gently, though I was only half-awake when I felt his hand on my skin.

"Phyllis," he whispered in the room in the house with dark blue carpet and white sheers covering the windows. "Are you awake?"

"Mmm-hhh . . ." I answered, not wanting to be taken from sleep.

"I need to tell you something."

"Mmmm." I turned onto my side and snuggled into his warmth. "Okay."

"I just had this absolute sense of calm come over me again. It was like the Spirit of God reminding me again that Geoffrey came to this earth for a purpose."

I burrowed my cheek into the mat of hair on his chest, happy to have the warmth of this wiry hair, this little pillow against my face, sleepily happy for the sweet man by my side who was open to things of the Spirit.

"He came to change the course of events for us."

"Mmmm," I said, unable to comment more intricately.

"There's no need for guilt or sorrow about his death on either of our parts."

When I heard the word "guilt," I momentarily snapped out of my groggy state, not so sure David's vision related to me as well as it did to him. It was then I thought about Christopher in the next room, the baby sleeping in his crib who was caught between a rock and some hard places. His birth had been overshadowed by his hemophiliac brother's complicated life; he'd been squeezed between our incessant worry about Geoffrey and our sometimes afterthought duty to our second-born child; and then, he'd just lost the brother who had been his constant companion.

"We need to adore Christopher now," I whispered into David's neck.

He stroked my hair, curved his hand around the back of my head, caressed it gently.

"All babies need to be king or queen." I spoke in finely threaded whispers, not wanting to wake Christopher. "And this is his first chance to have our attention, undivided, unadulterated with our fear for his brother. The world must feel slippery to him, only twenty months old. It's like I can't

Family Planning

UNITED STATES 8¢

hug him enough or tell him enough how happy I am that he stayed with us, stayed in my body when everyone, including me, thought he was on his way out."

"We may never have been brave enough to try a second time," David whispered.

"Mmmm . . ." I answered, feeling sleep's tentacles wrapping around me again.

::

Las Vegas, Nevada / January 9, 1971
My dear daughter, Phyllis,

On this Saturday afternoon, I am warm and comfortable on a winter day in my New York Life office at Fourth and Bridger Streets. Contributing to my enjoyment is piped-in music, to which I often listen. While busy at my desk, I became aware that a familiar gay and lively little march tune was being played. This is a tune that I first heard while you performed as a stately and pretty Rhythmette for Las Vegas High School. And I have liked the tune since.

This music stirred me and I stood up and marched around my office for a minute or two, then I thought of you and how dear you are to me. Then, at breakfast this morning, I listened to the Beethoven music on the little music box you sent us. I listened each time with pleasure and pride as I thought of you. Tender thoughts came to mind, deep feeling in my heart, and tears came to my eyes. So, dear girl, I am impressed to tell you, while possessed of my faculties, why I love you.

Why do I love you? From the day you were born, May 11, 1943, you have brought me happiness and some good fortune. On that very day, I won a hundred dollar savings bond in a payroll check number drawing at McNeil Construction Co., where I worked in the office. Later in the day I remember going to the hospital and seeing a delightful baby girl with her lovely mother. Both of you thrilled me with the sight. Here are some reasons why I love you:

I love you because you are one of my precious daughters.

I love you because you are a good wife to David, who is a man of excellence, and a devoted mother to your children.

I love you for your gaiety, your happy smile, and zest for living.

I love you for your sense of decency and good character.

I loved your playing of the piano to entertain me and the persistence you showed in developing your fine talent.

I love you because you have love in your heart, and show kindness to the timid, the lowly, and some not-too-successful people in life.

I love you for your common sense and the way you take tough breaks.

I love you because you listened to and applied some of the fatherly counsel I gave you.

I love you because you have been a delight and a joy to me in more ways than I can tell.

With sincere love,
Herman E. Nelson, your father

:: In the Attic with St. Francis ::

After a night of turning the bedsheets into a choppy sea while playing more torture games in my head, I woke to the day of summer solstice— June 20, 2002. A clear day. A stunningly bright day. I was still an emotional prisoner in the infamous attic in Denver, but when I looked out at the tops of the trees from my third-story perch, they seemed to be singing about sunlight. Something in their greenery seemed hopeful. It was solstice, after all. The turn of the seasonal wheel seemed the perfect time to stop feeling sorry for myself.

Not having thought of it for years, I suddenly remembered how I'd once loved stamp collecting. As a young girl, I used to order postage stamps from the back of comic books. When the postman brought the envelope stuffed full of canceled stamps and I grabbed it out of my mother's hands,

 I ran to my room, retrieved my maroon-colored album, spread everything on a card table, and spent hours looking for the right square for each stamp. Licking the back of transparent hinges, I attached stamps to the pages and swooned when I found the pretty ones from France, Hungary, and Madagascar. The sight of them had made me long for those places and those stamp makers who understood such beauty.

I showered and dressed. Almost excited about something for the first time in
months, I ran down the stairs and outside
to the garage where most of my belongings were stored. Searching through several
stacks of boxes, I found the one marked
"Yearbooks and Stamp Albums." I opened
the dusty box, pulled out two even dustier albums, then carried them back
upstairs where I wiped their covers with a damp dishtowel. In the green
album, I'd begun a collection of U.S. airmails, and in the blue one a hap-
hazard collection of commemoratives with no rhyme or reason except that
I'd always loved beautifully engraved stamps. When I was a young mother,
I'd often waited in line at the post office with a child in my arms and one
or two at my side for the express purpose of buying a block of the latest
commemorative. For some unknown reason, I hadn't made much of this
pastime to my family. Not that I was secretive, but I wasn't sure they'd
appreciate my private pleasure in such small pieces of perforated paper
and glue.

Turning through the pages of the green album, I marveled at the huge
amount of history each page evoked—the nation's and my own. Something
about the airmails had always fascinated me, maybe because an airplane was
a modern Pegasus, a chance to fly up, up, and away and disappear into the
sky, ah yes, into infinity.

Before too long, I found myself opening cupboards in the attic, searching for the phone book and turning to the yellow pages to locate a stamp
shop—an endangered species. Voilà! I found one in Old Aurora on East
Colfax, not too far from where I was staying. It didn't take too long for the
shop's philatelic expert to talk me into buying one of the first three airmails
printed in 1918. The particular stamp that attracted my
attention happened to be the uninverted, much more
common, right-side-up version of a very famous stamp
known as the Inverted Jenny. It was a blue "aeroplane"
printed against a red background.

"I wish I had the money to buy the real thing," I told him.

"It only costs about $950,000, give or take a few dollars."

"Last time I heard, it was $800,000."

"Depends on who you talk to," he said, "but the price is definitely going up. It was a printer's mistake, you know." He opened a drawer and brought out a folder filled with specialized plastic pages. "You'll need some of these to keep your stamps safe from heat and time."

"That's fine with me."

"You know, only one hundred out of some two million were printed upside down. If the misprint had been caught, it would have been considered "printer's waste" and tossed into the circular file. But it was accidentally sold over the counter by a postal clerk who'd probably never seen a Curtis JN-4 biplane or even an airplane, let alone had any knowledge of right-side up or down. It became collector's gold immediately. When the guy who bought the first ones saw what he had, he went back to the post office and bought a whole sheet."

Mistake = Gold. See, I said to myself as I wrote out a check for more than I should have been spending. *Learn from your mistakes, people always said. If only I could emerge from the Pacific Ocean of mistakes, misturns, missteps, mistrials . . .*

"Hope you can afford the Inverted Jenny someday," he said as I gathered my purchases, purse, and car keys. "I hope you can, too," I said. He laughed. "When you're ready, the other two 1918s will be waiting for you."

"Sure." I smiled. I'd foolishly spent over a hundred dollars for the one I'd just bought. I wouldn't be back anytime soon.

Back at home, I arranged my new airmail next to the old ones: the six and sixteen cent. Then I flipped through my collection, past the likenesses of Orville and Wilbur Wright and the words: "6 cents Air Mail, United States Postage, First Free Controlled and Sustained Powered Flight by

Man." There were Wrights in my family tree, and the brother in the foreground looked as if we could be related, something about his nose and the set of his eyes. "They're not the right Wrights," my brother, Steve, who loved genealogy as much as I loved stamps, told

me when I'd asked. One of his hobbies was to discover the famous people in our family line—Harriet Beecher Stowe, Elbert Hubbard, William Howard Taft, Richard Warren on the *Mayflower* (though he wasn't sure about him), even Anne Boleyn—and lay claim to the more impressive, go-getter ancestors. This did pump up our outlook on the family tree, I admit.

But why, I wondered after the green album lay closed on my desk, do my brother, my sister Elaine, and I spend this time with the dead and the inanimate? Maybe they were paying homage to our unredeemed ancestors, but what was to be gained from placing postage stamps on black pages with crystal clear pockets? Was this yet another escape from reality? When I pulled on the metal chain on my green desk lamp to put more light on the subject and when the bulb glared rudely yellow, I decided this was, after all, a dismal way to spend the evening, a bunk method of outwitting loneliness.

Concentrate. Persist. Back to business. You're never satisfied, are you, Phyllis? You always want more than you already have. Why do you need more to be satisfied? There's always the next corner. Maybe this is your problem with relationships, maybe with your life.

To avoid turning out the light, turning back the sheets, slipping into bed, trying to sleep and failing because those dragons of despair lay in wait with their jaws clacking, I lifted the cover of  the blue album. The book fell open to the page with the *Poste Italiane* St. Francis and the U.S. block of stamps. There he was with the birds of Bevagna flocking around him. Best friends. This stamp must have commemorated the famous speech he once gave, the one where he told all who could hear to praise their Creator, the One who'd given them feathers for clothing, wings for flying, all that was needful. Birds of the feather. One of them reminded me of my once-upon-a-time canary, Charles, who'd sung as if there were no bars on his cage. Maybe I should buy another one. A companion in the attic.

I'd always liked St. Francis. He saw the sacredness of life in swallows and crickets—his brothers and sisters. And he didn't consider this world to be evil but rather a sacred ladder for making our way back to the Creator. "The happiness that I expect," something I remembered him saying, "is so great that all pain is joyful to me." Would that I could be St. Francis who could comprehend the true glory of the Creator and know that all things are for our good. Even our sadness.

I paused to look out the window at the salmon sunset—all those little fishies swimming in schools across the western expanse of sky. And I wished I could stay still and watch the last of them swim into deep blue, then purple, then gray, then black. I wished I could stay focused until that happened—sit still at my desk, calm and peaceful, my swivel chair facing the window, both feet flat on the floor, calm, my hands on my thighs, my blue album lying open on top of my desk, a swatch of eternity outside the window for the taking. Instead I thought of the time in the seventies when David and I had gone to New York City in early October and just happened to visit the Cathedral of St. John the Divine on the day of the Blessing of the Animals, a legacy from St. Francis.

We'd sat side by side in a pew, wide-eyed, awed by the wonder of animals coming down the aisle to the music of "Missa Gaia" played by the Paul Winter Consort. The mass celebrated the whole Earth as sacred space. We witnessed a giraffe, an elephant, a horse, a cow, a zebra, a woman carrying a snake down the aisle, a young boy carrying a parrot, all of which seemed like a procession to the doors of Noah's ark, except the animals didn't come in pairs that day. Crowds of people waited on the sides of the cathedral, holding their dogs and cats in their arms and on leashes, waiting for their turn to receive the blessing.

Afterward, we scuffed through autumn leaves singing "Autumn in New York," and then we made let's-pretend-we're-socialites love at the Waldorf Astoria, David in an invisible bowler hat and me in a just as invisible fasten-it-around-your-neck bow tie. "I love you," he said as his finger traced the skin above her lips. "I love you, dahling," she said. "How lovely to be just you and me, my love." He smiled.

In those days I tried hard to be the consummate homemaker, the gracious hostess, and the dedicated community volunteer. In 1974 I'd been enlisted by the Junior League of Salt Lake City to compete in the Gorham

Sterling Table Setting Competition. I'd won a trip for two to New York and the Waldorf Astoria. I'd chosen a bird-nest motif: crystal goblets with impressions of swirled straw in their stems, centerpiece nests filled with collectors' eggs, handwoven place mats. When I didn't place in the national competition, David walked me back to our room, hand on my back, trying to soothe my creative wounds.

"Your table was too subtle for the judges," he said, rubbing my shoulders to ease tension. "They don't care if you wove the place mats yourself. They're just interested in showcasing their silverware. Don't take it so hard."

Birds. St. Francis. Charles, my departed canary. Tomorrow I'd definitely buy another one. That would be my next step forward.

I closed the album and looked out the window beneath the eaves one last time. The fish-scale clouds swimming through the pinkish orange had faded away, making me ask myself about the business of commemoration—the way people chose a proud moment and stopped time with stamps and statues. Time never stood still.

What had I commemorated out of my own life? It seemed I was addicted to memorializing the mistakes and the harsh things that could impale me. Once in a while, I'd savored the proud moments—reading stories to my boys when they were young, grinding wheat with Brad for homemade bread, organizing a neighborhood Christmas party every year, accompanying two of my boys on the piano while they played their guitar and violin, driving Brad to endless soccer games. But I'd been better at dissecting the underside of compliments or the people who seemed to avoid me after a reading of my work or a solo piano performance—those worst-case scenarios most likely manufactured by anxiety. I wondered if it were possible to "think differently," as the Dalai Lama said in those magazine advertisements.

A commemorative stamp was one picture from history, not a moving picture show. A memory was something grabbed from the river. When held in the hand, it wasn't part of the flow anymore.

:: The Precarious Edge of Life ::

I was pregnant again and, after the fact, made an appointment with my ob-gyn to ask him if it was all right to have another baby. He said because we'd had a normal child, it would be safe to try again. Then, after a few more questions, he realized I was already pregnant.

"Why did you come and ask me if it's all right?" he asked, exasperated, refraining from using the word "foolish," even "foolish Mormon who feels this bizarre pressure to have a big family," which I suspect might have been on the tip of his tongue. Salt Lake City had a great divide between Mormons and non-Mormons/Saints and Gentiles. Arrogance and disdain could be found on both sides of the fence.

I attended a church talent show one evening in March, having been asked to play a piano solo and accompany a singer of arias. As I sat on a wooden bench in the chapel, listening to a violinist play a Vivaldi sonata, the baby in utero kicked like a wild man, almost as if responding to this particular music, almost as if anxious to get out and romance the world with his own violin. When the piece was over, the kicking stopped. I wondered what might be in store for this child.

We had no tests performed pre-baby as sonography was uncommon at the time. On the 28th of May, 1971, Jeremy Scott Barber was born at the

University of Utah Hospital. Immediately screened for hemophilia while I was still in the hospital, we were informed he was free and clear. The long wait we'd had to endure for Chris's diagnosis was a thing of the past. I wanted to leap out of my hospital bed and dance on the ceiling with joy.

I'd been born in May. David and I were married in May. And, even though Geoffrey died a year earlier in May, we now had another son to bless our lives in this once again merry month of May.

I savored this black-haired, charming baby who smiled and bleated. Holding this lamb of a child felt like holding my own heart. He'd suckle for a few moments and then something else would catch his attention. It was as if he heard music or something urgent in the air, as if he were a gypsy listening for the call of the road. Thank God for a baby in my arms again, a well baby no less, my little Jeremy Scott. The world seemed to be returning to some kind of normalcy.

Christopher, though, showed signs of feeling overshadowed and excluded. The competition began. One of our hardest challenges as parents was to prove to both boys that they were on equal footing, that they both mattered more than they'd ever know, but I was oh-so-happy to hold this second-chance baby, to kiss his head and his cheeks and his thumbs, to blow on his tummy and make him laugh like ten Happy Buddhas when I changed his diapers.

::

The Uintahs in eastern Utah. A Saturday morning. David and I were hiking with Chris and Jeremy—a weekend getaway, a chance to spend time together. We both loved to be outdoors as often as possible in our busy lives and wanted our boys to love it, too.

"These new boots are killing me." David bent over to loosen the laces of his unbroken-in boots while the sun baked the path and the rocks. No rain had fallen lately. Dust covered the leaves of the bushes and the toes of our boots. The heat was closing in and wrapping around our necks. Streaked with sweat and caked dirt, I pulled bandanas out of David's daypack. We took turns wrapping them around the boys' necks kerchief style.

Three-month-old Jeremy rode on my back in a baby carrier while David helped Chris over rocks and sometimes boulders. This wouldn't be a long hike, as little legs could climb only so far. And little boys could be carried only so long before parents wore out.

Chris picked up a rock flecked with pyrite. "Sunshine," he said, massaging it as it caught sunlight and glittered.

"Fool's gold," I said. We scrambled over squared boulders and stubbed our toes on the everywhere rocks. "Lovely gold that glisters, isn't that the Old English way of saying that word?"

"What's that smell?" David said as Chris danced down the slide of a slanted slab of sandstone. I'd never smelled this smell before. It had a way of inserting itself. "Do you think it's a skunk?" Chris picked up more rocks and threw them to either side of the trail. Rocks. The best toy. Running, bending, picking up stones, little Chris shouted at the sky as if someone were up there listening.

"It doesn't smell like a skunk," David said. "Smells like six skunks and a dead weasel."

"Six skunks slunk sideways shushing Sally," I challenged.

"Six skunks slip sidewise squirting sizzling skunk sauce," he challenged back.

"Six skunks, six skunks," Chris chanted as he jumped up and down on top of a boulder bigger than he was, jumping on a one-foot square surface.

Out of habit I flinched, wanting to protect him, wanting to lay a mat of sponge on those rocks, but then I remembered he was normal, that his blood knew how to clot and even if he fell, his bruises would heal and his body would fix itself so he could run like new again. He was Superman compared to his older brother. He had nothing to fear. I felt this flow of air through my lungs, this chance to breathe free because this child wouldn't break so easily, because he could stay with us for a while and not turn into a uni-bruise or turn blue permanently. He was almost three years old, a few months shy. Geoffrey had been almost the same age.

Chris jumped off the rock and landed on two strong legs. He turned to climb up the rock again. "Six skunks," he said. His arms shot out to the side to check his balance.

"Superman," I called out as he steadied himself.

"Six skunks is harder to say than seven skunks," David said. "Six skunks slide. No, six skunks skitter sideways."

"Six skunks," Chris said, jumping up and down, a kangaroo boy. We all jumped up and down to play Follow the Leader, Monkey See Monkey Do. Baby Jeremy laughed behind me. I reached back and tickled his head of jet-black hair. It was then that I saw this thing I'd known I'd have to see sooner or later.

It wasn't discernible in the beginning. It seemed a mass of jelly, but then there was a head that told me this was, or at least had been, a goat. The head recognizable, the rest of the body had caved in. The bones were mixed up and its stomach had been hollowed out by time and weather, if not another animal.

"Ooh," we all said together, pinching our noses. David led us out and around the wreck of a goat. I took Chris by the hand and hurried him past the carnage so he wouldn't have to look at this awful thing, so he and all of us could be spared the sight. But when we hurried past the remains and climbed up and away from the smell, I said, "David, could you watch Chris for a minute, and maybe even carry Jeremy for a little bit?"

"Sure," he said, helping me lift Jeremy from my shoulders and working his own arms into the baby carrier. Then he lifted Chris and wrapped him in a great squeeze.

"I'll be right back."

"What's up?"

"I need to go back for a minute. The goat."

"Really?"

"Yes. Just a minute."

I knew I needed to look at this thing called death. I needed to stare at it. I was afraid of what it was, afraid of Geoffrey's death. As I stood over the last of this creature once known as a goat, I saw how part of it was liquid, part of it dried to dust, part of it tangled with bones that looked like sticks. I stared at its eyes staring back like glass, yet turning into something else. I didn't want to be afraid.

Everything was decomposing into another element—dust, air, water.

This crumpled heap of flesh was transubstantiating, as if this goat were a river at its source, the melting of snow. The changing of bones, blood, and flesh. The process of life and death in front of my eyes. The goat was. The goat had been. The goat was no more. But there was something else here, not entirely a disappearance as I'd once imagined death to be. There was something quite simple.

I looked up the trail where David held Chris in his arms and carried Jeremy on his back. I watched them laughing. Chris wriggled to escape, to resume his game of climbing rocks and jumping off. David lowered him to the top of a flat-topped boulder. As Chris used all fours to climb down from that, I took one last look at this goat no longer a goat and soon to be something else. I wondered about death and this exchanging of elements. It was quiet. No struggle. Extremely simple.

Simple after all the machinations to stay alive, to keep the food in the cupboards, to stave off death, to outsmart the Grim Reaper. As I took one last look, I felt a strange, rare bit of peace. How simple that this goat was gone and yet still here in new gases or substances dried and reshaped and passed onward or elsewhere.

"Six skunks," Chris shouted in a big voice in those big mountains.

"Six skunks skitter," David shouted back.

::

After resting two days in Lincoln at the home of C. J.'s ex-in-laws, the business of divorce hit me square in the eyes. No pictures of C. J. hung on the wall anymore, though she pointed out where they had been. The room in which we slept was the same room where she and her husband used to sleep when they visited. It had been rearranged, she said. When we were ready to leave, the soon-to-be ex-mother-in-law hugged C. J lovingly and yet distantly. As the bit players were leaving the stage, her soon-to-be ex-father-in-law gave C. J. a perfunctory kiss on the cheek. "The weatherman said something about severe thunderstorms and flooding along the Missouri River," he said. "Be careful." She seemed uncommonly quiet as we slipped through the soaked streets of Lincoln onto the back roads toward Prairie Home and Elmwood. Divorce. Division. Termination. Dissolution.

How could either of us come to terms with this radical severance of closely connected things?

At Plattsmouth, the sky looked like an overblown balloon ready to burst. We inquired at Brown's Family Inn, but the room rate was too high. Renting rooms hadn't been part of our plan, and we had approximately 1,650 miles to go. As we walked toward the motel's double doors to find a gazebo in yet another city park, the rain let loose and pounded the ground hard. The owner called after us to wait a minute. "I do have a new banquet room," he said, coming out from behind the counter. "You could unroll your sleeping bags in there." But after we followed him down a long hallway where he unlocked a door to a cavernous hall, the smell of carpet glue blasted out.

"Not a good idea." He reconsidered, thinking of options. "How about a room with twin beds if you pay seven dollars for the cleaning?" When he handed us a key, we thanked the man profusely for his generosity, but when we were alone, neither of us had enough energy for making small talk. In our room, we said little while we brushed our teeth, showered, refolded clothes in our panniers. Lights out, each of us trying to disregard our demons, I realized my main battle was whether or not I should keep going further into the heart of this nightmare.

After a restless night of troubled sleep, a petty argument broke out when I turned on the TV to check the weather. Should we watch the forecast, as I said, or should we just get out into the weather and deal with whatever was in the cards, as C. J. said? Realizing the argument was petty and that nothing was that important at that point, I switched off the TV, but not soon enough to avoid the tornado warnings traveling across the screen.

We pedaled through shiny wet streets, too close to morning traffic, too much splashing. We followed Highway 34 past VFW Post 2543 and Stan's Hometown Bakery, dropping down to a toll bridge, riding past graffiti on a cinderblock wall: "When You Die, You Go 2 NEBRASKA. GO BIG RED." We rolled over the steel girders spanning the swollen Missouri. A tug passed below.

The road stretched into swamplands where last year's cattails had burst, spewing their cotton. We passed another billboard: "Iowa—You Make Me Smile." But the shoulders on Highway 34 weren't paved anymore. They were hard-to-navigate gravel. Freight trucks roared by, unable to afford any margin for error. Rain, rain, and rain. And more rain.

In Red Oak, Iowa, we stopped at a bowling alley to ask if we could stay in an obscure corner of the establishment. "No, but you might try the fire station." At the fire station: "No, there's no place for women to sleep here." "Do you have any other suggestions?" we asked. "Not really." But as we turned toward the door, one of the firemen took pity. "Maybe I can make a call for you," he said. He dialed a number and asked the minister of the Red Oak Methodist Church if he had a place for us.

"I can't believe you've lasted this long," the minister said when he answered his door wearing house slippers and a dark blue velour robe over his clothes. Subtly, he gave us a quick once-over—the tall, statuesque woman with gray-streaked hair flattened ugly by a bike helmet and the age-less cheerleader with sunglasses hanging from Chums around her neck. The odd couple. Mother/daughter? Lesbians? Weirdos? Then he reached for the keys hanging from a nail by the door.

"Follow me," he said, leading us down a flagstone walk. "We've had awful weather for a couple of weeks now, and old-timers are saying it's the worst May in Iowa since 1903. You can roll your bikes inside those double doors and leave them in the foyer. Sleep wherever you need to," he said, showing us the social hall that seemed the best option. "Use the rest-rooms to wash up, and pull the door tight when you leave in the morning."

As we settled into the sanctity of this house of worship and nestled deep into our sleeping bags, sounds of high-volume wind ripped around the cor-ners of the church. Branches scratched the stained-glass windows. As the fury of the storm grew, we could hear frail tree trunks snapping, giving way to a force larger than themselves. It sounded like tortured angels, dead saints, and sinners flying through the chaotic air, nightmares wrangling with the furious wind.

::

She had a name. In my dream I heard him speak her name: "Audrey."

He kissed her, and as they kissed they invited each other to come inside each other for tea and sympathy. He sat on the edge of her bed while she stood in front of him and unbuttoned her blouse. His hands waited for the last button and for the blouse to fall open and for the bra holding her in place to come undone. He reached for her breast and touched the mother-of-pearl skin as if it were rare. She slipped her skirt past her hips. He touched her navel, the connection to all mothers. He kissed her belly and nibbled her skin. I watched this from the deck of a sailboat sailing past this scene on a sea of gentle water, the sun shining on my skin. And I made love to the sun that caressed me, its heat penetrating me as nothing else had ever penetrated me.

I awoke.

I was lying next to this same man, who was my husband. I listened to his deep-sleep breathing. The night flooded warm through the windows. I reached for the tips of his fingers. I wanted him to touch mine back, just the very tips, just a brush of skin, and tell me he loved me. There was no response. I wanted to roll him over bodily, all five feet ten of him, and exact a promise: "Always and forever." I'd hold him for ransom if he couldn't promise. I'd tie him to the bed.

Instead, I turned my head toward the window.

Is love like the weather, ultimately unpredictable, no matter how fancy the forecasting equipment? I want to tie love up in a neat package and decorate it with a pretty sky-blue ribbon. I want to tie up this man so he'll always be mine, but this man next to me is changing, not unlike the weather. He's not something that will ever be neat and tidy. That's not the way things work.

The day before this dream had been my thirtieth birthday. When he took me out to dinner and we both ordered lobster, which we rarely ordered, even on birthdays, he told me I was the woman he loved most of all. *I like to be loved most of all, don't I? Silly me. As if there is a "most of all" when we're all made of the same matter. But can't I make any or every thing work if I close my eyes and wish upon enough first stars and say enough prayers?*

Outside, a crescent moon dangled in the sky, and black branches brushed softly against our bedroom windows and against black night. Gentle wind. And I wondered about God's love. The wise ones said it was con-

stant if you trusted it. "Depend not on the arm of flesh," a scripture somewhere said. So, why did people keep looking for more love if God's love, all
the love that ever existed, surrounded them every day and every night like
the air they breathed?

*Even in his sleep, David looks hungry, like he's never been fed enough
no matter how many meals he's been served. Maybe it's his genes. His testosterone. Maybe it is beauty, pure and simple. Or maybe he doesn't love himself well enough. Is there another way besides duality—Either/Or, This/That,
Better Than/Worse Than, Loved/Unloved? Is there another way to hold love
other than possessively?*

When we both woke to a beautiful May morning and to the sound of
quails in the backyard, I scratched his chest where the hair always matted
when he slept—his favorite place to be scratched. "Funniest thing," I said.
"I had a dream about you and a woman named Audrey. You were making
love to her. It was so real I could have reached out and touched you like
I'm touching you right now."

"You and your dreams," he said, pulling me close to him, putting my
head to rest on his shoulder, pulling me long against his side.

"Do you know any Audreys?"

"Keep scratching my chest, will you?"

::

In labor once again. Number four. The epidural didn't take. It seemed, in
the swirl of fog in my mind, that the anesthesiologists were trying something else that wasn't taking either. My body was too tired to respond.

Nine months earlier, David and I'd been backpacking at Mirror Lake in
the Uintahs. Clear skies in the forecast, we didn't include rain gear. But
after three miles of hiking, the intermittent rain turned into a downpour.
We'd pitched our tent as fast as we could before we turned into pond creatures. After stripping off soggy clothes, zipping inside our sleeping bags to
stop shivering, and after a few lame attempts to write a best-selling country song—"Please release me, let me pee," "Ruby, if you take your love to
town you'll drown"—a love child was conceived while rain fell long into
the night.

During that pregnancy I knew tiredness I'd never known. Thirty-two years old and caught in the web of industry, of being necessary, of being important to people in the community and at church. Caught up in the hysteria of busyness, thinking I was important: mother of two, chairman of the Junior League Heritage Cookbook project; member of and fund-raiser for the Utah Symphony Board of Directors; composer of musicals for my church. I was busy, busy, caught up in the search for kudos and entrapped by the notion I was irreplaceable. I was the little train that could. I was exhausted.

Doctors and nurses circled in hazy loops around my bed, poking me with this, prodding me with that. A monitor jumping with green lines blipped up, but mostly down. The baby was coming, but nothing had numbed the feeling of this baby shedding his womb. As he headed for open air, I felt him pushing my soft bones apart—unplanned natural childbirth. As soon as the baby's head crowned and his body separated from mine, I lost consciousness.

When I opened my eyes, I heard disjointed words from somber voices. "Blood pressure." Mumbling. "Still dropping." I caught glimpses of serious faces half-covered with paper masks, green monitors, and hookups like octopus legs everywhere. A feather-light thought floated across my mind, but I couldn't catch it. All I could see was an unsteady mosaic: people, green scrubs, hooks holding a curtain that slid back and forth, slow movement. A joker in me suggested I ask who was ahead, "the Dodgers or the Yankees?" though the World Series was months off and the thought too wispy to connect clearly to me or my brain. I had no will. Absolutely no will to will anything. No will to be anywhere else. No will to wonder.

This was a friendly place where no voices at the back of my mind directed me to do something or told me to improve or be better or try harder. I liked this feeling of not having to do or say or be anything. It must be nirvana. Or heaven. Maybe I'd arrived, except this seemed to be a hospital, and there were no tunnels with lights anywhere that I could see. Only people in paper masks, green scrubs, and machines everywhere. Heaven wouldn't have such things. This was a seductive place. *Warm. Like floating on an air mattress in a world-sized pool.* But I couldn't stay here. There were things to do. Places to go. *There's your child somewhere, wait-*

ing for you, your last child. You must get back. Now. Pull yourself back to where you were before all of this. And I paddled slowly through the warm water of my mind to the edge of the pool where I caught hold of the metal ladder and pulled myself out. Climbing. Dripping. Suddenly shivering, aware of myself shivering beneath the covers of this foreign bed with people like dragonflies hovering over me.

Tomorrow you're scheduled for a tubal ligation. They're tying your tubes for good. No more Russian roulette. No more blood running wild or multiplying and replenishing the earth. Tomorrow you can rest. Your job of giving birth is done. The fertility clinic will be boarded up. Finis. Complete.

::

"I don't like monogamy," David said to me three months later in the middle of a hot night, no breeze, the air too still.

"What . . ." I moaned, groggy, "are you talking about? It's four in the morning."

"I need to talk."

Though I would rather have stayed in a ball on my side, I stretched out of the safe fetal position and raised up on my elbow. "You whisper such things while I'm in a deep sleep and expect me to be rational?"

"I don't like the idea of just one woman and just one man, of being tied into a limited, narrow way of life. The sexual impulse crosses boundaries. We're all one. We're not separate. Making love makes me feel charismatic and whole, not small or imprisoned."

"A narrow life?" I asked, trying to unscramble what he'd just said.

"It's too constricted. Not that I think promiscuity is the answer. A man should be responsible for his sexual encounters and be willing to make a contribution to that woman's life."

"There's a beauty in commitment to one person." I knotted the sheet in my hand. "When you can be happy with one woman or one situation, you can be happy with everything."

"Right. See the whole world in a grain of sand."

"Why did you ask me to marry you?"

"I'm not sorry I married you." He paused. "Don't take this personally, but I don't think it's immoral for a man to love more than one woman at the same time, or for that matter for a woman to love more than one man."

"I'm not supposed to take it personally when my husband says he has trouble with traditional marriage and I'm the one he's married to? Get a life." I doubled my pillow over to raise my head higher.

"What if we tried a more open marriage? Let some air into our lives and our minds? Our ancestors practiced plural marriage. According to Joseph Smith, it was the higher order of things."

"Like how he said a woman's salvation depended on her being sealed to a righteous man, the higher up in the pecking order the better?"

My left-hook sarcasm settled into silence. Off in the distance a train whistled its melancholy whistle from the west side of town. The sound always carried in the middle of the night, too much city traffic during the day to hear anything but the lull from the ocean of motion around us.

"Maybe if everyone were practicing plural marriage," I said, trying not to wimp out of this conversation, "I could deal. But they're not. Some people might be sneaking around behind closed doors, but they're not practicing plural marriage."

"But that's the whole idea . . . to take responsibility for the women you're attracted to and want a relationship with. It's better than affairs and casual sex."

"But you haven't even tried traditional marriage, not really. You're always preoccupied, bent on making a million dollars and living a larger life. We live in *this* world, *this* time, *this* house. It might seem small to you, but who else has more than that? No one needs more than one woman or one house. What's so good about many?"

"It's in the feeling of freedom and fulfillment of the universal need to connect. Without the sexual impulse, most people would end up alone and isolated, though I admit, you can't spread yourself too thin."

"And what, my dear David, is freedom?"

"The right to choose the way you live your life. The right to decide about the boundaries of your behavior, as long as you don't injure others."

"You're kidding yourself. Cultural boundaries are part of life."

"The way most marriage is practiced reminds me of how small some people make life."

"You just want an excuse to follow your penis around like the rising sun. Every time it comes up." I pressed the top of the alarm clock to light up the face. 4:45 a.m. "Let's get some sleep."

He reached over and messed my hair playfully. "That was a cheap, small-minded shot. You know I'm loyal in my own way. If you could trust that I totally love you, things could be better between us."

"Why should I trust you when you make your own rules? Time for sleeping. I'm tired." I turned my pillow over and puffed it fat. "You're stuck in one point of view, the Get Out of Jail Free point of view. Nobody to report to. Situational morality."

"And you're not stuck in yours? You're not beholden to the approval of your parents and brother and sisters? Your friends?"

"Good night, David."

"Look . . . I'm trying to be honest with you. Would you prefer it if I lied to you?"

My pillow was damp. My neck was stiff. I thought about the definition of insanity, how it happened to people trying to solve problems the same way over and over again and getting the same results over and over again. Dilemma: David was a good man, at least, deep down, he was a good man. He was the father of our children. A good man would Choose the Right, wouldn't he? And the Right was to have a committed marriage and a deep loyalty to family. Wasn't it? Things would change, wouldn't they?

The Meaning of Goodness

I carried Brad everywhere in a Snugli, a secondary womb of yellow corduroy attached by soft straps to my shoulders. I couldn't stop kissing the top of his head and patting his white-blonde hair. He was always with me, even at the kitchen sink paring potatoes. He was a tiny, elflike, wispy baby, almost too thin. Maybe my body had been too undernourished, too busy, too tired to give him what he needed in utero. But I would protect him now. I wouldn't leave his side. Except for this one particular day when I asked David the tough question.

"Are you or aren't you?" I sat beside him on a Saturday morning before he rolled out of bed. "Please don't lie. I'm not blind."

"Yes," he said, since there was too much available information hanging out in the air for him to tuck it back inside where no one would notice.

"I can't take this anymore." My eyes filled up. "We have a brand-new baby plus two other children."

"I don't mean to hurt you. You need to believe me."

"Tell me something." My whole world wasn't whole anymore. Nothing was in its right place. "You can't deny your current involvement with Melanie, but when I had that dream last year about a woman named Audrey, was that another affair?"

He looked to the left of my chin. "To tell you the truth, I almost fell out of bed when you told me your dream and said her name. I knew you knew, even if you didn't know you knew."

"How can you keep doing this?" I grabbed the sixth Kleenex from the box. My nose was red. A crumpled pile of sopping tissue proliferated on the bed. "Tell me what's going on. We have a new baby, and this is killing me."

"I've been coming apart at the seams." He pulled the covers up over his shoulders. "In the middle of every night, I wake up sweating after dreaming of sex with another woman. During the day I fantasize about the same thing. I know I can't explain it, but the only time I don't feel totally stressed, when my muscles aren't tense, is when I'm sexually aroused. I've had trouble for years with, you know . . . I stayed with Audrey one weekend when I was in the Bay Area. Maybe because I wasn't in love, I could sustain an erection for what felt like the first time. You can't imagine how that felt. Being with her was only a passing thing, but it helped me feel less frightened about sex."

"A passing thing, you say. But what about our intimacy? Why can't we solve this between us? And now Melanie. Why her?"

"I haven't always volunteered everything, but I'll tell you the truth if you ask me a question."

"So . . ."

"You're right." He wrapped himself in a cocoon of bedcovers. "Melanie and I were working on a committee together, we took a hike in Parley's Canyon, and she invited me home and asked if I'd make love to her—she was lonely. But it was a mistake. I promised myself I'd never again make love to someone I didn't love."

"It wasn't anything, you say. That sounds like a line from a movie." The pile of crumpled Kleenexes grew higher. "How am I supposed to feel while this is going on?"

"I feel totally shut down. I've been having a hell of a struggle with all of this," he said. "The strange thing is, I still love you very much."

That stopped my flow of words.

"You need to understand. I'm trying to keep our family together at the same time I'm dealing with these feelings." He folded his pillow double and punched a place for his head. "Maybe I shouldn't have married before all this was worked out."

"Fine time to tell me, Lucille."

"It's not about you, Phyllis. It's certainly not about not loving you."

I lifted my fist. I wanted to hit him. Hard. Hit him in the jaw and knock some sense into his head. I wanted to shout until my hurt could be heard all over the neighborhood: "Traitor, traitor." Instead, being of partially sound mind, I said, "You take care of the babies. I may be back and I might not."

I roared through the house, a forest fire raging. My red-hot anger burned wide as a mile. I jammed my backpack with two water bottles and a package of Fig Newtons, screeched out the driveway and down the street, oblivious to everything peripheral. I wanted to scream out the venom, louder than anyone had ever screamed. *Not now, Phyllis. You're driving a car. There are other people in the world. Calm down.* I still managed one puny scream in between stoplights, but my voice sounded thin and insubstantial. Why couldn't I be a banshee and fill the air with unchained, hateful noise all the way to Millcreek Canyon?

I parked askew, not caring if anyone needed to park there, too. I headed up the first trail I saw, one of the most difficult trails in the canyon where I often hiked, one I'd never tried before. It was unrelentingly steep.

If I can get to the top of this . . .

I batted pine boughs, stumbled on rocks, and valkyried my way up the side of the mountain. I bent over when I couldn't breathe. I stood tall and pulled my shoulders back to open my lungs. *Bastard. Breaker of promises. Doesn't your word mean anything?*

When I reached the sign that said I'd arrived, I was a force to be dealt with. Nothing would mow me down. Nothing. I stood at the top of the ridge large as a Titan with the city below diminished to mini-doll-house size. Daylight glinting off tiny windows. Ants in cars. All those people lived in an anthill. They were ants. They meant nothing. It was all sound and fury. Nothing meant anything. Not even people's promises. I stretched my arms as wide as they'd stretch. I leaned back. I felt the heat of the brilliant white globe above shining on my black hair. I begged it to fry my brains dry, to sear my heart so it wouldn't hurt anymore. *I want everything to be clean. New. Pristine again. I want my family to work the way it's supposed to work.*

The house was quiet enough when I returned, everyone well tended, but I didn't speak except to Chris and Jeremy or to Brad when I changed his diapers. After the children were fed dinner, given baths, and put to bed, I disappeared into the downstairs laundry room. Discouraged all over again, I sank to my knees on a pile of dirty sheets while I waited for a batch of diapers to finish washing. *Help me deal with this, God. I have a brand-new baby. I have no place to go.*

When the washing machine paused before the spin cycle, a thought that could have been one of those still small voices people talk about came into my head. "Don't be afraid," it said. "Your husband has huge needs he's battling. Pay attention to *your* life. Focus on what *you* need to do. Not on him."

Amazed at the clarity of the words I'd never have strung together on my own, I picked up a stack of folded diapers, carried them upstairs, and decided to talk to David for the first time since morning. Sitting on the bed with crumpled sheets covering his feet and two pillows at his back, he was reading a book. He looked up with brooding, questioning eyes. His skin looked gray.

"I prayed." I set the diapers on the dresser and quieted myself as I stood on the wooden floor in my bare feet. I slowed the flow of words that wanted to rush out of my mouth, the words that weren't my words. "I didn't know what to do," I said, "so I prayed. Then I heard an answer. Something told me you have huge needs."

He flattened the open book across his knees, cautious about listening.

"It said for me to put my attention on my own life right now and not be hurt by your personal battles. That's what it said."

He blinked his eyes to slough off some tears. He didn't speak.

"I'm not sure I can do this." I leaned over and patted his hand. "But I'll try. Believe me, I couldn't come up with an idea like this, so somebody's on your side."

He sat in a silence, full of feeling I couldn't interpret, then took my hand, stroked a circle on the knuckle of my longest finger, and looked off in the distance.

A week later while Chris and Jeremy were off at school, I strapped Brad into his blue vinyl car seat that hung over the back of the passenger seat and drove south on the winding road at the base of Mount Olympus, the most imposing mountain rising out of the Salt Lake Valley. I felt surrounded by its divine majesty. This was Mount Olympus, home to the gods.

"I want to be good," I said out loud. Brad looked over as though I'd been talking to him. I stroked his cheek. "I want to understand goodness, Brad. I want God to help me."

"You know nothing of goodness," something inside me said too quickly. I slowed the car and pulled to the shoulder. I wanted to hear this something clearly. *Is this me? Is this God?* "You know nothing of goodness," it said again.

I listened intently. I'd lost the most valuable thing a wife could have—the honor of a faithful husband. In my thinking, I was no longer a treasured woman, a valued partner, a respected member of any community, let alone the Mormon one. I needed to make the world fit together again.

"You hold tightly to one thin sliver of goodness," the voice said, "and you blind yourself with this sliver, this mote in your eye. You need to experience the darkness to understand the light. Live life instead of holding onto an ideal of it. Don't be afraid of the shadows. You can't understand goodness because you know too little of the wide spectrum. How can you be good when you're hanging on to such a paltry version of what might be?"

Who knows what happened in that moment . . . that moment that felt like a road to a dark Damascus. I didn't know if it happened because of my brush with death at Brad's birth and the fact I'd never be a mother again, or if it was a brief acquaintance with the reality of the Other. I didn't know why a voice spoke to me about the nature of good and evil. Dark. Light. Me. God. Satan.

"Stop performing for everyone else and dancing to their tune. Go inside yourself. Be aware of who *you* are and what it is *you* feel. You are my child. You have something unique to give."

I looked over at my infant son who had fallen asleep, his head bent awkwardly to the side of his car seat. Beautiful, tow-headed Brad. I looked at the vista of the Salt Lake Valley between the Wasatch and Oquirrh mountains. No pollution. A clear day that heightened the senses.

To be or not to be an adventurer who dares step out on her own? To be or not to be an obedient lamb who follows the rules, no questions asked? Sheep are safe in their flock. Maybe sheep are smart. But I've been attached to clichés and secondhand faith. I've been lazy, riding on other people's coat-tails. Maybe I'm addicted to belonging and bowing to community require-ments so I can belong. And yet, does being an adventurer mean being out in the ether all by myself?

I signaled with my left blinker, turned back into traffic, and continued south to Little Cottonwood Canyon where there were more mountains, precipices, peaks, cliffs, ravines, all those metaphors for conquering or surrendering to life. The valley stretched out below this ridge. Thousands of homes. Houses. Streets. Streetlights. Traffic moving. Stopping. I wasn't part of this endless hive at the moment. I was up here on the side of Mount Olympus speaking with the gods.

I'll do it. I'll resign my community positions. Get out of everything so I can spend more time with this beloved baby. I almost lost him, or better said, he almost lost me. I'll let go of the illusion of becoming a full-blown concert pianist. Music isn't enjoyable anymore. My perfectionism is strangling me. I'll start with something simple. Something unweighted. I'll start writing. My father always wanted to be a writer.

And there was rain in the west. And sunshine in the south. Dark clouds and white clouds. Day and approaching nightfall. Light. Dark. Clouds. Sun.

::

I was on my knees, planting flowers in David's backyard. I wanted to return his kindness for providing a place for me upstairs in the attic. It was the end of June in 2002, late to plant tender things that close to the bru-tal heat of July. I was determined to transform this yard, which had been neglected since he moved elsewhere with his girlfriend. Maybe I had a need for uniformity just now, forget passion. I was planting mostly purple flowers. I even bought a trellis for the purple clematis I hoped would do well in this spot where I dug.

I heard sparrows chattering, a nice enough sound, but somehow it was like a switch that transported me too quickly to a place of longing—a long-ing to hear the cooing of quail, a longing to see their bobbing topknots flipping from side to side when they ran. I had this primordial connection to birds, especially eagles, hawks, swifts, canaries, and the humorous, breathtaking quail whose feet moved like propellers when their babies skittered after them. When we lived in Salt Lake City on Lincoln Circle in the neighborhood I so loved—the place where we raised our family—I remember watching them, laughing, pointing them out to the boys and to David.

Something resembling a squall was blowing into my head, something full of low pressure. It filled my body like tornado weather and settled like lead from the skies. It didn't move. It filled my lungs and veins. *Please. Not this weather again. Lead me not into temptation.* I pursued the roots of a dandelion with the forked digger and a renewed determination. *Deliver me from the evil of despair.*

But then I thought of the Little Milton song I'd heard just yesterday: "When the blues come knockin,' you better open up your door." *Don't fight it, Phyllis. Let the melancholy in. If you resist, it'll keep knocking until it busts down your door. It'll shout at you. It'll say you're not worth much. It'll ask you why you're bothering to keep on.*

My hand cramped. I'd been holding the digger too tightly.

What's with this storm system, this recurrent bad weather, these twisters constantly forming on the horizon?

I added another weed to the pile, took off my garden gloves, and massaged the palm of my right hand. There was a bunched muscle in the middle. Almost a ganglion. And there was a blister agitating my third finger. A redness talking back.

You're all by yourself. Again. There's nobody here in this big house except you stuffed under the eaves of a steeply pitched roof. You and your computer. This is the good life? Your sons haven't called since Memorial Day. They don't call unless you call them. Out of sight, out of mind. The phone hasn't rung once. Yes, it has. No, it hasn't. Stop harassing yourself.

I'd tried everything. Prescriptions. Therapy. Prayer and meditation at a convent in Minnesota. Self-help books. Buddhist books. A crazy bicycle trip of a thousand miles. Travels to Greece, the Yucatan, Slovenia, South America. I'd even tried shamans in Peru and Ecuador, attempting to heal myself by understanding the wisdom of the Land of the Condor as opposed to the Land of the Eagle—the United States. And the wisdom of Pachamama, mother of everything, Mother Earth, the round woman of matter.

After Spinner and I washed up in Minnesota, I moved to Park City. I wanted to return to Utah, which felt like home and where I could be close to my younger sister, Kathy. I bought a condo in Old Town, found a job at the Expanding Heart—my friend Joy Barrett's metaphysical gift shop—and signed up for a trip with some like-minded, mystical-traveling, Park City women. This group traveled to Peru to study with a shaman in Cusco.

The day we hiked above the Pisac ruins, we passed groups of Quechua Indian families in their colorful, backstrap-loomed shawls. When we'd hiked for about an hour, all of us, under the direction of Theo, the shaman, stopped to do a "heart" exercise with a partner—exchanging feelings about who we thought each other was. As I looked in my assigned partner's exquisitely shaped, Madonna-like face, I projected my sadness onto her. I told her how I saw a world of hurt in her eyes. She looked puzzled. The proverbial tears gushed out of me as we sat across from each other cross-legged, Indian style, holding hands, all of this above the Urubamba Valley, El Valle Sagrado, patchworked by patterned fields and rimmed by vast green terracing in the heart of the old Inca Empire. As we parted, she squeezed my fingers gently.

"Why are you so sad?" Theo asked me after we returned to hiking, his magnificently brown liquid eyes penetrating my deep black aquifer that kept sending up tears.

"I've lost everything I love," I told him in view of the unbelievably green mountainsides dotted with men in round felt hats wearing black pigtails and working the fields. "I don't want to be alone anymore."

He guided me inside a crevice of tall stones, laid his hands upon my head, and gave me a blessing, much like the blessings I'd received as a young girl from my father who'd been granted the Melchizedek priesthood from an unbroken line of authority in the Mormon church. That authority was said to have been restored by Peter, James, and John to Joseph Smith and Oliver Cowdery. I felt the power of Theo's blessing moving through me, then realized that this most ancient of rituals must exist as if it were a net cast over the entire earth, that it had survived in the most unexpected places.

Two weeks later, I visited a shaman in Otavalo, Ecuador, with another group of spiritual explorers. He prepared a ritual ceremony for us in his spacious round lodge built of thin stalks of small trees and capped with a fire hole in the ceiling. As each person stood on the dirt floor next to a crackling fire sending smoke skyward, he gave individual blessings with the aid of strong condor feathers he kept in a long, leather sheath. When it was my turn to walk to where he stood by the fire, this shaman, as beautiful physically and spiritually as I believed Jesus must have been, pulled out the tiniest of downy feathers from a packet tucked inside his sheath. It was as if he needed the most fragile gift a bird could give. His words for the blessing were spoken in the native tongue. I had no inkling of their exact meaning, but I felt the presence of a pure spirit. I also felt a new birthing inside me, a new desire to turn my face toward the light again. In fact, when I returned to Park City, ready to jump back into life on all fours, I met Bill, fell in love, and married him four months later. I was never going to be alone again. *Feat accompli.* But the truth of the matter was: the cycle of the seven lean years hadn't been completed.

Face it. I freed the roots of yet another weed. *You're hardwired on both sides of the family.* Those Scandinavian ancestors didn't get enough light in winter. Long nights. Overcast skies. Those Welch forefathers and mothers were good at making poetry out of the sorrow of being themselves. They'd been famous for singing from their toes and hearts and for mourning the sadness of this earthly travail.

While my mother came from more solid stock, so it seemed, I loved my father's family with a passion. They had soul in spades, the real thing. They knew how to feel all of life deeply and richly. They could laugh. They could cry. But my father's grandfather, a good Mormon man of Danish descent, hung himself in the garage. In the family photograph he looked solid enough, though a bit nonplussed in the midst of so many children.

My father's mother, a dedicated Mormon woman who sang for Franklin Delano Roosevelt and a national radio audience at the dedication of the Hoover Dam, was sent to the Nevada State Mental Hospital for a year. Diagnosis: melancholia. She'd given birth to six children and had been bounced around the West by a husband who couldn't keep a job: Brigham

City, Logan, Salt Lake City, and Price in Utah; San Diego in California; Ely, Ruth, Boulder City in Nevada; Malad and who knows where else in Idaho. The fact that she was a gypsy by situation rather than nature and that her husband had an on-again, off-again romance with alcohol must have gotten to her. The family story goes that after one year in the Sparks hospital, the resident doctor telephoned her sister, Helen. "Please," he said. "Come and take Hortense home. Nothing's wrong with her, except she's dying of a broken heart." You could say that Hortense's life failed her or that she failed her life. You could say she suffered from melancholia, if you're inclined to compartmentalize.

My father decided to finish his life on a different planet without actually moving there. At age sixty-five, he had a nervous breakdown, had to be subdued, and was taken to the hospital for a week. "He was just telling everybody things he hadn't been able to say for years," a consoling cousin said. For twenty years after that, my father listened to his own tune. If anyone told him to mind his manners, he sang loudly, "Blow the Man Down." He was free, at last, from the rules, the shoulds, the oughts. Free from my mother's advice about how he should act. You could say he suffered from senile dementia, if you're inclined to tidy diagnoses.

I assessed how many more dandelions needed to be dug out of this nearly defunct flower bed. And then I wondered why something was called a weed or why it was called a flower. Weeds had flowers. My favorite flower, the calla lily, was a weed in California. *Who decides what's a weed or whether or not it belongs in the garden anyway?* I dug deep into the neglected hard clay soil, deep to the tip of the dandelion roots.

My lungs are made of clay. They're heavy. My heart's trying hard to keep beating, but it's clay, too. The whole grid's down. My body's turning the blues kind of blue. There's no place to catch a breath of clean, clear, unadulterated air.

A snail crawled along the concrete edge of the flower bed, oozing a shiny path behind itself. It reminded me of seashells, water, ocean, of how waves pulled away from the shore, then rushed toward it and curled and rolled and crashed and then pulled together again. Endless motion. Endless breaking. Endless knitting back together. Nothing but motion. It was always moving. Never static. Never definable.

Over the years, I'd tried to label myself: creative with a vivid imagination, bright but flawed, normal with a spin on it, gifted with a string attached, unipolar, quadruple-polar, an aesthetic artist, a highly sensitive woman, someone unafraid to talk about life from the down side or maybe even someone with a weak mind touched by madness. Even now I wondered if I were mad, plain and simple, ambushed again by this melancholy while my trowel loosened the ground. *Why not go to a doctor for a diagnosis? But why ask someone else to put a sign on your chest?*

Weak hearts. Weak knees. Weak minds. Did unrelenting sadness mean a person had a weak or sick mind? Did it mean a person was mad? And what did madness mean anyway? Maybe it was a word that took on too much just as the word "love" took on too much. Madness could be a curse, but it could also be a kiss from God, couldn't it? A chance to know the full spectrum of humanity, a chance to feel the condition of being tied to the moon and tides and the pull of the ocean waves, back and forth, in and out. It took immense strength to love so deeply and to sorrow so sadly. Maybe weakness had nothing to do with it.

Maybe my tribe and I had been asked by the Someone who assigned tasks for this earthly experience if we'd volunteer to hold the place for the depths and heights of human feeling: the musicians, the painters, the sculptors, the writers. Didn't every human being play a particular role on the stage to show others what it was like to be that particular part of human: the delirious, the clogged, the malignant, the bent who couldn't straighten, the straight who couldn't bend . . . so many combinations and variations, each variation with its own variation. It was perverse to think everyone should fit mid-spectrum. Fitting into something was an illusion. We fit one moment; we were misfits the next.

All I knew was that I was full of too much feeling with no place for it to go. I wasn't solid flesh anymore, but spongy beneath the surface. Ninety-eight percent water. I wished I could come to a definitive conclusion about whether I was well or sick or whether I was a gift or a hex or a bad seed.

It seemed a curse to have a mind that could behold so much and feel so much, then to watch it turn against itself and devour itself trying to figure everything out.

Be still, mind. Be still and remember the quail with the bobbing top-knot running across the yard and beneath the pine trees in Salt Lake City. Remember Theo's blessing and the second blessing of the softest downy feathers. Listen to the sound of the leaves on the tree that's giving you shade, the sprinkler watering the yard next door. Be still and behold the beauty. Behold the lilacs and the lilies that toil not, neither do they spin. Behold the buds of new things. Hold yourself like a sleeping baby. Be still. Listen when the blues come knocking. And be still.

::

We were riding through Hell that day, even if the map said Iowa. The wind blasted everything and everywhere bleached-bone dry. While I battled split asphalt and broken pieces of concrete, the evil wind churned mercilessly. My bike and I crept an inch at a time up a viaduct that arced over trains carrying grain to market. Waging an intense contest with the wind, I finally reached the top where I could roll down the rest of the high-profile viaduct. Back on level ground, I thought the wind would let up. But instead, it suddenly shriveled the contact lens in my left eye.

I blinked rapidly to moisten the only lens I'd brought with me, then held my eye closed to prevent it from drying to an insignificant flake of plastic. It dropped as if it were a falling spider onto my lower lashes. Jamming my fingers against the lens and slamming my brakes, I stumbled to a stop and a dismount next to a battered highway sign. My bicycle loaded with my home away from home crashed to the ground.

Ahead as usual, C. J. looked over her shoulder, turned around, and biked back to where I stood. Her wind jacket rippled like a flag on a sailing ship on a stormy sea. The loose strap around her tire pump chattered at high speed.

"Why don't you keep going?" I said, then put the lens on my tongue to reconstitute it, health standards be damned. Down-deep cranky, I felt like shouting at her for always being ahead. Was she trying for some kind of Olympic medal? I most assuredly didn't have to have one, I felt like telling her. I could have blamed her for the wind and everything else. Instead I said, "Please, please ride ahead. I'll meet you at the first convenience store in the next town."

"We should stay together," she answered with a strange calm in her voice, knowing the end of a rope when she saw one. "I could draft you."

"Should've, would've, could've." My voice edged close to hysteria. "Today is save-yourself day. I can't keep your pace. You shouldn't have to keep mine."

"But we need to stay within range of each other," she insisted. "For safety's sake."

"I'll catch up with you, but stop waiting for me. It's driving me nuts." My tone of voice was as brittle as the cold wind.

"I'm trying not to go too fast." She wouldn't quit. "Ease up on yourself."

"I know, I know, but I feel too much pressure when I see you waiting for me at the top of every hill."

Without a further word, she set her lips, sat back on her seat, and pedaled away at adrenaline-stoked speed. I stood there, not one whit interested in putting my feet to my pedals. I felt a horrific anger swelling up inside, something like a Bitch Goddess in her awful splendor spewing poison when she spoke words, even when she thought thoughts.

I pulled my bike from the edge of the highway, not caring if the panniers were dragging in road crud and turning gray. I folded into a cross-legged position, two elbows crushed into my knees, two fists smashed against my cheeks. People driving by might have seen a picture of defeat, but none could have guessed that the Bitch Goddess was performing a hysterectomy of the inauthentic niceness in my body. The wind flattened the toughened, strawlike grass in which I sat, some of it old, some of it new. Anger flooded every cell.

The Bitch Goddess didn't mess around. Tangling with her was like hanging on to a bolt of lightning, and suddenly my nice life felt like stuffing in my ears and mouth and body, like too large pimentos in skimpy green olives. *Do unto others. Treat them as you would have them treat you.*

"A nice girl. A nice woman," people often said of me. "Lovely, sweet Phyllis." Right now, I hated niceness, maybe because it was often a whitewash spread over the top of fear. I hated dysfunctional language—the kind that masked real thoughts, that heavy, velvet-cloth drapery language meant to dampen and stifle real feelings. *Always say the right thing. Choose the right. Be kind. Bland, passive, harmonious ad nauseum. Nobody wants to keep company with Endlessly Nice People. Nice equals something to the far left of real, even interesting. Something dismissible.*

A yellow and black diagonally striped sign stood above me, a warning sign of some kind, but I didn't care. How luxurious to let the Bitch Goddess rage—a primal matriarch, a combo of Lillith/Artemis/Freya. This awful magnificence was ten feet tall with iron shoes and legs like tree trunks. The Boss of the Universe, nobody messed with her, and I mean nobody.

Why did you have to do a stupid thing like get on this bicycle and suffer in rain, wind, thunder, lightning, at the edge of narrow shoulders on narrow highways while huge trucks threaten your life? My legs ached. My back and butt hurt. My crotch was almost raw. I'd been forcing my body onto that bike every day. It needed rest and laughter and touching and pillows and nice linens. I lay back on the prickly grass, arms spread-eagled to the side.

The universe wasn't cooperating. It wasn't ratcheting things down to fit my capacity. It wasn't helping me with miracles or transforming me into some kind of Lance Armstrong or Eddie Merckx. Didn't I excel at everything I undertook? Couldn't I figure out any problem—an unhappy marriage, even an intimate relationship with a crack addict? Why couldn't I ride a bicycle across the United States? Couldn't I just will my way across and over and around everything?

A bird swooped up and down and around the choppy current. A bird being a bird. I suddenly sat up, crossed my arms over my knees, and hugged myself tightly. I'd been conning myself with my need for power over something and my delusions of grandeur. I lifted my head to the sky, noticing how the birds and the clouds were tumbling thoughtfully, not chaotically, and how the wind wasn't an enemy to clouds and birds. I saw the pinpoint of C. J. at the top of the last hill I could see. I picked up my helmet and rebuckled it.

::

On the eve of my birthday, we tried hard to keep our spirits up at a steak house in Griswold, Iowa. We avoided speaking about boredom, no break from pedals turning over and over again, no break from each other, my snoring problem. We even tried a few lame jokes. Comrades. Together. Onward. But we didn't have anything new to say.

"These restaurants are all the same," C. J. said, twirling her fork clockwise.

"Yeah," I said, straightening my knife.

Stilted silence. C. J. drank some water. I tapped my shoe.

"Maybe I'll call Spinner's parents," I finally said, trying to keep myself upbeat. "I told them I'd call them at least once during the trip."

I found a pay phone in a dim, narrow corridor.

"Hi," I said when Spinner's father answered. "It's Phyllis. I told you I'd call, so here I am. Calling."

"Aren't you back in Denver?" he said, real surprise in his voice.

His question confused me. "No. Why would we be back in Denver? We're at a restaurant in Griswold, Iowa."

"But Spinner told us you'd gotten in trouble. That you'd called him to come and get you. We sent him three hundred dollars to help out."

"No," I said, still confused. "We're fine. We never asked him to come and get us. Besides, if we did get in trouble, I always have my credit card with me."

"He said somebody stole your bikes with all of your stuff."

"Nobody stole anything," I said, the dawn slowly coming over me that Spinner had pulled off another of his brilliant scams, a Good Samaritan scam, no less. He'd done the same thing in different variations a countless number of times, telling his father his car needed a new radiator, tires, or fan belts, telling him every kind of hard-luck story that his father wanted to believe because he'd lost two other sons to alcohol and suicide.

The Meaning of Goodness :: 129

"But Spinner said you were in trouble," his father insisted, not wanting to hear me.

"Thank you for your willingness to help us out." I didn't know what else to say. "But we *are* in Iowa."

Stunned by Spinner's elaborate gyrations, I couldn't even try to imagine what his father felt.

"I just wanted you to know we were okay," I stammered. "Hope everything's good at your end."

"Well," he said, still assimilating this new set of facts. "Be careful."

"Okay. Talk to you later."

I stood in the hallway for at least a minute. I took a deep breath and held it, then went into the ladies' room to wash my hands and splash cold water on my face. When I looked in the mirror, I shook my head. "What is going on with you?" I said out loud to my weary reflection, which offered no answer.

"You'll never believe this one," I said, easing back into the booth and the permanent bowl in the vinyl.

C. J. was furious when I told her the details. "How could he do that to us? That's the lowest thing I've ever heard of." She slapped her napkin on the tabletop. "If you let somebody use you, that's one thing. But he's not going to use me, that son of a bitch."

"I wish I could believe he wouldn't stoop that low, but what are you going to do about it?"

"I'm calling him and giving him a piece of my mind, that's what. What in the hell are you doing with a loser like that?"

"Heaven only knows that answer, but it's not that simple. Okay?"

"It is that simple," she said. "Wake up. He's an unbelievable jerk."

We biked back to the Sleep Well Motel. My mind besieged with thoughts about winners and losers. The righteous and unrighteous, superior and inferior, saints and sinners. Weren't we all people passing through with one degree of strength or another? Weren't we all manifestations of the Divine, all on a journey back to the Divine? As much as I suspected Spinner was undoubtedly a loser, I wanted to believe he was more than that. He must be unbelievably humiliated to be so bound and tied and yoked to his addiction.

The motel owner in Griswold knocked on our door early the next morning—my fifty-third birthday. "Morning, girls," he said when I answered, hiding myself and my pajamas behind the door. "Just thought I'd tell you about Highway 92. It's the old Mormon Trail and great for biking. Not much traffic and long, gentle hills."

"Thanks for thinking of us," C. J. called from her bed across the room.

"No problem," he said. "And I think it might clear up for a few hours today. Wouldn't that be nice?"

"Nice?" I mumbled when I closed the door and sat on the lumpy mattress to pull my socks on. "Nice, he says? Little does he know." When I stopped mumbling and looked up, there was C. J. standing next to me in her pajamas, holding a white envelope and a box wrapped in purple paper.

"Can I give you a birthday present before we go? I've been carrying it since Fort Collins."

"That's impressive," I said, working my finger beneath the glued flap of the envelope. "Be with those who help your being—Rumi," the front of the card read. I paused at the thought. *Who are the people to best help you with your being? Do you learn from all kinds of people, or is it a must to hang out with shining examples?* When I opened the box, I found an earth goddess pendant wrapped in purple tissue.

"She's the one who's supposed to inform your dreams," C. J. said.

"She's not a voodoo doll for people who snore?"

"I wish." She laughed.

I hung the pendant around my neck. "That's beautiful," I said, taking a long look at my bicycle partner, my fellow road warrior. "I guess you know you have a friend when you go through some rough times together," I said carefully, placing my hand tentatively on her shoulder, a small truce. "Thanks for putting up with me."

"I hope it's your best year ever," C. J. said. "Starting right now."

"Yeah. Right."

"I said 'starting right now.'" We both laughed.

After the morning rain shower, the clouds hung sticky until eleven. Finally, they blew elsewhere and revealed the fact that, yes, there was a sun in the sky. We passed fields of bright yellow dandelions against new green, pig farm pastures (ah, the awful smell), copacetic cows, swelling hills, breaks of earth with small creeks, isolated trees, stands of trees. Good earth. Mid-America. Iowa. Good people.

Biking along the sparsely traveled road, I imagined I could still hear the sounds of wagon trains heading for the Territory of Utah, the State of Deseret with the oxen, the horses, the squeaking of the wheels turning through the ruts and the uneven ground on the way to Zion. I imagined my great-great-grandfather, Charles Wesley Hubbard, crossing Iowa with his first wife in 1847 in the first company of pioneers heading for Utah. Charles Wesley didn't make it all the way to Utah with that company, however, because Brigham Young asked him to stay behind and build a flour mill at Winter Quarters for those who would follow. He and Brother Brigham might have had a discussion about this problem on the very spot my bike was now crossing, stopping here to camp for the night, puzzling about how best to proceed with the migration. Or, he might have been sitting astride his horse on this trail, directing a wagon to keep to the right where the terrain would be more cooperative. He was renowned for his ability with horses. I felt ancestral pride. I felt good. I felt strong. My body responded to the demands of the hills and even to a spill when I tipped over once. I took it all in stride. I got back on my bike with no excuses and without feeling sorry for myself. This day, my birthday—a day of cycling at its best.

The hills were equally balanced. The sun shone. Sparkling day. Sparkling streams. We rode as if in the perfect movie. Everything in order. Everything effortless. For a few glorious minutes, I felt whole, unified, not separated into pieces.

About twenty-five miles out of Griswold, in a barely there, scanty collection of buildings, we stopped at the C & C Diner, a community-owned restaurant. "Ten people put in $800 apiece to make this place happen," said Barb Schroeder, who was managing the restaurant for the day. "The

C & C stands for two Connie's. And I guess you know you're smack dab on the Mormon Trail, don't you?"

"My great-great-grandfather may have broken bread in this place," I told her. "May have stopped for water over there by that stream."

"There's a sesquicentennial wagon train coming through this summer. Handcarts, too. Some big commemorative celebration."

"I should come," I said. "I'm related to members of the wagon company and to those Danes who pushed handcarts when their green wood Conestogas fell apart. The Nelsons. The Jensens."

Back on our bikes, I sang the "Handcart Song" I'd learned as a young girl in Primary: "Some must push and some must pull, as we go marching down the trail. So merrily on our way we go, until we reach the Valley-O." And I thought more about the ancestors who'd come this way caught by the spirit of the Latter-day Saints in the 1830s, moving from Massachusetts to western New York to Ohio to Missouri to Illinois and to Utah with the infant movement called Mormonism; the Hubbards from New England, the Wrights from Illinois who were baptized by Hyrum Smith, Joseph Smith's brother, in the Mississippi River; the Evans and the Davies ancestors who were converted in Wales, the Danes who followed. All of them walking or riding on this trail—the family tree packed into wagons and stout shoes and heading for Zion.

These were the stories I'd teethed on. Always the pioneers and their great sacrifices. The selfless pioneers. This was deep in my bones and my blood, the notion of sacrificing and pledging one's life to the Kingdom of God.

:: The Iron Maiden Cracks ::

My husband touched the small of my back. He caressed my hips while I tried to cling to the world of sleep. Suddenly I pulled myself to the edge of the bed. We'd been married for thirteen years, and I was crawling away from him, inching away, a bit at a time.

Love. What was love? And sex, what was that? It meant too many things. It could be a place for abandon and recklessness and giving up your mind. Yet all I could think about when he touched me was that I didn't want to give in to that touch. I didn't want him arousing me anymore. I'd given over one too many times. I rolled out of the covers and ran to the bathroom for air.

He followed me. He stood behind me and cupped his hand around my breast. "You want me. Don't try to run away." My autonomic responses were waking, my genetic impulse to procreate being aroused. I found myself trembling at the touch of his fingers on my nipple.

"It's a lie between you and me," I forced myself to say. I rested the palms of my hands on the sink tile. "Things dried up a while ago. You want other women, so go take them. Go have what you want, but don't drag me along just so you can have everything you started with. I don't want you. I don't want your body. Leave me alone."

He pressed his maleness against my back side. I felt gooseflesh on my arms. "Just because I'm attracted to other women doesn't mean I don't love you."

Why couldn't I be calm? Why couldn't I be cool? Why couldn't I tell him to go away and leave me alone? Too much excitement rising in my body, that sap, that juice, whatever it was that was the source of all fluids.

"Go find someone else. Things are too messy between us. Too many botched attempts." I wanted to say that we didn't have a big enough heavy-duty pink eraser, that no matter how hard we rubbed, we could still see the pencil lines.

He bit into my neck and planted three tiny kisses on the lobe of my ear. "I want you," he said. "I've always wanted you."

"That's not enough anymore." I reached for my bathrobe on the hook of the bathroom door. "Like I said, things are too messy. We've blown it too many times. I just want a clean slate."

I broke free of his hold and directed my arms through the purple sleeves of my robe. Tied the sash in front. Hoisted myself up to the bathroom counter. Let my legs hang over the edge, swinging them, and humming a nondescript tune.

"There's not a clean slate anywhere in this world," he said. He wrapped his hand around my shoulder. "All the air's been breathed before. All the water's recycled."

"It's too messy." I moved away from the province of his hand.

"But isn't there such a thing as forgiveness?" He examined the shadow of his beard in the morning light. "For a woman who talks about faith, you don't have much."

He looked small in his nakedness, his penis at rest, unengorged, hanging quietly. He was a man. No more. No less. A simple man with testicles, pelvis, a hairy chest, arms, legs, and a head and whatever else.

"Actually, the way I figure it," I said from my perch on the counter, "if you cling to the bad things that happen, you'll have something to talk about. Something dramatic. People love a shocking story. A whispered, closely told shocker. They try to hide their fascination with your bad luck or judgment while secretly congratulating themselves on their lot in life being better than yours. Or they feel hip and privileged being around someone who's been there, done that, and knows all about bad luck. Don't you think?"

"You'll never be happy. You don't want to be happy. You're too attached to the sad, cynical story of it all." He took a T-shirt out of a bathroom drawer and pulled it over his head. Then he grabbed his running shorts. "I couldn't make you happy if I tried, and believe me, I've tried. When are you going to lighten up?"

"Iron Maiden. Adagio Alice. Pavanes for dead princesses. That's my style." I smiled against my will and forced a laugh. And then the forced laugh turned into a real one. He rolled his eyes back, slipped his sweatband onto his forehead, and kissed my cheek quickly. The bathroom brightened.

::

The belly dancing began innocently enough.

My sister, Kathy, and I decided we needed more time together. We'd grown apart. Taking a class seemed the answer. I felt some responsibility, after all, to be a caring sister to my sister who was toying with scissors and her roots. Make no mistake, we'd been well instructed about the righteous life: serving the Kingdom of God, serving others, serving our families, although Kathy didn't have a family yet. The trouble with the choice of a belly dancing class was that Kathy had an amazing, drop-dead physical body and didn't need the exotic for ornamentation. I'd always been rail thin, called "Philly Bones" and "Skinny Minny"—five foot nine in the seventh grade with a flat chest, acne, braces, and eyeglasses. I, at age thirty-four, was the one who got hooked. There we were at the YWCA in 1977, every Tuesday night, learning big and small hip circles, the step-hip move, Egyptians, belly rolls, and snake arms. At first I felt like a camel dressed in a chiffon skirt. But as the weeks passed, a sensuous, sensual, earthy Woman stepped out, much more than skin and bones.

"This is about being female," the teacher said. "This is about giving birth, giving life, about being the woman who conceives and ripens and bursts." My body grew rounder, even as she spoke.

I signed up for every class I could—other Middle Eastern dance classes at the University of Utah and at small, discreet dance studios. I attended workshops, even one in Las Vegas where my parents still lived and where my dance friend, Patricia, and I stayed for the weekend. Thank goodness my father had always loved dancing. They expressed a polite interest and didn't roll their eyes when we walked out the front door carrying costumes and bags of noisy coin belts and beads. At the Las Vegas Convention Center, an Iranian drummer gave me the name Anoush, which he said meant "Beloved." I enjoyed being Anoush. I learned all the rhythms one could play with zils. I bought more scarves and coin belts and a sequined bra. Back in Salt Lake, I performed one night at the Grecian Gardens restaurant. The earth rose up through the soles of my feet.

After a brief period of unemployment, David was now teaching corporate law at the J. Reuben Clark Law School at BYU. He'd been asked to step down from his position as executive vice president by the new president who'd originally sought his counsel. He'd been shuffled into a small office with free rent for three months and had brooded after hours in our dingy, unfinished basement. In the interim, to make ends meet, he decided to beef up the law school outline series he'd started at Stanford. Flying back and forth to California, David spent many weekends at his partner's house in Los Alto Hills. He also spent many late-night sessions with his partner's wife, who listened to him pour out his troubled feelings. Gradually, David grew convinced she was the only one who could understand his double bind. In addition, she and her husband were experimenting with marriage lifestyles.

When David tried to explain this in our continuing sensitivity sessions back home, none of it made sense to my common sense. But being a Taurus who was stubborn and loyal beyond the point where loyalty was a virtue, I still looked for ways to stay in the game. I wanted our marriage to work. We had a family to raise. I'd signed on for eternity, nothing less.

David was commuting to BYU in Provo four days a week, and somehow, someone on the law school faculty heard that I'd been dancing and asked if I'd perform at a faculty party. They weren't an insular bunch, as some might expect. Several of them smiled with abandon and clapped their hands to the doumbek drumbeat and the wailing sound of the oud. Most asked polite, intellectual questions after I danced. I told them of my serious interest in folk ethnography.

Just beginning to publish my writing and encouraged by editor Paul Swenson, I wrote an article, "What Does a Nice Girl Like Me Get Out of Belly Dancing?" for *Utah Holiday.* The photographer took exotic pictures in my backyard with veils, zils, bare midriff, and bare feet. I was a new woman: a well-mannered, buttoned-down, and zipped-up community volunteer/good neighbor by day, exotic dancer by night. When the avid belly dancers had parties for their friends, I swirled in the twist of my veil, openly enjoying the art of the earthy feminine and the loosening of my boundaries. I loved the feel of undulation and swaying. I loved moving from the inside, feeling what it was to be a woman with a pelvis, breasts, a stomach, and a womb.

I also attended dream analysis groups, women's groups, sweat lodges, solstice celebrations, Native American ceremonies. At each new event, I met a wider circle of intriguing New Age women. A certain recklessness filtered into my life, a sense of the oyster opening wider and having more than one pearl inside. David and I spent evenings with friends in their Japanese bathhouse, complete with a steam room and massage table. We dipped in hot tubs with other friends. We attended a Tom Jones party complete with a roast pig, no utensils allowed.

When I taught belly dancing at home, Chris, Jeremy, and Brad peeked around the door frame to watch women floating scarves through the air and practicing the elemental step-hip. They stared. They giggled. I taught neighbors from my Valley View Ward and also women in the LDS Relief Society in Grantsville, Utah, a small mining/agricultural town to the west of Salt Lake City.

Each week I drove past the Great Salt Lake, catching glimpses of the huge blue expanse, the seagulls, the bleak salty sand where no trees grew, the towering Oquirrhs, the Kennecott copper smelter. Some of my students' husbands worked in those copper mines. How we ended up having belly dancing lessons in the church's cultural hall I don't remember, but the women had arranged everything. Week after week, they arrived in their leotards, puffy scarves tied around their waists, and the zils I'd ordered from a catalog attached to their fingers with elastic. I brought my boom box each week and filled the hall with the sounds of the Middle East. Definitely an unusual activity for the Grantsville ward house, but no one could claim it wasn't uplifting or cross-cultural.

"It's about the joy of your body, which is your temple," I told the class. "When you dance, tell the story of who you are and what matters to you. This isn't about being a cabaret dancer, which of course some of us might like to be in our wildest dreams." Everyone giggled as if they were little girls playing dress up. "It's about you."

We became fast friends, dancing every week together, laughing, enjoying this new kind of sisterhood. One of the students arranged for me to ride the big bucket down into the mines with her husband and some other miners, all of us dressed in slickers and souwesters to protect us from the water dripping everywhere as we descended into the earth.

"My wife loves your dance class," her husband said, grinning as if suspecting wildness beneath my fingernails. "You think maybe us husbands could see what you girls are up to?"

"You know you're not allowed in Relief Society," I teased him. When the bucket hit bottom, he gave me a royal tour—trains into tunnels, maps of the mine, locations of offices. Several weeks later, I received an invitation to perform for the Grantsville Chamber of Commerce, apparently attended by many of the students' husbands.

"Of course," I said, lulled by the pleasure the women had shared. I took a modest costume, made an agreement with myself to dance conservatively, and, as I drove to Grantsville in the dark, I turned on the light to recheck myself in the mirror. I didn't want to appear too made-up.

When the music announced my entrance, I whirled into the room, surveying these men as I did—their faces above their Salisbury steak dinners, their neckties, their collars, their various heads of hair. Suddenly, as I clanged the zils in a 5/4 rhythm, I couldn't see any individuals. They all become Church Fathers staring at Salome as she danced. When I framed my face with my silver-threaded veil, their somber faces blurred. The joy and playful innocence I felt with the women wasn't in the restaurant that night. My smile plastic tight, the balls of my feet grinding the grunge on the floor, I wished I would have worn a long-sleeved shirt and workout pants and done aerobics for them. I decided to cut the last section of my dance and make a pretty bow. I found my coat immediately, said the necessary good-byes, and hit the road back to Salt Lake.

I never went back to Grantsville. The lessons were cancelled. I was never told what happened, or who, if anyone, ordered the moratorium. Maybe the men got a whiff of too much liberation for the sensible women in their lives.

::

Still walking the line inside of Mormonism, paying my tithing, attending church regularly with our children, serving my neighbors, still keeping the Word of Wisdom regarding tobacco, drugs, alcohol, and caffeine, I also decided to be a good partner to David and blow out some of the cobwebs.

David being bored with the predictable social life of Salt Lake City, we tried Werner Erhard's est and lectures by Ram Dass; we signed up for Marriage Encounter sponsored by the Catholic Church; we read *The Dancing Wu Li Masters* and *The Joy of Sex,* even though my face glowed a maddening red when David asked for a copy from behind the cash register at the Cosmic Aeroplane bookstore. While vowing to be a cosmic adventurer myself, I still tiptoed. Trying to open my mind, I remembered hearing that if your mind's too open your brains will fall out.

I consulted the Bible, the *I Ching,* and the *Tao te Ching,* not knowing which was the wiser oracle. And yet I wondered whom I was accommodating: David or myself. Thus began a giant seesawing, a series of mental acrobatics to make this fit into that. A good marriage, I'd been taught, was the responsibility of the good woman who endured to the end. I bent as if I were a pretzel, determined that everything could work if I tried hard enough. And not without a large measure of angst, I considered not being involved with Mormonism any longer to take the pressure off our marriage. Round pegs. Triangular holes. I bent and swerved and swayed and arched and scrunched and stepped aside, whatever motion was necessary to keep the show on the road. Bottom line, how could I help David get what he needed? How could I stop getting sadder and sadder?

I met a new friend in one of my new women's groups—Ariel, who was in the goddess line of work. She believed she'd received a call from the Divine Goddess and was working on a book about the Mayans and their mysteries. Sometimes I thought she was brilliant, inspired, and the embodiment of love; other times, I felt as if I were a pawn in her game of self-proclaimed goddess, who needed followers to be a goddess the way a king needed subjects to be a king.

The day our friendship became friendship for life, we spent the afternoon sitting on a floor in her home, cross-legged and facing each other, both of us sitting on meditation pillows, quietly holding hands and looking into each other's eyes. She had intense blue eyes, this blonde, blue-eyed Scandinavian with milk-white skin and a sense of destiny. She knew I didn't know what to do with all the pins being knocked out from under me. She'd invited me to spend the afternoon.

"Just be with me," she said. I wriggled my hips to find the most comfortable sitting position. "Notice the fidgeting. Notice the nervousness, the way you want to be somewhere else."

I breathed deeply. *How does she know I'm nervous? Am I that obvious?*

I took a different grip of her hands. Readjusted my fingers and steeled myself to get through one minute of looking into her eyes. A purple velvet cloak draped Ariel's shoulders. Royalty. Queenly bearing. Self-possession. First I blinked to moisten my eyes. Then I blinked them self-consciously, and then too infrequently, which caused a rash of even faster blinking. My goal became to maintain at least two minutes of stillness in this small room with incense, an altar, and candles.

This was too intense. I wanted to laugh, to play dodgeball, make a let-me-out-of-here move. But I straightened my back. Breathed. Didn't look away. I willed myself to focus on her eyes fractionated by tiny specks of crystal. Light behind the irises. Light seeping through the lids of her eyes. I willed myself to look, really look into someone's eyes for the first time without any thoughts about romance or what might happen next. As I gazed intently, her eyes became chameleons. What they seemed at first was not what I saw as I looked more closely. They were changing entities. Living things. A wisp of one thing, then a hint of something else. Windows of the soul. Eyes that were an organ so much more than the external cornea, aqueous humor, pupil, iris, and lens. Eyes hooked up to so much else I couldn't see. Timelessness in her eyes. Centuries passing between us.

Finally able to sit in peace with my friend who wanted me to acknowledge the goddess energy in myself, I straightened my back again. I wanted it to be yardstick straight. Regal. I wanted to give back what she was giving to me. "I can't believe you'd take this much time with me. That you'd take this whole afternoon just to be with me."

She smiled calmly, the Mother of the World. "Of course I'll take this time with you. You are a beautiful being." She squeezed my hands and continued to look straight into my eyes. "You are a fawn. A gentle deer who frightens easily. The world is a brutal place for someone as sensitive as you are."

"I still can't believe you'd sit here with me like this," I said again, this time my eyes filling with tears—the flow of water for parched earth. But as we continued to sit in each other's presence and sift through layer after layer of what it meant to feel oneness with another human, the tears dried. We still held hands and breathed deeply. Circuitry. A traversal with no starting or ending point. We sat this way until time didn't matter, and when time became real again, we'd been forged together into an everlasting link. A section of chain.

I left that day with the awareness that no one was home for anyone. Everyone, especially me, was too busy grasping, looking everywhere but to their own circumstances.

::

How many years had David said, "Let's have an open marriage?" Maybe ten. Maybe eight. To him, closed meant claustrophobic. No room to breathe. "Give me openness. I need space," he said from time to time. It felt as though he kept jimmying with the church key and working the hole bigger and bigger. It felt as though he kept pushing, pressing, and asking my permission for something to which I didn't want to give permission. Maybe he'd press me so hard I'd open the gates. I wasn't invincible. I wasn't an oak, but more a willow that bent when the wind blew hard.

The man was a gardener. An eastern European immigrant who spoke broken English. I'd gone to southern Nevada in the spring of 1982, just before turning thirty-nine, to do research for a novel. He worked at the house of a family friend who'd said he'd be out of town but that his house was mine to use anyway.

It wasn't about attraction. It wasn't about love. It wasn't about truth or infidelity or anything magical. Maybe it was more about two people floating through the vascular walls of space, neither feeling tethered anywhere. It wasn't a temptation. It wasn't even exciting. It was a resignation, me tired of trying to fit inside a marriage that didn't feel like a marriage, tired of being asked and asked and asked to go against my inclinations. It was an anger at David's insistence that I be other than who I was and other than what I cared about. It was about what I saw as his inability to see my worth and his unwillingness to address my desires when I'd tried so hard to meet his. "I forgive you," I'd said after his indiscretions, his sowing of wild oats, hoping things would be different if he had more breathing space. But when I gave it to him, he took more. A camel in the tent. He needed too much oxygen. Too much air.

"Men aren't meant to be monogamous," he'd said more than once.

Monopoly—one owner. Monotonous—one tone. Monochromatic—one color. Monochord—an instrument with one string. Monocle—an eyeglass for one eye. And so we struggled: one of us wanting togetherness, the other running from the shackles. How could we change the dance? Or how could we end this one? Except we were married forever. Time and *all eternity*. He'd promised. I'd promised.

After a supper we shared, the gardener sat on the patio, smoking. He surveyed his handiwork with a slow turn of the head. Cholla cactus. Sage. Creosote. Barrel cactus. I walked outside and sat on a green and yellow webbed lawn chair.

"Nice evening," I said.

He didn't say much. He took a last drag on his cigarette and stubbed it into the ashtray on a table between us.

The sunset was spectacular—salmon eggs, salmon gills, speckles of blue, mackerel sky. So many fish in the clouds. So many eyes. Fluttering color.

He held out his hand. "May I make love to you?" he asked. His direct-ness caught me by surprise. What was he saying? He was asking *me* to make love with *him?*

I sat there for a moment, not saying anything, weighing whether or not I was ready to take the dare. And it was a dare. Should I or shouldn't I? Could this really be *me* considering this possibility? I'd heard a Sunday school teacher say that adultery was next to committing murder when it came to sin. I'd be breaking the covenant I made to remain pure for my husband. *Dear God, is this really happening? I can't be here doing this. Never. Ever.*

As if I were in a trance that had been arranged before this meeting, I lifted my hand to his, almost as if he and I had agreed on this many life-times ago, as if we knew this thing was to happen on this night. It wasn't love. It was an agreed-upon thing. An initiation. A moment when the prin-cess opened the locked door and stepped over the dark threshold into the cavern. The darkness. The sleeping dragon inside. We walked into the bed-room where I'd decided to sleep. There was an acceptance that this thing needed to be done. He'd been assigned; I submitted.

I'd slept with only one man, had made love to only one man, was still loyal to one man who didn't seem to want my loyalty. And now there was this ritual to be followed, this christening, this birth into something other than I had been. There was this thing that needed to break the logjam, the ice jam, the impasse.

He helped me unbutton my blouse. He helped me undo the metal but-ton on my Levi's. He slipped his hand beneath the elastic on my bra and caressed my back. Held it like a baby's back. We sank onto the bed. Then we were falling and falling into a black hole, me holding onto a doll and kissing his plastic face in the whirl of stars and space.

"God," I pled silently. "Why am I doing this?" I felt a scream lodged in my throat. I felt the man's physicalness rolling over on top of me. In my mind, I pushed him away, even as I lay still and allowed him to grope for my arms and shoulders. I was scrambling after God who was walking away from me, his back turned. *This isn't me, God. This isn't me breaking my cov-enant of chastity. I'm not betraying all the things I'd ever hoped for—Mother of Zion, true and faithful wife. This is someone else.* I had no idea who this man was as he rolled away, back to the bed that wasn't his or mine until he got up to go to his own room. Nor did I know who lay here in my body.

When I saw him in the yard as I packed my car for Salt Lake the next morning, we didn't kiss. We didn't say good-bye. Just nodded our heads. No hard feelings. No feelings at all, except for a sense of myself being a hollowed-out container. I had little connection to this strange body walking away from that stranger, having done something my mind couldn't believe I had done.

You were supposed to save yourself for your one and only love. Now you're the dreaded bruised rose. You're not worthy of anyone's love now. You're not a good girl anymore, or even an honorable, noteworthy woman. You've failed something essential inside yourself.

But maybe, just maybe, you are someone who is incredibly brave to break yourself to put yourself back together again.

Or maybe not. Who are you?

::

I'd grown tired of counting cornfields and barns. A farm was a farm was a farm was a farm. They were endless in Iowa, as were the words that rolled through my mind while I rolled and rolled over cracked pavement, scattered gravel, and the remains of the long gone. And there were the words hounding me, the hounds of heaven:

Loyalty. Integrity. Purity. Sacred. Pure. Holy. Let. Light. Shine. Before
men.
Restlessness. Boredom. Satiation. Betrayal. Shameful. Unworthy.
Bruised. Broken.
Family name. Honor. Forever. Mother. Madonna. Virgin. Whore.
Good. Example. Always.
Sigh. Weary. Fed-up. Aberration. Blood. Purity. Pure in heart.
Separation. Flock.
Family. Family. Family. Everything. Eggs. Basket. One.
Good girl. Bad girl. Blight.

::

Sin. Error. Degradation. Broadcast. Magnify. Attack. Defend.

Stones. Throwing. Blood. Drawing. Stones. Holding. Turning.
Dropping.

Pride. Goeth. Before the fall.

Opposites. Attract. Everything. Rises. Falls.

::

Emerging. Subsiding. Gain. Loss. Pendulum. Swinging. Broken.
Fix. Mend. Repair.

Perfect. Perfection. Perfecto. Perfectability.

Broken wings. Soaring. Falling. Shelter.

Hammered. Chiseled. Refiner's. Fire.

::

Pure in heart. Strength of ten. One. Many. One. Many. Up. Down.
Stand. Fall.

Carousel. Carnival. Carnie. Sideshow. Main. Tent.

One. We are all One.

:: The Doves Descending ::

David didn't register any seismic shock when I told him about the gardener. He sat at his desk, surrounded by stacks of files he'd made for every idea and theory that came to him at 4:00 a.m. I felt as if I were a young girl coming to Daddy to tell him she'd proved something, that she was a Big Girl now, that she wasn't a scaredy-cat. I sat in the chair next to his desk and crossed my legs at the ankles. He raised his bushy eyebrows and said, "Really." He was quiet, then looked up at me as if looking at his wife for the first time ever. He tilted his head.

I cleared my throat. "You've wanted me to be more open-minded, you know."

"That's true."

"Are you happy now?" I asked this question with an edge in my voice.

"Are you happy now?" he answered.

I shrugged my shoulders. I couldn't admit I had things to learn. I also couldn't say out loud that the shattering of my vows, my promises, my ethics, and my loyalty seemed a harsh sacrifice. Because he subscribed to a different set of ethics, David didn't understand the magnitude of this sacrifice.

"Different people want different things," I said. "My mother and father. You. The Church, society, the Sixties, free love, the Seventies, open marriage, people with closed minds, people with open minds. Whom should I listen to and why should I listen to everybody else anyway?"

"What do you want for yourself?" He put his hands flat on top of his knees and turned to look at me directly. "What's important to you?"

"I want us to be happy." Open palms. Tented eyebrows. Slight pleading in my voice.

A pause from David. A consideration of evidence. A look at me. A look away.

"Let's make this agreement," David said, fiddling with a letter on his desk. "If I don't like who you're involved with, I'll say so. Same with you. If you don't like someone I'm with, then tell me. Checks and balances."

"All right," I said. "That seems simple enough. And we won't lie to each other or hide anything, will we?"

"No." he said.

"Do we need to shake on this?" We both laughed.

Not long after our deal was struck, after eighteen years of battle over what the LDS church meant in our marriage, we pondered whether or not to end our involvement and withdraw cold turkey. David told the powers that be at the law school that he was struggling with whether or not he should stay in the Church. The man to whom he reported told him to be patient and prayerful and to come and see him again later. After many weeks, days, and hours of angst, I finally decided that not being involved with the Church on a daily basis was a good idea because, plain and simply, it didn't work for me if it wasn't working for other members of my family.

As a couple, we'd never fit comfortably. The religion of our birth was always a sore subject surrounded by too much tension. I was tired of sitting without my husband at church, of dragging my children to church to sit by my side unwillingly because they knew their father was home alone. Too much edginess. Besides, Lady Chatterley had lain with the gardener. Both David and I could be excommunicated or dis-fellowshipped should someone in authority choose to shine a light on our doings (though I felt I could justify mine on the basis that I was trying to keep my marriage intact). Maybe we could find something that would bless our lives rather than create problems, something that didn't claim to be the only truth or the only answer.

Christopher, our fourteen-year-old, was surprised, especially at me who'd always been the stalwart. "It's like we've been going along for all these years believing one thing," he said, "and now you throw it out the window."

It wasn't so hard on Jeremy, who'd often resisted church as if he were oil on top of water, or on Brad who'd just been baptized under the wire of our decision. But Chris went into his own tailspin. He'd been a believer as I'd been a believer. I told him he could go to church if he'd like, but he said no, not without me. I didn't know what to say, wandering in the dim light of a hazy territory looking for the best path. I'd relinquished my position as Mother, Guardian, Guide, and Stay. Chris flailed, even floundered, as we both struggled to reinvent ourselves and what mattered.

::

For a while I lost my reason. Having done what I'd done, I didn't know who I was or what I wanted. I was thirty-nine, still a mother and a wife, and yet a foreigner in my own body. I'd blown up the walls within which I'd lived my entire life. As they tumbled down I became drunk with the craziness of it all.

I decided to take an MFA in writing degree at Vermont College, a low-residency program where I'd only visit the campus twice a year for a two-week stint. I was ready to take a writing career seriously. After hours at the residency, in a most minimal fashion, I experimented with drugs with some of the students. I'd never had an alcoholic drink or a cup of coffee or tea until then, age thirty-nine, and I thought, as long as I'd broken some of the bigger rules, why not this one? *Why not go all out while I'm on the loose? Get some experience. Make my own judgments as to what's good and bad or useless or helpful.* The shy one felt bold. She needed realignment.

Luckily, I knew my physical self well enough to know when I'd gone too far. One of the students was generous with his stash of pot and his high-grade cocaine. Even though I stopped using before I ever got started, I was still caught in the world without walls. I was used to boundaries. I was off the beaten track with no trail of bread crumbs to follow home.

While David continued his involvement with several different women, I had an affair with both a professor and a student during my first residency at Vermont. I was available. I was a woman with a scent men could smell. I wanted to understand this chemistry. To be this chemistry. It was all new, self-conscious as I'd been when I was young in the fifties and sixties. Sensuality. Sexual power. A new toy.

Every six months while I was away at Vermont College, I became wild and free and wanton (the word my mother would have used to describe a woman like me). I thought I was in love two or three times, though maybe I had to think I was in love to do what I was doing. I rationalized my affairs because my husband said it was okay and because I didn't lie or hide anything from him. This was our contract.

After graduation, I continued on as a teaching assistant at Vermont and, twice a year, continued to see the man I'll call Alex, who'd been a fellow student in the program. When I was back in Salt Lake City walking around Lincoln Circle at night, past my neighbors who'd settled into their beds, I gazed wistfully at the different phases of the moon, Alex on my mind. "I love you," I said passionately to the constellations in the sky, which I hoped would carry my message where it needed to go. But what was love, I asked myself sometimes when only the wind answered back.

::

One summer, David taught law school for ten weeks in Bridgeport, Connecticut. The whole family moved East, where we spent weekends in Manhattan and at the beach where I enrolled the boys in sailing classes. On the night before we were supposed to drive back to Salt Lake City, Alex called and wanted to see me.

"Do you mind if I see him before we go?" I asked David.

"We're supposed to leave at five in the morning. Don't you think you should stay around and finish packing?"

"But I haven't been able to see him this summer. I never get to see him in Salt Lake. Your extramarital women live close by. Wouldn't it be all right?"

"I guess so," David said as he folded his clothes into his suitcase, obviously not happy with the inconvenience of this request.

"Is this a problem?"

"No. Go ahead." His body language said something else.

I packed and cleaned until Alex arrived, parking on the corner so my sons wouldn't see me leaving. But he was late. Very late. Ten thirty. Originally, I'd said I'd be back by one o'clock, but I telephoned David from the restaurant where Alex and I had a late dinner to say I'd be later than that. I didn't return until four in the morning, though I planned to use that last hour to finish packing my bags and do what was necessary to depart on time.

"So where in the hell have you been?" David stood outside in the driveway. It was still dark. He was tossing luggage into our van. "How can you be so inconsiderate when we have a cross-country trip to make? Find your own way home."

He stormed into the house, led the boys outside—their hair bed-mussed and their clothes barely buttoned, told them to get in the van and pushed me away when I tried to climb in. "I said find your own way home." He handed me my suitcase, slammed the van door, and backed out of the driveway where I watched my family disappear down the street and onto the freeway ramp.

Stunned, I dragged my luggage to a pay phone where I called an old friend with whom we'd spent time that summer. She picked me up, took me to her home, offered to lend me money for a plane ticket, and drove me to the bus station the next morning. As the bus rolled along the freeway toward JFK, I cursed David, but also myself. *Who is this catastrophe? Do I have one shred of intelligence left?*

I was home in Salt Lake when the family van pulled into the driveway. After I hugged the children, who didn't seem to have a clue (who knew what David told them?), and after a terse greeting between David and I as we carried the bags to everyone's room, he and I looked at each other. We couldn't keep straight faces. We burst into laughter. Then we were belly laughing. We couldn't stop. We were hysterical. Tears rolled down our cheeks. He wiped his eyes with the back of his hand.

"All's fair in love and war," I said, looking for a tissue to wipe my nose.

But the comedy was brief. Too much of my life was in my head anymore—pining for someone hundreds of miles away. This was taking my mind away from my obligations and pleasures at home, and leading this fantasy life wasn't doing anybody any good. Loving someone in my thoughts messed with loving someone in the present. I didn't want this anymore. I wanted to be with the one (or ones) I was with. I wanted to love my husband. I wanted to pay attention to our children, who watched from the wings as the drama of David and Phyllis unfolded. I couldn't handle this business of open marriage. It scrambled my brain.

Unfortunately, David still wanted the same arrangement. When I asked him to end his involvement with the woman who'd once been my friend and who no longer was, he said he couldn't. He felt spiritually bound to her. "But I want this to be about all three of us together, not just me and her," he said. "I love both of you."

But finally I was free enough to say I didn't care what he wanted. I knew I couldn't live this way. I knew what was important to my well-being. However crazy I'd been, however immoral, however rebellious, however I or anyone else needed to label my behavior, I realized I needed certain boundaries for myself, certain ways of living to stay healthy emotionally and spiritually. Our three sons needed a mother. They didn't need someone off in her head living a make-believe life. I was practical. I had some common sense left. I said that was it for me. We discussed the possibility of divorce, then let the discussion lie like a sleeping tiger.

::

On Sunday evenings, I'd been invited to join a group of writing students from the University of Utah at François Camoin's home, the man who'd been my most influential writing teacher at the U. We left our manuscripts in a drop box in Orson Spencer Hall, read the manuscripts beforehand, then critiqued each other with long faces of wisdom.

One evening, François and James Thomas talked about starting a writing conference at the encouragement of Dolly Makoff, owner of Dolly's Bookstore in Park City. They asked if Kate Woodworth and I would like to be involved. Flattered, I said yes, and so did Kate. The four of us had many meetings with Dolly to prepare for the first Writers at Work Conference in June of 1985 at the Yarrow Hotel in Park City. Some of our featured guests were Harriet Doerr, who'd just published *Stones from Ibarra;*

Bernard Taper, a feature writer for the *New Yorker*; Michael Curtis, an editor for *Atlantic Monthly*; Carol Houck Smith, an editor from W. W. Norton; Gwen Head and Marlene Blessing from Dragon Gate Press near Seattle; Nat Sobel, a New York agent. The success of the conference amazed us. We decided to do it again the following year, James as director.

Coming out of my position of noncommunity involvement, I became engrossed with putting on the next few annual conferences, being asked at one point to be president of the board of directors, then a codirector with François. Inviting writers on the cusp of fame was our intention (for the most part), rather than depending on the sometimes dinosauric and demanding already-famous. We invited a stunning array of writing luminaries, some of whom were just getting started, some of whom were established: Bob Shacochis, Richard Ford, John Nichols, Charles Baxter, Fred Busch, Mark Strand, Larry Levis, Charles Wright, May Swenson, Ethelbert Miller, Charles Johnson, Thomas Mallon, Dorothy Solomon, William Kittredge, Terry Tempest Williams, Al Young, Ron Carlson, Gordon Weaver, Jack Meyers, Walter Wetherell, Stephen Dunn, Stephen Dobyns, Alan Cheuse, David Lee, Ken Brewer, Rita Dove, who sang "My Girl" with our Motown group at the conference—First Draft and the Five Erasers (my son Chris on the guitar, Elaine Jarvik on drums, me on the keys, Penny Austin, Tom Hazuka, Scott Cairns, and Wyn Cooper who'd written the poem that would later become the lyrics to Sheryl Crowe's hit song "All I Want to Do Is Have Some Fun"); Gary Fisketjon, who was in the process of editing Hemingway's posthumous novel; Gerald Marzorati, an editor at *Harper's*; Alice Quinn, poetry editor at the *New Yorker*; Alice Turner, fiction editor from *Playboy*; agent Gail Hochman, whose client Scott Turow got his first big nod from the publishing industry while Gail was at the conference.

Those were the heyday years. In the second year, we laid Persian runners and placed potted plants throughout the parking garage maze of the Park City Resort Center to help people find the meeting rooms. Members of the Park City community provided free housing for our visiting writers, food for the hospitality suite, and gave total support to the event. Rick Bass, Pam Houston, and Alison Baker were discoveries at the conference—the hottest writing ticket in the West.

One year, when Tony Hillerman telephoned to say he couldn't come after all, I called Michael Curtis at the *Atlantic* to ask if he knew someone "cheap and cheerful," preferably a woman from the West. He told me there was a young woman from San Francisco who would be publishing a story with his magazine the coming February and that I should give her a call. I did. Her name was Amy Tan. She was most gracious. "Yes, I'd be pleased to come." I introduced her to Ai Bei, a writer from Beijing who was passing through Utah. We scheduled a panel on Chinese and Chinese/American writing. I assisted with a translation/publication of an Ai Bei novella, and Amy Tan was famous by the time our conference rolled around that June. NPR interviewed her in Salt Lake City. The Gap called her to see if she'd consent to having her face on sides of buses.

In March of 1988, David and I hosted an afternoon with Ray Bradbury to raise money for the conference. I was hip-deep in the whirl of writers who visited our home and gave readings to help us raise money—Anne Beattie, Terry McMillan, Tomie dePaola, among them. Heady times. Exciting times. I was a writer now. I was part of the writing community. I felt alive. And all of this was helping to cover the yawning hole growing larger in my marriage.

About this same time, David attended a law professors' conference in St. Louis. Late for a meeting, he grabbed a cup of decaffeinated coffee. One of the other BYU professors saw him with a coffee cup in his hand. "That's been bothering me," he told David later when they were flying back to Provo. "We're supposed to be representing the Lord's school."

"It's time for me to stop teaching at BYU," David said when he returned home from the airport and dropped his briefcase and bag in the kitchen. The boys asleep in bed, I was preparing their school lunches for the next day. He looked haggard.

"What happened?" I asked, sensing something major in the air.

"It's not like I really drink coffee," he said, "but I can't keep up the charade like this. Even if I am a teetotaler, if I *have* to be a teetotaling member of the Church to be teaching at the law school, then it's time I go in a different direction. I thought only Pharisees dotted their i's and crossed their t's and prayed in public places."

Both of us looked at each other in a now-wait-a-minute moment of recognition, neither of us saying anything about the other, more crucial problem that would have been a much greater affront to the university, the law school, and the professors.

"It's time," he said quietly, lifting his suitcase and taking it to the bedroom to unpack. "I won't be a hypocrite anymore. I hope you understand."

I didn't want to understand as I stood there spreading peanut butter and jam on whole wheat bread. I swallowed, feeling my slim connection to my metaphorical air supply being cut with a knife. *This is my last lifeline to my way of life. I don't want it to slip away. This is my tribe, like the Masai, Navajo, Hopi, Maori, and Ogalala Sioux have their tribes. God is my breath, my blood, my language, and my thought. I know about God in the way my tribe knows about God—charity never faileth, love one another, the Lord is my shepherd, the Word will abide. I don't want to be on the outside looking in. This is what feeds me, even if I pretend otherwise.*

I swallowed hard as I cut the sandwich in half diagonally. He'd said he was quitting his job at BYU. That was that. Standing there stuffing PB&Js into plastic sandwich bags, I realized it had been a matter of pride for me that he was a professor of law at the "Lord's University." It was evidence that we were in high standing within the structure of the Church. But pride goeth before the fall. He made the necessary arrangements to leave and taught part-time for a year before resigning completely.

As synchronicity would have it, David's parents appointed him executor of their estate when they needed to move to Utah to be closer to those who could help care for them. They gave him administrative control over the family property in Concord, California, which included several other properties his mother had acquired with pinched pennies. Never learning how to drive, she'd been blessed with a remarkable ability to walk for miles to find a deal or save a few cents. As a result, throughout the late eighties, David and his Legalines partner, Bob, assembled parcels surrounding the family property to create one contiguous piece of real estate. As extraordinary luck would have it, the Bank of America bought six blocks of Concord next to this property to build a corporate center. After a long string of negotiations, Pacific Gas and Electric bought David's parcel for a hefty sum. He now had a door through which he could escape.

But still, there was rotting in Denmark to consider, as Hamlet might say.

::

"I can't stop crying," I said to David after six weeks of nonstop crying jags. "I can't find a way out of this hole."

In the spring of 1989, I couldn't sublimate my feelings in busyness anymore. David had been listening to me weep, downstairs in his office in the basement on a beige sofa. I wept for hours, days, six weeks before we decided it would be smart to consult an expert to get a prescription for this untapped faucet.

"We had an agreement," I said to him. "You promised if I didn't like a relationship you were in that you'd stop. I'm not okay with the one you're in anymore. You're too attached."

"Sometimes people can't keep agreements."

"But you promised."

"I know. You're not saying anything new."

If I had to name one point where the melancholia took the upper hand as my response to life, it would be that time when my marriage showed no signs of repair. No sign of change after twenty-five years: David was still insisting his needs weren't out of the ordinary and that polygamy was the true order of things even though he hadn't suggested anything formal.

This was getting out of hand. This was insane.

"In the early Christian church there was a practice called the 'Descent of the Dove,'" he'd told me the night before. "Something outlawed in 200 A.D. Two people who loved each other would embrace sexually, not trying to reach a climax, but praying for the descent of the Holy Ghost. They'd be filled with the spirit. They'd open up and become expansive rather than closed and contracted. Things should be defined in terms of consciousness rather than moral rules. The spirit, not the law. Why can't people love each other and let love be the large thing it is?"

"I'm not comfortable with your relationship with her, and especially with the idea that she's some kind of spiritual wife. I'm your wife."

"But," he shifted in his chair, "it's like I've been getting downloads from Joseph Smith, like I have a psychic connection to polygamy. I feel that she and I were married by God, like we were ordained by the Spirit."

"The right to plural marriage was withdrawn in 1890," I say, my shield rising. "Besides. The first wife is supposed to have something to say about it."

He paused, almost as if he stopped long enough he could figure a way to get the prize. "But I care about her," he said. "I can't just break it off like that."

"Why not? I did it when you asked me."

"You don't understand."

"What part of the word 'no' don't you understand?"

This was the moment when I decided there was a hungry beast in the house, one that wouldn't ever go away, one that got bigger the more you fed it. This was the moment I gave up the notion that I could change David. He wasn't my clay to be crushed and shaped anew. His "needs" would always be first; his insistence that men were, by nature, polygamous, and that multiple relationships were acceptable, even ordained by God in the right time and place, would never end.

"Look at the Old Testament," he told me. "Look at Islam. Look at Africa. All over the world. It's not a strange or unusual practice."

The psychiatrist called my moods "aberrant depression," but prescribed lithium because of the story I told her about my father's mother. The one with melancholia. The one they said was dying of a broken heart. After the first appointment, David broke off intimate relations with his psychically/ spiritually acquired new wife.

:: In the Beginning ::

When you see a psychiatrist, your conversations remind you of things, of those tied boxes that have been sitting in your personal garage, unorganized and unnoticed, for too many years.

You start thinking about your beginnings, those things that shaped you, those moments commemorated in those old white-bordered snapshots that made you believe you were a certain way: the shyness in the photograph with your dog, Rocky; the full unruly lips stretched tight across your teeth covered with braces; the awkwardness of your oversensitive, skinny body that showed no signs of maturation; your near-sightedness corrected by the cosmic cat-eye eyeglasses that told the world you were stylish and hip. You wonder about those stories you've told yourself so many times. You wonder how your life became your particular life. Why didn't you make a few different turns along the way? Why did you respond the way you did?

Maybe I need to start before romance and marriage, maybe go back to the beginning . . .

One day, I must have been about nine years old, my mother was showing me how to shape a loaf of bread. She must have been feeling the need to teach some fine points of homemaking to her growing daughter. "The consistency of the dough will tell you when it's ready to be shaped into loaves," she said. "It will have a soft elastic feel." She showed me how to push the dough with the heels of her hands, back and forth, pushing and pulling it into a fat lump before flattening it again. "When you poke it with your finger and the fingerprint won't stay indented, then you know it's ready. Now you try it."

I stood on a low stool to gain the best leverage for the task.

"What was it like when I was born?" I asked her while I attempted my first kneading. The dough was a big challenge for my skinny arms.

"May 11, 1943. A great day in my life. Your dad won a hundred dollar savings bond that very day, so we figured you were a lucky child. But I had to hold you back for thirty minutes, tight inside the birth canal until Dr. McCormick arrived from an emergency call. I'm sure you didn't like being held back. You were always ready to get on with life and do it up big. I was so excited when D.M. got back and when you arrived, your arms flailing, rearing to go like you still are, all of your toes and fingers in place, a headful of black hair."

She watched me do battle with the dough. "Use the heels of your hands, not the palms. Here," she demonstrated, "like this." The muscles of her strong arms tightened as she pushed. "Now you try it again."

The heels did work better than the palms, she was right.

"Rose de Lima Hospital," she continued. "That's where you were born. Basic Townsite, Nevada. That was its name until they decided to change it to Henderson. I remember the delivery room doors opening wide as you and I were rolled into the hall. D.M. was with us. He removed his glasses and gloves and stopped to shake hands with your anxiously awaiting father. 'It's a girl,' he told Herman. 'What do you think of that?'"

"'It's a girl?' your father asked when D.M. made his announcement. I remember how he tried to hide his disappointment, but the tears came anyway. It wasn't that he didn't love girls or you," she reassured, looking gently at me because she couldn't touch my shoulder with her dough-covered hands. "We already had Elaine. He was crazy about her. But, you know about Douglas who was only three years old. How he died the summer before you were born. Died of iliocolitis for want of penicillin in the Ely hospital. Your dad must have been hoping for a replacement, I guess, and just couldn't hold back the tears. Don't get me wrong. He adored you. But there's something about fathers and sons."

My thin young arms were aching from the effort to tame bread dough.

"Here," she said when she saw me running low on steam. "Let me spell you off."

"I wept all through the pregnancy with you," she continued while I rolled little snakes from the stray pieces of dough. She leaned extra hard into the large blob of pre-bread with the concentrated strength of her arms, upper back, and shoulders. "I couldn't get over Douglas going limp right while I held him on the way to the hospital. Me sitting there in the passenger seat and your dad driving as fast as he dared. I kept trying to get hold of myself after he died," she confessed, "but the tears kept coming."

I can imagine those tears seeping down into her womb, making things moist there, dripping into the incubator where my tiny hands and eyes and toes were forming. Blue lagoon, blue haze, blue bayou, blue womb. Thora Jane Mickelsen Nelson had used a moist, slow method of preparing me for life. Tears—a given. Tears—a style of responding that I inherited. Easy tears constantly rising to the surface—my legacy from both my mother and father.

People said I looked like her: the shape of our faces, our black hair that turned prematurely gray, our aristocratic noses. She had a noble profile, a regal elegance even though she was what most would call a simple farm girl born on the west side of the Grand Tetons in Tetonia, Idaho—an immigrant from Denmark for a father and for a mother one of the beautiful Hubbard girls, known for her embroidery and skill with raising chickens. My father always called Mother his queen.

Maybe that's what I've been waiting for—someone who loved calling me his Queen of All and Everything.

"In the next few months," she continued as she sprinkled more flour on the counter to keep the dough from sticking, "your father got over his initial disappointment. He really doted on you. Before he went away to war, he was tickling your chin and tossing you up in the air and patting your head. He was a good father. A loving man."

When I think about him now, I remember how I adored the man with the sparkling blue eyes. Even now, when I look at his picture in the dark sailor suit with the white piping on the collar and the sleeves, the one I keep on a shelf of the bookcase next to my desk where dancers dance on the mobile, I still light up as if I were a little girl wrapped in a string of Christmas lights. I can feel that age-old response, the sheer joy of my daddy smiling back at me, even if it's only from a black-and-white photograph. How I loved my daddy.

"But he heard the call of duty," she said. "There were war cries. It was 1943. Soldiers and sailors and pilots were needed. But he didn't have to enlist," she said with a trace of bitterness in her voice. I took over kneading again. She greased the bread pans with Crisco smeared on waxed paper. "He was twenty-six years old and had two children. He didn't have to go. But you know your dad. He felt a surge of national pride every time he listened to the radio, Edward R. Murrow, Gabriel Heater, Churchill's speeches from England. He still gets a lump in his throat when the flag passes him at a parade or when he sees it waving over the post office. He needed to play his part."

She showed me how to roll out the dough into a rectangle with a rolling pin, fold it in thirds, then turn it over to make a rounded top before tucking in the ends. "He sent a note to the Clark County Draft Board to ask when he'd be drafted. He passed his physical with flying colors and was given his pick of duty.

"Feel this bread dough now," she interrupted herself. I'd poked the newly made loaf, and sure enough, my poke hadn't stayed indented in the dough. But I remember getting bored with breadmaking and kneading and the extra flour she kept asking me to sprinkle on the counter. I wanted to go out and play with the neighbor across the alley, the only other Phyllis I'd known at that point in life—Phyllis Thomas.

I can still smell the bread we baked together that day, maybe combined

with all of the bread my mother baked in that gas oven while we were grow-
ing into awkward teenagers. She tried to nourish us well when we returned
from school. Golden loaves. Crisp tops that had a hollow sound when we
thumped them. Melted butter and honey drizzled over the hot bread. Maybe
I should start making bread again. I can feel the consistency of that dough
even now, the moment when I could no longer leave a thumbprint on its sur-
face. Consistency. What does that mean? The condition of adhering together;
firmness of material substance, the dictionary says. I think of the material
substance of my father, a romantic at heart. He'd been landlocked his entire
life. I imagine that he had dreams of himself standing on the deck of a ship
steaming toward faraway ports of call he'd only read about. His life of grand
adventure to that point had been found on bookshelves at the library. He
chose the navy, the sea.

By Christmastime, Herman Evans Nelson, named Herman after a
great-great-uncle who'd been an officer in the Danish army, was on his
way to basic training in Farragut, Idaho. I was seven months old when Dad
moved us to Idaho Falls in between winter storms. That way, he figured,
Mother could be near her sisters and her own mother. They could help her
with her babies. Her brother Lloyd, one of her six brothers, helped her find
a job teaching in a one-room school in Sage Creek, but no one had time
to babysit this baby full-time. Sit by the baby. Stick around the baby. Walk
and talk this baby. Dance and prance with the baby. Everyone had a farm
to tend, chores to finish, a full plate of their own. One of the things my
mother told me that day was that I was a little like a football, spending a
day here and a day there—a grandmother, a great-aunt, a neighbor—and
finally, she was forced to toilet train me at eleven months so I could be
taken to a scratch-and-bite nursery school where babies my age weren't
supposed to be.

I can only imagine that occasion being a great contest of wills. In my own
infant way, I probably began resisting her even then, testing whose will was
strongest. I was like she was, after all. And I must have puzzled about the
disappearing things in my life, why I saw so many new faces, why my daddy
didn't peek around the corner of the door to make me laugh. Except, maybe,

too, my wondering was my mother's wondering at why she'd been abandoned by her young husband and ignored by her family. Who knew where her feelings ended and mine began?

In Idaho, my mother tried hard to do right by her two children. With only one year of college on her resume, she tried to be a good schoolteacher, but she'd been thrown back with her well-meaning but uneducated parents of ten children. They didn't encourage her to further her education, read books, or discuss ideas. They knew their code well: how to farm, how to get up with the chickens, how to work, work, and work hard, how to worship at the Mormon ward house on Sundays. Everyone was supposed to carry his or her own weight. Solid folks. Good, physically strong people with strict rules about caring for one's self.

According to my father's notes that my brother Steve compiled, in August of 1944 our father was sent to the Pacific on the USS *General Howze* troop ship. He loved the moment he sailed under the Golden Gate Bridge with two thousand other men reporting for duty and cruising to Hawaii where he saw the remains of the USS *Arizona* in Pearl Harbor. Two months later, a Fireman 1/c, he was assigned to the USS *Caliente*, AO53, an attack tanker that carried aviation gasoline, oil, grease, and tanks of oxygen, acetylene, and other supplies to ships in the Seventh Fleet. When his ship harbored at Ulithi, he watched the *Mississinewa*, a ship anchored a few yards away from his own, burning and sinking after an attack by a Japanese midget sub that had entered the harbor when nets were opened for a freighter to pass through. He also heard destroyers in the harbor dropping depth charges, later learning they'd sunk three enemy subs. At this point, Daddy must have reconsidered the romance of the seafaring life.

I can picture him leaning against the ship's railing and thinking about inches and yards, the grand design, and whatever had he been thinking to leave his wife and children to fare for themselves.

In December, while we were decorating a Christmas tree with popcorn and paper chains in a small farmhouse in Sage Creek that belonged to Uncle Lloyd, Daddy sailed to Okinawa where he was caught in a terrible typhoon, "waves rising as tall as the mast of the accompanying cruiser, strong enough to roll back the deck like the lid on a sardine can." Acetylene tanks and drums of oil and grease broke loose and gyrated wildly across the deck. Some of the smaller ships beside them sank in the violent seas. A few days later, probably while we were roasting a chicken from Grandma's coop for Christmas dinner, he celebrated his newly renewed life by "dancing the polka with a sailor named Hlasnik. Back in the safe harbor of Ulithi, we danced on deck to the music of an accordion. Merry Christmas, one and all."

With the coming of the new year of 1945, Daddy sailed through the Surigao Straits and enemy fire to fuel one of the fleets in the Philippines. He watched bombers drop bombs on Panay to protect the tankers. In August, after the *Enola Gay* dropped another bomb called "Little Boy" on Hiroshima, the uss *Caliente* and Daddy sailed to Japan where he toured Tokyo, Yokohama, and Yokosuka in a jeep with Guy, another one of my mother's brothers who was an army MP. Daddy bought a Japanese rifle, "relinquished because of the terms of unconditional surrender." After the treaty was signed, his ship sailed on to Tsingtao on the coast of mainland China to take oil to Chiang Kai-shek. He rode in a rickshaw and heard children saying "kome-sha," "give me something." Others tried to procure business for their prostitute mothers, and the idea of children pimping marked him as deeply as watching men die. That was a story he repeated many times during his life. Finally, he returned to Idaho Falls, where he tried to live among the farmers to make Mother happy. Because she was an Idaho girl, she wanted to stay near her brothers and sisters and what she understood. But the weather was cold. My daddy was a man who loved books and ideas and warmth. His constitution was delicate. He had a young family to support and time to make up.

He took us all back to southern Nevada where he took a job as a salesman for New York Life Insurance. Boulder City had been built in the early 1930s to house the builders of Hoover Dam (then known as Boulder Dam). It was a federal reservation, a fortress hedged in by bare mountains that were black and full of minerals and chemicals. The important people—the engineers, Bureau of Reclamation administrators, contractors, and the

better educated—lived at the top of the hill in solidly built, desert-red brick houses. Our $500 house that had been brought in from Basic Townsite on a tractor-trailer was tacked onto the town at the bottom of the hill where we could look out the front window and see "B" Hill and the desert. It stretched toward Arizona to the southeast and California to the southwest where rows of tower transformers marched across the desert. To the north, this no-man's-land was dotted with craggy lava boulders and dark outcroppings. Daddy must have redoubled his efforts to protect his young family. He had more mouths to feed now, as my brother, Stephen, had been born—a son at last.

The years that followed were good for our family, even though I was unconsciously stuck with the notion I'd been cheated of something undeservedly when Daddy had other things to think about besides me. That notion sat like lead in my belly, this little princess subterraneously negotiating a way back to her throne—playing the piano, winning spelling bees, getting top grades, trying to fill an unfillable hole, begging for attention from the father who now seemed so distant, the man she loved more than any other except for God, whom she also believed was her father.

In the meantime, he was elected to the city council and also called to be bishop of the Boulder City Ward of the Church of Jesus Christ of Latter-day Saints. Our church, the great equalizer because of Christ's teachings that we should love one another and that all humans were equal in the eyes of God, was the centerpiece of our lives. Our harbor. Our safety net. No questions asked. People loved "Herman," always saying what a nice, kind, gentle, and sensitive father Elaine, Steve, and I had. He blossomed during these years, directing the building of a new chapel for the ward, receiving kudos for his quality service in the insurance business, fathering one more daughter, Kathy, who looked just like he did and whom he unequivocally adored. I remember feeling jealous of the attentions he gave her, and yet I also had big affection for my new baby sister, who livened things up around the house. Then, somehow, something got to him, maybe the night he got a phone call to come quickly, one of the ward members had shot himself in the head. Being the sensitive man he was, he handled the details himself and didn't ask for anyone else's help.

That story was a seminal one for me, even though I only overheard it in bits and pieces and may not have the facts aligned. To me, it seemed that the night he returned from that task, he was a changed man. Granted, that may only be my storyteller's penchant to point out a particular moment in time as THE *turning point,* THE *agent of change,* THE *height of the tension.*

Not long after that, my father asked to be released from his church position. He said he needed more clients for his insurance business, which meant a move to Las Vegas. Even at eleven, I wasn't convinced by this reason. But move we did to a house at the south end of the town that was still small in 1954. Our new home was a yellow stuccoed, thin-skinned, two-story tract house that faced the never-ending desert once again. Dust storms assaulted the windows. Day after day, jets from Nellis Air Force Base streaked across the sky leaving contrails imprinted on pure blue and sometimes breaking the sound barrier—a sonic boom that shook all the glasses in our cupboards.

My father seemed more nervous in this place. Pressure seemed to be building inside him after he left the town where he'd mattered. When he couldn't play the game and get bulldozer-aggressive as insurance men are supposed to do, he spent more and more time at home where his bookshelves were lined with self-help books about confidence and how to get it.

We all seemed more nervous as he labored in the front yard wearing his pith helmet, trying to make grass grow while the wind blew the seed away, inside in his study reading *Think and Grow Rich,* and trying to pay the bills that became harder to pay. As he became freer with his hand and sometimes his belt, I became more liberal with my smart-mouth comments. One time at the dinner table, he slapped me hard across the face, stinging the skin, making my cheek salsa red. My mother threatened to leave him if he ever did that again. Nervous mother. Nervous children. Nervous me in this uncertain place—a lost and displaced princess who didn't like her further fall from grace.

Maybe my disappointment was filtered through my mother's disappointment, but it seemed as though the first father who went away to war never came back—the one who told me how I was good luck because of the savings bond, the one who tossed me in the air, and blew raspberries on my belly. I kept waiting for that part of him that went away and never came back. This other man was distracted. He seemed worried. His little princess Phyllis could annoy him. Maybe he was the same man but not the one I wanted him to be or who my mother wanted him to be.

Maybe I've never stopped hoping to find the first daddy somewhere.

:: Two Thousand Kisses Deep ::

High above the hood of our car, a hawk swirled with the current. David leaned forward, his eyes skyward as I oohed and ahhed over the marvel of that bird of prey floating on the invisible ridges of thin Colorado air. It understood the physics of ether and the avoidance of gravity.

Though I didn't want to leave our home in Salt Lake City, David, Brad, and I had moved to Colorado in 1990, while Chris and Jeremy went off to the Northwest to attend Evergreen and Whitman colleges. David had been traveling back and forth between Salt Lake City and Summit County, Colorado, to take care of an investment he'd made in Silverthorne with his business partner. The high mountain ranch property needed to be developed and sold before it drained off the money David had made in Concord after splitting the profits equally with his brothers and sisters. He needed to protect our newfound riches.

"We need to move to Colorado," he'd said one night as I sat on the edge of the bed removing my shoes. "I can't keep traveling back and forth."

"You know how I feel about leaving Salt Lake . . . I've got so much going for me here. A writing network. The kids' friends. All of our friends."

"I know, but even though you're happy here, I've never felt like Utah was my home. I'm just not like most of the people here."

"So you've said many times." My voice could be caustic. Like lye.

"It's just killing me to live in two places." Then he looked at me with narrowing eyes. "But I guess if you have to, you could stay here . . ."

Lines of demarcation, lines in the sand. The silence was pungent, almost putrid with resistance as I carried my walking shoes to the closet. But, caution here. That was our family we were talking about—our family we'd promised to keep together at all costs.

"I guess if we have to, we have to," I finally said. I pulled my nightgown over my head. "There's still Brad to think about."

"And there's something else I need to tell you." He stood on one side of the bed. I stood on the other. "You know I don't want to keep anything from you anymore. I've met a woman over there who's really stressed out. She's in an unhappy marriage, and she's developed MS, probably because of all the stress. I wanted to help her out, so I've been sharing some information with her on relaxation methods."

I could feel the sympathy card being dealt. I braced myself as we pulled back the bedcovers and put our pillows against the headboard to serve as cushions for our backs.

"She's really been down," he said from across the bed, both of us still standing.

"That's all well and good, but your idea of helping someone out is different from mine. You always think you're in love. I can hear it in your voice."

When he didn't answer, I exploded. "This is ridiculous." I walked around the end of the bed—a banshee unloosed again, feeling like the agonized female spirit bewailing the coming death of something she loved. "When will this end? When are you going to put our marriage first?"

"Maybe we should just get a divorce," he said.

"Fine with me," I said quickly, buckling my armor. "I'll keep the Salt Lake house, my friends, and my niche. You take an apartment in Dillon. Done deal."

A long moment of silence settled over us as we climbed beneath the bedcovers to sit side by side—upright and stiff.

"Let's think this over," David said. "This isn't a decision we should make right now. We've made it through a lot of ups and downs, you know."

I sat there rigid—a wooden woman who needed someone else to operate her arms and legs. My skull felt numb. And then, in a moment of levity, I thought how maybe I really was a numbskull. I laughed to myself, though didn't let it show.

"There's Brad," I said. I slid down under the covers onto my back. "I don't want to finish raising him without his father."

"That's true."

"Maybe we should hang on a while longer. I know your relationship with this woman isn't platonic. Maybe you can pull back from your involvement."

"When we both step off our soapboxes," he said, sliding down beside me, turning out the light, and putting his hand on my shoulder, "we still love each other, don't we?"

"In our own strange way." I turned out the light on my side of the bed. "We just can't agree on what it means to be married, can we?"

"No, we can't," he said.

As if habit were greater than any subject matter, we leaned into each other for our ritual good-night kiss—a rather stilted peck, not without feeling. We'd been at this juncture too many times to let this one be our Waterloo.

But then, unable to keep my mouth closed as I rolled over to find sleep, I said, "Is this stalemate or checkmate?"

His exasperation cut through the darkness. "You don't know when to quit, do you?"

"Neither do you."

After twenty years of living in Salt Lake City, we had a huge garage sale and packed up our household in a gigantic U-Haul truck to head for bigger mountains: 9,300 feet, Straight Creek Drive in Dillon, Colorado, next to the Continental Divide, Loveland Pass, and the forest primeval where a mountain lion took down a jogger the first week we were there, just snatched him from the dirt road where he was on a training run for the high school track team.

While David worked night and day to pull his property development together, my life had became one of supporting Brad at his soccer and basketball games. I cheered his every move. I ran the concessions stand for both soccer and basketball. I also helped create an artist series in Summit County with the energy left over from Writers at Work, then dedicated the rest of my time to my writing. Within the space of four years, four books were published, all of which had been in the works before I left Salt Lake City: *The School of Love, And the Desert Shall Blossom, How I Got Cultured: A Nevada Memoir* (which won the Associated Writing Program's award for creative nonfiction our first spring in Colorado), and *Legs: The Story of a Giraffe*, a children's book. After my book of short stories, *The School of Love*, received a rave review in the *New York Times Book Review* "In Short" section, the director of the Vermont College MFA in Writing Program called and asked if I would like to teach for them—the same low-residency program from which I'd graduated in 1984. It proved the perfect job to alleviate the loneliness of exile in the mountains of Colorado. A perfect blind.

As the hawk floated above our car that day on lonesome Highway 40, I knew that David's and my strongest, and maybe only, connection to each other at this moment was our youngest son—Brad, Bradley, Birdley, The Bird (an appropriate name for his skinny legs and thin body). He was a talented athlete like his father, and we were returning from a high school soccer game in Steamboat Springs.

A magpie perched on a fence post, eyeing roadkill. The hawk in the sky faded from view.

"David," I said, as we descended the steep grade out of Rabbit Ears Pass, "I've been understanding, haven't I?" I'd resisted this subject for the trip over and for part of the trip back, but this question had been eating at me. I'd tiptoe carefully. "I know you're seeing her again."

"Does it help to discuss it? You know how far we get on this subject."

"But aren't problems supposed to be solved?"

"Yes, they are," he said. An antelope leapt gracefully over a fence into a cattle pasture. "But this is a hard one. I'm having a very difficult time financially. Bob and I are running into lots of snags with the property. And this woman helps me feel like the world isn't such a hard place. I feel more passionate and alive. And frankly, with her in my life, I feel even more love for you."

"But David," I said, a big truck with an extended cab passing us at eighty miles per hour as if it were a mach one county sweeper. "This has been going on for years now. You tell me you love me, and then you want me to be understanding and flexible and Buddha-om-like, but nothing changes. Why don't you just admit you don't want to be with me anymore?"

Silence.

"I keep hoping you'll wake up one morning and say, 'Everything's okay now. Been there. Done that. Don't need it anymore.'"

Again, he didn't answer. I listened to the tires on asphalt, then saw a doe standing patiently at the edge of the highway, waiting for us to pass. I spotted a fawn in the gully behind her, nosing the grass that grew roadside. *Why are the bucks always absent? The fawns and the does out grazing by themselves? What is it with the male species?*

I broke the silence. "I need someone who puts me first."

"Is this the real crux of the issue?" he asked. He turned on the radio, which broadcast sheer static until he turned it off, but then the car seemed as though it were standing still while the scenery raced past. "Can you trust that you're loved, even if you aren't the only one?"

"Prove it to me. Come in my direction. Halfway. At least halfway."

"You want me tied up at the door, don't you?"

"That's an idea," I said, half laughing, though I couldn't keep hold of the humorous perspective. "I want you to give up something you want just like you've asked me to do."

"We both want something we're not getting, so we're stuck. How can we get unstuck?"

"Look," I said, pointing my finger at a large bird lying at the edge of the road. "There's a hawk. It's been hit. Maybe it's alive. Stop the car."

David braked. I waited at the edge of the road for a pickup to speed by, then crossed the now quiet highway lined by a barbed-wire fence and sage being bent by wind.

It was a red-tailed hawk, unmoving, no blood anywhere. It was still until the wind picked up one of the wings slightly, as if encouraging it to fly, beautiful in its silence, in its stillness.

"Come on, Phyllis." David rolled down the window. "I've got a meeting at six."

I couldn't move, being so close to a bird of prey that was impotent and so like me, stopped on this highway, wings down, dreams broken, the wide sky called marriage that I'd believed in and that had held so much promise for me and my children, the wide sky failing me and the hawk. I'd been so sure something would change and that time would heal the wounds and that God would intervene and make everything all right.

I walked back to the car, slowly, as if I were alone on a hiking trail rather than in the middle of a highway, even though no cars were in sight. "Open the trunk, please."

"Why?" he asked.

"I have an old dress I was taking to Goodwill. I need it."

"Why?" he asked again.

"I'm taking that bird home."

"What for?"

"I need to. Please pop the trunk."

At the sound of the latch unlocking, I walked to the back of the car, pulled out a dress in which I'd danced, even danced wildly once upon a time. I carried it across the quiet highway and covered the beautiful bird and his red tail feathers. It was a whole bird, nothing missing, almost as if it had a heart attack or had glanced off a fender. I tucked the dress around its wings and gathered it into a bundle that I carefully placed in the trunk of our car.

"That's illegal, you know," David said as I slid back into the car. "You could get a fine."

"I didn't shoot it," I said, buckling my safety belt. "It's a gift from Mercury."

"What are you going to do with it?"

"I'll bury it eventually, but I want to save some of the feathers as special gifts, especially the tail feathers. It's not every day something like this just drops into your life. You know how some of my friends are into sweat lodges and Native American ceremonies."

"If you say so."

And for one entire day (the next day after Brad helped the Tigers of Summit High School win their soccer game), I dismembered the bird. I cleared the dishes and laid the morning's newspaper over the top of my butcher block. This was no small bird. I gathered scissors. Pliers. Even a hammer.

As I held those implements of war in my hands, I felt many impulses: bold; angry like a thrasher and a hacker must feel; reasoned, rational, scientific—the biologist I'd once been in high school lab. I assessed the attachment of the wing to the body. The task wasn't going to be easy. I felt on the edge of mad science, as if I were someone uncontrolled, sawing through that modified forelimb—those membranes, muscles, and sinews. I was at one moment a cave person, a woman fighting for survival in the wilderness of her kitchen, and a woman preparing sacrificial gifts for a few friends, her sons, but maybe mostly herself.

The red tail wasn't a challenge, but when I tried to separate the wing, it was attached with a sinewy, gumlike string or muscle thick like catgut. Those ligaments or tendons seemed stronger than anything I'd encountered before. The bird was no barnyard chicken I was preparing for dinner. I sawed back and forth. I pressed harder, then harder until I made a small slit. The sight of the unnatural gash and the thick pink fluid caused me to cringe. But I'd gone too far to stop.

The knife dulled rapidly. Its edge gummed as pinfeathers stuck to the steel and to my fingers. I felt as if I were being tarred and feathered. But still, there was that need to divide and conquer. I used the full weight of my shoulders. I pressed harder and deeper.

This was not the beautiful bird up in the sky, I reminded myself. These were the remains. These were only bones and tendons and science in front of me. These were feathers that would have been crushed by the wheels of a Dodge Ram carrying livestock to market. I was preserving these feathers for my friends. Still, I was the Destroyer. The gluey liquid wasn't like blood I'd known. It covered the newspaper and the edges of the butcher block.

My wrists and forearms and fingers and fingernails were covered in the essence of blood that was sticky and pinkish. I smelled the smell of dismemberment and destruction as if I were on a battlefield and the bones that were meant to be strong were being crushed by my will to survive. Beyondananda—that was where I wanted to be with that bird and its wings as they cracked and split apart. Except, the bird seemed closer to life than death. Still wet. Still supple. The sun hadn't sucked its bones dry yet.

There were hundreds of thousands of feathers—each shaped differently—some ends pointed, some rounded, some shaved close to the shaft, some curving outward. Each was a microcosm of flight, of soaring, of modern aviation. Pinfeathers, tiny down feathers. Strong exquisite quill feathers. I marveled. Each served its tiny usefulness, each was an integral part of the whole of the bird that could soar and be something so mysterious.

With the hammer, I pounded the rim of the wing until I separated the strongest, longest, and most exceptional feathers. I placed each on tissue next to the red tail fan: for special people and ceremonial occasions. I wrapped the package carefully and put it in an empty dress box from a Denver department store. I carried it to a safe place in the garage. I tied it with a string and hoped the Division of Wildlife Resources wouldn't come searching for this lost bird. I hadn't shot it. I hadn't hunted it. But I hadn't left it to its natural process of decay, either. Had I committed a crime?

The feathers safe in a box, I folded newspaper over the carcass and prepared the bundle for burial or for the trash or for a sky funeral. I couldn't think of what was best at that moment. All I knew was that kitchen, that mess on my hands and under my fingernails, those changing elements.

::

We sat side by side on Olympic Airlines. We were flying back to Athens on our return from Tel Aviv, the Israeli National Basketball team also on board. David and I had taken a month away from Colorado to go on vacation—the Nile, the Sinai, to Petra, and to Jerusalem where we'd flown in a private plane with a former Israeli fighter pilot to get an overview of the place where Jesus walked, where Hasidim beelined through the Christian Quarter with their heads bowed and an Uzi clutched tightly to their ribs, where eleven Jewish students had been killed by a bomb a block from where we'd eaten lunch.

We'd been at each other's throats the majority of the trip. Same subject. His I-have-to-have-this. My I-have-to-have-it-otherwise. There was no denial on the Nile, or on the Sinai, or in Petra. No pretending. The cards on the table, this was the bottom-line summit meeting.

The tour bus had been our battle headquarters. Our Waterloo. Our Armageddon. Everyone on our tour knew something was wrong, even though we'd spoken in whispers and wore pleasant enough masks. But our passionate discourse could be felt, if not heard.

Luckily, there were distractions: the middle-of-the-night hike up Mount Sinai where we witnessed the sunrise and the vast purple cloud cover over the mountains below and remarked about Moses being smart to choose that place to talk to God. We'd danced with the crew under the boat's canopy on the Nile, frolicking to the music of a one-stringed violin and a doumbek; we'd flown to Abu Simbel and the mammoth pharaohs carved in rock; I'd taught the six other women in the group how to belly dance on the shores of the Red Sea and scavenged the local markets for scarves, skirts, jingling coin belts, and zils for a command performance. We danced barefoot in the sand, starting out seductively, clinking our zils in perfect rhythm for a few measures. Then we broke out in girlish giggles, bending over in gales of laughter while our Muslim tour guides watched the forbidden scene covertly behind the screen of palm fronds. And best of all, I danced with a Bedouin in a Bedouin's tent in Jordan. Our hypnotic, reed-like movement to the sinuous music of the oud and high-pitched drum bound us together in a trance, as if we were making the most exquisite love without ever touching. Thank God for those distractions that kept David's and my battle fire at a minimum.

But now we were whispering heatedly again while members of the basketball team stood in the aisles, their bodies crammed, their heads crunched against the ceiling, their legs too long to sit comfortably. *What was it like to be so tall, so out of measure with the average world? But then everything seemed out of measure, out of balance, out of kilter.*

"When are you going to pay attention to the fact that I'm your wife?" Tears I'd come to despise filled my eyes.

He shrugged his shoulders, beleaguered by my dog-teeth-on-the-ankle pleading and my need to have resolution to this issue. He crumpled the empty bag of peanuts and poured the last of the ginger ale into his cup of nearly melted ice.

He wasn't the most handsome of men, though I'd always found him appealing. He had a slight build in a well-conditioned body, but his face sometimes seemed puffy and hinted at old-age jowls. A fringe of scanty thin hair stretched behind his ears. His skin was pale and freckled. Some people were surprised when they learned he was my husband. They said we weren't a match. But I'd always loved his eyes, so intense, and his quick, bright mind that could venture into so many different arenas. I'd loved this adventurer of the spirit, trying to break through his limits, trying to understand why people did the things they did. He was certainly the most intense, as well as the most interesting, man I'd ever known.

"I've tried to be like Jesus with no judgment," I told him, though he'd heard this line before. "But I'm turning into an obsessed monster, always looking for clues. Those dead giveaway signs. The quick smile of a beautiful woman. The wink. The stare. Obsession dictates my world, and I'm sick of it. I feel powerless, except to say good-bye, but why do I have to say good-bye to my family I love just because you put your needs first? What's a partnership about anyway?"

It was as though my words were raindrops pelting a window, as though David had a wall in his brain that blocked him from grasping my logic, or that I had an electric fence in my head that protected me from grasping his. Somehow, I didn't feel like myself sitting by his side. I'd turned into a green-eyed stranger—unable to dance to my own music, haunted by that jealousy, that anger, that ineffectiveness, that need to be loved, adored, and cherished. Maybe it was all a sleeping princess dream. Maybe I couldn't have what I wanted, which was "my way," and my way was the right way, wasn't it?

"Phyllis, there's one thing I'm certain about," he said, pulling a wrinkled time schedule from his shirt pocket. "I don't think anyone should force another person to agree with him. It must feel like I'm doing that to you. But it's like I prefer chocolate ice cream and you prefer vanilla. That doesn't make me wrong and you right. It's what makes you, you. And me, me. I need to accept what I am and not be ashamed. Both of us need to accept our experience and not judge the other. But it's clear you'll probably never agree with my point of view or truly understand it. What do we do now?"

"Right now, the plane's going to land." I heaved a big sigh and leaned my head against the back of the seat. "We need to decide what we're going to do for the day." He checked the times and distances on the schedule. "Looks like we don't have enough time for the boat to Santorini."

I traced my finger over the timetable. "Delphi looks possible."

"Delphi sounds good," he said, refolding the schedule with too-tiny print. "I've always wanted to see it. Sound good to you?"

"Definitely." Though the thought of one more place to sightsee was not the most welcoming one at the moment.

The tour bus to Delphi was two-thirds empty. Off-season. The other passengers kept at a distance, possibly sensing our uneasiness, our subterranean war, though we'd exhausted our arsenal. We were tired of talking. Tired of engaging in no-win battles. After we arrived, the others scattered and disappeared. It seemed the whole of Delphi was ours for two hours.

We wandered on the barren path, commenting on the port far below where centuries' worth of boats had toiled upstream from the Aegean and about the gnarled trees whose hard-earned greenery had been shaped by centuries of heavy rain, fierce wind, and drought. As we approached the seat of granite in the Temple of Apollo where the Oracle was supposed to have given her enigmatic answers to unanswerable questions, the day turned hotter and the air seemed to quiver, almost as if it were a gelatinous substance.

"It feels like the air's full of wide wings," I said, looking up, sensing.

"Something does feel different," David said. He pulled his cap from his back pocket to protect his bare head. "I'm not sure what."

"I'd like to stay here a while," I said. "You don't mind, do you?"

"No. I'll look around. Where should we hook up?"

"I'll wait here. About a half hour?"

The rocks jutted out everywhere as if determined to protect this place from anyone who would do harm. I wondered about the others who'd come here: shepherds, goatherds, seekers, kings, generals, gladiators, poets, mystics, people who believed in the unseen, people who did not.

As I stood before the Oracle's place of divining the unhearable and the unsayable, I again felt the subtle presence of large wings in the air, their steady movement, their fluttering. I felt my mind opening up, my ears becoming finely attuned. Rather than holding my breath, which I sometimes did when I felt unsure, I felt it falling into synch with the subtle breath of that place. Almost unbidden, from an unconscious place in my mind, I asked a simple question.

What is love? I asked silently. I waited for a sign of someone or something to appear on the granite outcropping. The wind played around the angles of the rock. Teasing.

What can I do to know love, to express love, to be love? I'm tired of being caught up in my own world that keeps knocking me on the sides of the head. I'm tired of the self-pity. The sadness. I want to know real love. I want to get outside the prison of my self that seems so demanding. Help me know love. Tell me how, Oracle.

As soon as I thought the last three words, I felt a stronger beating of the wings and a rush of wind. Almost as if they rode on the wind into the labyrinth of my brain. The words swept through quickly, as wind will do. Deep, strong, ancient owl words.

A mystery is a mystery. And then the echo. *A mystery is a mystery.*

We flew over the Atlantic that night, the windows blackened, everyone curled up however they could in their seats to find sleep.

::

I remember writing this song on Clarkson Street in Denver in 1996. Spinner and I lived in the upstairs. Jeremy lived in the basement. I'd found a new jazz piano teacher, the amazing Eric Gunnison, to pursue my neverending fascination with weaning myself from the written pages of music:

I believe in love, Sometimes, sort of, maybe.
I believe in love, When it looks like my kind.
I believe in love, When the cards are stacked right,
> Love, love, love, love, love.

::

I believe in love, When your face is open.
I believe in love, When your heart is showing.
I believe in love, When I'm sure you love me,
      Love, love, love, love, love.

  ::

A mystery is a mystery is a mystery,
A mystery is a mystery is a mystery. . . .

  ::

Are the straw that breaks the camel's back and the last straw the same thing? I wasn't sure. I shouldn't have, but I invited her to lunch—the woman in Summit County where David, Brad, and I now lived, the woman who was sleeping with my husband. We gave our order to the waiter and then chatted about the weather and the office where she worked with David and the trouble in Israel (wasn't there always trouble in Israel?).

"So, you wanted to talk to me," she said, her fork poised over her salad.

"Yes, I did." I took a bite out of my Reuben. I'd gained twenty pounds since we moved to the Colorado mountains.

She lifted a grilled piece of chicken to her lips, the lips he'd been kissing whenever he could find the privacy. She was younger. A blonde. Attractive, though not especially so. Because I was the enemy assessing the enemy, I decided there was something insipid about her, something weak.

"This is a small town, you know," I said. "And we have a son in the high school. I don't want people smirking knowingly around him. Or around me."

She looked annoyed rather than repentant. I'd hoped for a bit of repentance or understanding in her eyes or in her mouth. No sign.

"You know, we only have this last year until our last son graduates from high school. I was wondering," I said. I sounded desperate. Inane. Weak. Somehow these were the wrong words. "I was wondering . . ."

"Wondering what?" she said, putting the last piece of bread on her plate and tearing it in half slowly.

Why do I do this? Why do I think I can say anything that will make a difference? Why am I coming from such a weak position to a woman who's taken the wrong position, according to most standards? I know I'm gaining weight. I know I've been nonresponsive to David in bed. Why do I feel apologetic, and how have I lost my right to ask for my rights?

I hesitated. I chewed methodically. *She'll be a shrew someday, even if she's blonde and hot for love right now.*

"Well," I finally said. "Couldn't you and David wait until this school year is over. I'll probably be leaving then, and you two can do what you want. But now, couldn't you just wait?"

She studied me from across the table. Cold. Icy. But maybe she was afraid. Maybe she was summoning up her courage, too. Maybe she had no use for my tepid requests that reminded her of her compromised position.

"That's not what David wants," she said, looking me directly in the eyes.

If I could have spit in her face, I would have. If I could have slapped her or called the police to put this nuisance in jail, I would. But that was not my style. I was a lady at all times and at all costs. I'd been trained to be polite. But at this moment, I hated this woman and all the women who needed to have their vanity stroked by the attentions of men, women who thought husbands were fair game, women who betrayed other women (forget the gullible male and his ego and forget the fact that I'd done the same thing).

But I couldn't say anything. It was like there was a closed and locked door in front of me. But wasn't I the wife? Didn't that count for something? Two ends against the middle. Was that what that meant?

Six months and no changes later, it was Labor Day night. After she called our home, which she'd never done before, David asked if it would be okay if he went to her house. She needed to talk. He'd be back by ten. I said okay even though it wasn't. He didn't show up the rest of the night. The next morning, I was blind with the pain of accepting the inevitable. I got in the car. I sped through Frisco and Breckenridge, sped over Hoosier Pass in my four-wheel drive, made a screeching right turn at the Mosquito Gulch turnoff on the way to Alma. I didn't care where I was going or whether I got hurt. I climbed higher and higher and ended up on the thirteen-thousand-foot pass between Leadville and Alma. The old stagecoach road. The one with massive boulders for pavement. Me driving insane. I could feel broken pieces of heart rattling around when I traversed over the half-submerged boulders.

The big trouble happened when I reached the summit. After blasting through a thin layer of snow on the east side, I suddenly found myself plowing into two feet of new snow as I crossed over to the Leadville side. The snow on the east side had melted in the morning sun where I'd driven up, but not on the west.

It would have made a great movie: inches at a time; royal weeping and wailing. I couldn't see the edges of the road. Tears clouded my eyes. Too much snow. A two-thousand-foot drop to my right. Forward was the only choice. It was as if the back end of the car was made of rubber. It fishtailed every time I put my foot to the gas pedal. I crept. I bargained with God. If I didn't die coming off the top, that would be a sign that my life was worth living.

Out of nowhere, a man in an SUV came driving up the snow-covered road and honked his horn for me to let him pass. "No way will I drive any closer to the edge," I got out of the car and told him. "If you want to get around me, you'll have to move my car out of the way yourself."

"They shouldn't let women drivers up here," I heard him mumble as he climbed into my car and negotiated sliver-close to the edge. "Stupid woman," he said getting back in his car, making no effort to speak softly.

The man wasn't dealing with a mere car here. He was dealing with years of pent-up rage and frustration. Years of trying to adapt to David's needs and not having him recognize mine. Was I playing the victim? Yes. I knew that, but I didn't care. Stubborn woman? Yes. Stupid woman? Possibly. How could anyone with brains have stayed in that marriage for that long?

When I arrived at the bottom and rejoined paved road, I knew our marriage was over. I knew things would never change and that I'd reached some kind of impasse that required another solution. Maybe I had no faith, but this thing between us had become a torture chamber. Time to leave. Time to say good-bye.

Funny thing happened when I said, "You do what you need to do, and I'll do what I need to do," and when I moved to Denver into a condominium with many windows and lots of light and where I could remain in close proximity to my sons, yet stay out of the town where that ice princess lived and kept seeing my husband. David told me he'd help me every way he could. He also stopped seeing the princess. Stopped cold, though I didn't know it at the time and didn't care.

:: Filling the Void ::

I needed someone. After all, I'd lived with three sons and a husband for thirty years. My nest wasn't just empty. It had been obliterated.

I met him in July of 1994. After a separation of nine months, David had picked me up from the airport after I'd taught for a semester at the University of Missouri as a visiting writer and after I'd finished my two-week stint in Vermont. He'd volunteered to drop me off at my place in Denver—an old mansion converted to five condos in Park Hill—and I sensed he was hoping I'd be happy to see him. But I was determined not to need him anymore. We hadn't gained any ground. I was still angry over the losses, the betrayals, and his insistence that he couldn't change. Besides, something in me wanted a bold stroke. "Boldness has a stroke of genius in it," Nietzsche said. A rebel part of me still felt like riding a Harley in a blizzard in a leather jacket and chaps, no helmet, wind blowing my hair every which way, me not caring how fast I drove or whether I crashed.

With David standing behind me, my bags in his hands, I unlocked the door to my condo. Startled, I saw canvas drops covering the living room floor and a house painter standing on a ladder. The contractor had promised to be finished with the job before I returned from Vermont.

"Hi. I'm Spinner. I work for Jack," he added as if reading my mind. "I was supposed to be finished before you came back, but the job's bigger than we expected. Sorry."

"I'm glad it's getting done," I said, most of my attention on the unspoken dynamics between David and me.

"Do you want to go out for an early dinner?" David asked. We stood next to each other in the doorway of the room that smelled of turpentine and paint.

"I think I'm too exhausted. Maybe another time. But thanks for picking me up. I appreciate it. A lot." Being valiant, he carried my bags to my bedroom. I gave him a good-bye peck-on-the-cheek kiss—casual enough to get my message of unavailability across.

"Catch you soon," he said. Then I heard my door close, his footsteps descending the hall stairs, and the sound of the heavy, bulky front door snapping to a close.

When I became aware of Spinner again, I saw an attractive, somewhat bashful man in his midthirties dressed in painter's whites, paintbrush in hand, and hair streaked with paint. My immediate impression: a simple man, organic somehow. A man who could be happy driving a long-haul tractor-trailer. I'd grown weary of paralysis by analysis. Of intellectualizing relationships. Of battling with David over his repressed needs. I felt a pull toward Spinner immediately—some animal kind of magnetism. That he would be part of my life felt like a done deal the minute David closed the downstairs door, our thirty-plus years together neatly summarized in the click of the latch.

Spinner painted my condo for a week, though I think his boss, the contractor, kept him on the job to make me think he was providing more service than he was. This justified the outrageous price he'd quoted and which I'd agreed to pay. As far as the contractor was concerned, I was a single woman with three Persian rugs and a concert grand piano who reeked of naiveté and unconsciousness about matters of the world—that is to say, a sitting duck.

I fixed lunch for Spinner every day. We sat down and ate at the dining table—me fixing food for my absent family. We had heartfelt, intimate chats. "I have a lot to make up," he told me. "I screwed up my marriage, my chance to be with my daughter." This was something I could relate to. People often told me their troubles.

Two weeks after the painting was finished, Spinner telephoned to ask me out to dinner. I was in a reckless mood. I said yes. But as we ate dinner at the nearly deserted Italian restaurant I'd recommended, too early in the evening, nothing seemed right. I became all too aware of what must have sounded like my high-blown, intellectual diction. I loved language. I loved to philosophize. Spinner had barely finished high school and had one semester of dissatisfactory college experience. In my usual effort to wrap myself around a situation, I shrank my sentences to converse simply.

He didn't seem comfortable either in his dress-up khakis or in the emptiness of the restaurant with its ghost waiters standing against the farthest walls. Of course, I was sixteen years his senior, having lied about three of those years because I couldn't bring myself to say, "I'm fifty-one years old." But as we drove back to my place and began to relax, I knew I was tired of walking to the edge of the ocean, putting my toe in the surf, and running back to safety. Something in me wanted to run into the water, sans clothes, surrendering to the waves that would carry me where they would. We sat on the coral-colored sofa in the living room to recapture our lunchtime rapport.

"I've made lots of mistakes," Spinner said. "I'm trying to make up for them."

"Haven't we all?" I said with conviction.

"I spent a year in prison," he said out of the blue. "It was when I had a drug problem," he added.

"I guess a lot of people get in trouble because of drugs," I said, unshocked and calm. "I've made mistakes, too. I . . ." I paused. "I may have been responsible for my son's death."

I waited. I held my breath, surprised at myself and at the words that had jumped out of me, as if there were a serpent inside injecting its poison into my system and that this poison wanted out. This was my black secret, the one I thought I'd laid to rest twenty-four years before this moment.

Because Spinner didn't say anything, I kept talking. And the story, from deep inside the locked closet inside my chest where the serpent lived, came pouring out. *Why am I doing this, telling him this tale I've relived a thousand times? This story that's been unspoken until now? Is it because he shared his sins with me? Is it so he won't feel badly about what he's done when he knows someone else shares the same territory? Or could it be that I want forgiveness?*

He touched my face gently. "I'm sorry." His eyes were those dark brown eyes that looked as if they were small, still ponds almost hidden by over-growth in a thick forest.

We slid to the floor onto the dark blue Persian rug in front of the glass-covered gas fireplace, removing each other's clothes, bruising each other's face with blind kisses, and lying together as one: two sinners doing pen-ance, their voluntary act of contrition.

As the music on the stereo became audible again, I heard myself saying, "I love you." Who knows what I meant when I said those words, but they were the words that came to my lips.

"You don't even know me," he said. "You don't know anything about me."

But I let the words stand. For all I knew, I meant each of them. Some-thing about Spinner moved me. Gaping wide open with my own vulner-ability, I'd walked headfirst into his. Sitting next to him on the floor, I said, "I'm here to stay. Whatever you do, I'll stand by you." *Mother Teresa Phyllis. Woman Phyllis. Lusty me. Lonely me.*

When Spinner left, I turned the deadbolt in the door behind him. It was the loneliest sound I'd ever heard.

::

After that night of contrition, Spinner was elusive. He called and said he wanted to go on a bike ride, then didn't show. I called and invited him on a picnic, then he stood me up again. I was crushed. Since I hadn't had time to get established or make friends in Denver, his breaking of promises only redoubled my efforts to cross paths. I began calling him when he didn't call me. Maybe, to keep his options open, he showed up from time to time. We shared several afternoon delights that excited every hungry cell of my body. After all, I was a passionate woman who hadn't had physical contact for almost a year and who'd shut herself down to her husband who hadn't kept promises. I threw myself into the ocean without a life vest. I'd sink or swim, but I wasn't going to be tepid, shy, or reticent. I wouldn't mince one step or one word.

But early in August, when it became obvious I was more interested than he was, I struggled with the possibility of obsession, even possession: I must have/I can't have. But what was it that I had to have?

In a candid moment on one of his rare visits, Spinner said he'd promised himself he'd never say "I love you" unless he meant it. He had an ex-wife he once loved and a daughter whom he loved more than anyone on God's green earth. He didn't want to mislead anyone. I was impressed by his integrity. His honesty. Maybe someday, he'd feel like saying "I love you" to me. But by the end of August, my brain reported for duty. This was a no-win situation. I'd put my heart out to indifference. I decided to use what wits I had left to get out with some dignity. I'd swim back to the shore before the sharks started biting big time. But I was a slow swimmer.

Though I knew Spinner was smoking pot occasionally, I had no idea he was hooked on crack. About the time I decided to use my brain and get on with life, the telephone rang.

"I'm at a halfway house," he said, his voice sounding as if he lived in China. "I'm going down fast. I need help. Would you come over and see me?"

I jetted to the address he gave me—a halfway house on Wadsworth. He sat back on a tipped folding chair in front of the Arapaho House dressed in a wrinkled purple T-shirt and jeans loose at his hips. He seemed shy. Beat-up emotionally. Fried, actually. "I haven't slept in a week," he said. "Would you mind buying me a pack of cigarettes?" I was only too glad to bust myself down to the closest gas station to help him out of his nicotine misery. *St. Phyllis. Friend of the downtrodden. Committed to saving Spinner's life. I could help him find his way out of his deadbeat/loser sense of himself. I could love him like a king so that the god in embryo would hatch out of his scaly shell.*

For the thirty days Spinner spent in rehab, I arrived promptly for evening meetings five times a week. He'd asked me to be his sponsor, after all. The jaded counselors instructed the families and sponsors about the high failure rate of rehabilitation, but we each harbored hopes for our loved ones. When one of the counselors asked me if I was Spinner's mother, I answered, "Sort of," without letting on how deeply I'd just been offended. I made friends with the other "clients" and listened to their stories: a beautiful African-American high-fashion model who said she'd give anything to be reunited with her children; an alcoholic/heroin addict who'd been abandoned on a doorstep as a child; a rocket scientist with a doctoral degree. I brought flowers, books of inspiration, and thought I was doing the right thing, the genuine thing.

On the last day I visited, Spinner made an announcement: "I've fallen in love with Erica," he said. "You've met her. She's the one who doesn't say anything at the meetings. She's quiet." He was careful of my feelings. "I gave her some of the flowers you brought me. She needed them. I hope you understand."

Speechless, I immediately found my way down the long corridors with my heart falling out of my chest into my hands onto the floor—my bleating lamb heart. I drove up to the mountains, always the mountains for sustenance in hard times, as if they had room in their vast reaches to accommodate all sorrow. I drove to the edge of a high mountain lake. I sat. I slumped over the steering wheel. For all my effort, I had nothing. A raven flapped silently over the lake. *He never said he loved you. He didn't ask you to adopt him. Why are you asking a drug addict to make your life all right anyway?*

As soon as his time at rehab was up, Spinner moved into Erica's house, and the swim back to my own personal shore began. Twelve strokes, Australian crawl. Twenty strokes on my back. Side stroke for as long as I could stand it. Back to the crawl to make distance. *Don't try to find out where he is or what he's doing. Don't call his cousin. Let go. Let him out of your heart.* But I felt as though threads woven by a frenetic spider had circled, crossed, and bound me to this man and wouldn't release my arms and hands and legs that wanted to swim back to shore.

I signed up for jazz piano lessons with a local musician who played at one of the big hotels in Denver. He came to my condo for lessons. Through the weeks, he became increasingly insistent that I come hear him play at the hotel, that I have dinner with him, implicitly that I do more than dinner. After feeling his intensity getting out of hand, I finally told him "Good-bye. Sayonara. Thanks for teaching me to play the bass line in stride piano style." I was getting tougher. I'd look for another piano teacher.

::

How to recognize when you're the star of your own soap opera:

When you cry about the nice things people will say about you at your funeral

When you think you are all the sad songs on the radio

When you blame the next guy for your hemorrhoids, ulcers, and bad luck

When you think the birds are singing just for you or won't sing just because it's you

When you think the world owes you or when you think you're entitled to special privileges

When you keep wishing the world turned differently

When you suspect you're the star but aren't sure whether it's good or bad news

When the cast and the script revolves around you, when you can't laugh at the lines, and when you realize who wrote the script

::

As always, at the precise moment when someone has gained ground, the cat comes back.

Three months later, two days after Thanksgiving, Spinner called. I was shocked to hear his voice. To the core. "I want to come by," he said.

I didn't know what to say.

"Just for a minute."

I hesitated. Silence on the line. "Okay," I said, my voice subdued, noncommittal.

"Half an hour."

I didn't invite him in after I casually walked down the two flights of stairs to answer the door, both of us pretending not to see each other through the leaded-glass side windows and the front-door glass. I stepped outside.

"Come out to my truck," he said. We walked down the front walk, down three concrete stairs to the sidewalk, out to the curb and the shade of the gigantic elm. He opened the car door and picked up a small white box with a purple bow from the passenger seat.

"For me?" I said, totally surprised. I untied the ribbon and lifted the lid. "What is it?" I lifted a beautiful silver and turquoise pin from the soft cotton and turned it in my hand—a Native American symbol with two heads meeting in a near circle.

"I got it in Montana when I saw my daughter for Thanksgiving. It's for you."

"But why?" I blurted out.

"I want to thank you for everything." He paused and dug his hands deep into the pockets of his Levi jacket. "So thanks."

I wished I could have said, "Thanks, but no thanks." But I felt pleased as a little girl is pleased when her father puts his hand on her head and says, "You're a lovely daughter." I felt gratified to have left my mark, and yet I knew I was feeling too grateful.

"That's kind," I said, hiding the emotions rising inside. I turned toward the condo. "Take care of yourself now. Okay?"

"Okay," he said, then walked around to the driver's side of his truck, lit a cigarette, climbed in the cab, and started the ignition. Smoke trailed out the open window as he accelerated, driving into the afternoon, into the veritable sunset. *Good-bye, Spinner.*

Inside the door, I held onto the doorknob and took three deep breaths. I still cared, but I had overcome. I could now get down to the business of living my life with a strong will and good common sense. But the sun didn't set on that textbook farewell, the one my mother would have approved, the one I wanted to believe I could write.

A week later he called.

"I can't find work right now. December's a slow time. If you have any friends who need work, could you send them my way?"

"I guess my kitchen needs painting," I volunteered after a minute of mulling it over while we discussed other things. "But I'm not paying the contractor's price."

"I'll do a good job. On the side. Cheap."

We kept everything formal. He did his best work. He was, after all, a good painter, trained by his German–house painter father. As a thank-you gesture, I invited him to a Christmas party with some new friends I'd met. He looked stiff when he arrived—and pale, the circles under his eyes blacker than before. He seemed uncomfortable. If I'd known how to read signs, I'd have known he was using again, but he wasn't my business anymore. He left early. If I suspected he was headed for trouble again, I nevertheless said, "C'est la vie," when I closed the door and returned to my other guests.

Off and on during January, February, March, and April, we talked over the phone. Luckily, he could always get a painting job, though I wondered at the fact he never lasted in a long-term situation. Two weeks seemed his max. When we spent any time together, there was a cool distance between us, until one evening when the weather turned pleasant after a late spring snow. He called to ask if I wanted to go for a walk.

Bundled into a hat, gloves, and a parka, I joined him on the sidewalk in front of my condo. "Where's your hat and gloves?" I asked, then recognized the sound of motherliness in my voice. I needed to go to rehab to get over being a mother.

"Don't need either one," he answered, tucking his bare hands into his pockets.

We walked side by side, comfortable banter between us.

"Look at that moon," Spinner said. We both stopped and looked into the inky black sky with a thin crescent of moon hanging there a if it were a pendant on an invisible chain.

"You're a writer," he said. "What would you call that moon?"

"It looks like a clipped fingernail," I said.

"I think it looks like a smile." We laughed. Talking was easy. We crossed Forest, kept advancing toward the end of the alphabet, two streets for most every letter: Fairfax, Forest, Hudson, Holly.

"Things are good," he said. "I've been clean for two weeks now."

"Good for you."

We walked carefully around patches of ice, stepping into the street when the sidewalks hadn't been cleared.

"I'm really going to do it this time. I can make it."

I avoided turning my head. I'd learned to put a lid on my gullibility, remembering the stats from rehab: something like 5 percent of their clients, if that many, turned their lives around permanently. "Wouldn't that be nice?"

"Thanks for walking with me," he said as we turned back onto my street, a D street, Dahlia.

"No problem. It's nice to be out on such a night as this," I said. Then I laughed out loud.

"Do you know that's a line from a Shakespeare play? 'On such a night as this?' I can't remember who said it, but can you believe with all the city lights running interference, we can still see the thousands of stars surrounding the moon?"

"It looks like a cradle, too," Spinner said. "The moon, I mean."

"Yeah. You're right," I said as we arrived at the doorstep.

"I'd like to see a Shakespeare play sometime," he said, then brushed my cheek with the tips of his icy fingertips. I jumped.

"Oooh. Those are so cold. Do you want a hot chocolate or hot apple juice before you go?" After all, something about Spinner did feel different. His vitality maybe. More determination than I'd seen before.

"Sure," he said. He blew on his hands as I negotiated the door keys.

We climbed the stairs to no. 3, unlocked the upstairs door, and hung our coats on the coat tree. I sorted through my CDs, found some unaccompanied Bach cello pieces, and put them into the CD player. "These are beautiful," I told him, "even though I know you prefer Leon Russell. If you let them, they can take you to another time and place."

While I was heating water in the kitchen, I could smell a joint. I'd seen him light one before, as pot was a twenty-four-hour-a-day habit of his, but not in my place. When I returned with a tray and two cups of cocoa, I impulsively decided to stop being Mother and Angel, to stop putting on every brake in the book, to live a little, to take a few hits with Spinner. It was something I'd tried maybe twice before in my post-thirty-nine-years-of-age rebellion. I hadn't ingested a drop of tea, coffee, liquor, tobacco, drugs, nothing until age thirty-nine, and very little after that. I'd never smoked cigarettes either, except for a puff or two to prove my daring. But I didn't like the barriers I always erected around myself that kept me protected and safe, the way I did when I took banjo lessons from Jerry Garcia.

Tonight, I'll do this thing. Why should I always have to be a lighthouse, flashing warnings to everyone else? Why be such a prude?

The smoke burned my almost-virgin lungs. I coughed.

"Hold it in," he said.

I followed his directions until I couldn't stand the tightness in my throat. Then we sat back on the sofa. Waiting. Listening to the music. Entering wider space.

Rostropovich's cello sang to the wild floating of my mind. Cello. Mellow cello singing phrases, digging deep into the phrases of Bach, crushing the bow against the long strings, coaxing the voice from the belly of his instrument, the deep longing vibrating through the room. And our bodies were like music, our touching a continuum of sound as Spinner kissed my lips, my cheeks. I kissed his eyelids. We sank deeper into the cushy soft coral cushions in our first time together like this in seven months.

"I love you," he said, the light from the streetlamp crossing his face at a diagonal slant as he put his hand beneath my untucked blouse and caressed the small of my back. The words startled me, coming after so long, coming out of a distant corner of a foggy universe.

"I love you, too," I heard myself saying as Rostropovich descended the scale and ended the phrase on the lowest note of the piece. That deep note vibrated in my mind. And those words. Those words that could catch things in their net. I felt a hook of some kind sliding under my skin, pulling me toward some shore, and my mind struggled to say things it should say: *He can't love you. You know that. His mistress, lover, wife, girlfriend, and main consort is cocaine.* But my mind floated off again, dismissing the hook caught on a small piece of skin. *Big fish. Little fish. Which is which gliding through the water, held in place by water, weightless, no gravity, "I love you" coming from the top of the water on a shaft of light? I love you.*

When we resurfaced, I lay by Spinner's side, squeezed in the narrow confines of a coral sofa, our arms and legs tangled. His eyes were closed. With my eyes only, not wanting to move a muscle, I looked up at the egg-white ceiling he'd painted on a tall ladder, at the cornices on the molding, at the windows level with tops of trees and streetlamps.

Spinner can do this. He can do this, and I can help him. Take him to plays. Read poetry sometimes. He's starving for beauty. For the good things in life. We can do this. Things can be whole again. Spinner loves me.

"I love you," I whispered as I stroked his shoulder blade ever so slightly.

But do you really believe in love? It only leads to trouble. If you believe in love, I think it's only sometimes, sort of, maybe.

"I love you," I whispered again.

The Human Head Is a Cube

At the end of July in 2002, my good friend from Salt Lake City, K. C. Muscolino, telephoned me in my Denver attic. Because she knew I wasn't faring so well, she convinced me to attend a workshop with her in Helper, Utah. The class would be taught by Paul and Sylvia Davis, well-known Utah painters and sculptors. We'd be studying the human head. Drawing. Sculpture. I was a musician and a writer; K. C. was a photographer. We both thought this would be a good change for us. She wanted to expand her horizons. I wanted to be curious again.

I took Amtrak from Denver. The train pulled into Helper two hours late, the town that had been named after the extra locomotives hooked up to trains to help them over the steep grade in the nearby pass. K. C., who'd driven to Helper from Salt Lake, met me at the station, and helped me settle into my room in a cavernous building that had once been a flophouse for coal miners and railroad men. The first night I didn't think about the ghosts of those who'd been there before me.

That first morning, we learned triangulation. We were instructed to treat the human head as a cube. This would help us develop the right perspective and understand the geometry of the face. Learning that eyes needed to be placed at the midpoint of the cube was a revelation. Then we were assigned to draw the head of a fellow student's beautiful girlfriend. She was young, a bundle of pheromones, a sex goddess. He fawned over her. I think my jealousy mingled with my attempt to draw her face. The lines of her face in my drawing appeared somewhat harsh. We sculpted a young Chinese man, a park ranger in Capitol Reef National Park. When I shaped his head in clay, I felt as though I were caressing him. I wondered if he sensed the familiarity my fingers were enjoying as he sat in the center of the room and turned on his stool every five minutes.

During class time, I befriended another student—a doctor's wife who lived in an out-of-the-way Utah town with her retired husband. When we conversed over dinner that evening, I heard myself heating up the familiar narrative about my recent divorce that was killing me, about my failed first marriage of thirty-three years (the number thirty-three made me sound lovable, I must have thought), about the rough relationship with a drug addict, about not doing so well on my own. It was as if those stories had become tattoos. I was showing off my tattoos again. Looking into my water glass, I caught a quick glimpse of myself. I saw a crazed lady wandering through the streets, spilling her story like water to anyone who would listen.

I made an effort to change the subject. We talked about writing. Kathryn had attended one of the Writers at Work conferences where I'd spoken on a panel. She'd tried her hand at writing, too. She asked if I'd seen a book of essays by Margaret Atwood. "You must read this," she said. She went to her room, returned, and placed the book in my hand.

Not wanting to hear myself telling any thread of my story again tonight, I went directly to my room, changed into my nightgown, and settled in with the book. The lamplight was dim, but good enough for a few pages. Immediately, something caught my attention. "It's somewhat daunting to reflect that Hell is—possibly—the place where you are stuck in your own personal narrative for ever, and Heaven is—possibly—the place where you can ditch it, and take up wisdom instead." After I read this, I laid the book across my chest. I felt a slight sense of recognition unwillingly making an appearance. This was the first time it had occurred to me that I might be locked into the story I told over and over—as if I were locked into a seat on a Ferris wheel in an amusement park.

I didn't like the notion of myself wandering from listening ear to listening ear repeating the story about not being well-loved: somebody "done me wrong"; I'm a victim of men who can't understand me; I was under the thumb of a strong-willed mother who had to have her way, of people who didn't bother seeing who I was. I had thought of my story as unique. But lately it was eerily reminiscent of a blues song someone wrote a long time ago: "Nobody loves me. Nobody cares. I've got to walk this rough road alone."

The sheet over me was paper thin and ripped as I slid down and settled onto the plastic-covered mattress and the pancake-thin pillow. Sure, I thought. My father went away to war, but lots of fathers go away to war and come back changed. My mother went off to teach school and left me with people who cared for me half-heartedly, even ignored me, but maybe that was your mother's guilty slant on the story. Not the truth. Maybe I listened to her saying wistful things about my father. Or even resentful things. Maybe she'd been angry at him for enlisting when he had a family to care for. Her to care for. Maybe I'd been her unsuspecting confidante. Maybe I let the threads of her story weave into my own.

But what story?

My brain felt tired. I couldn't think about this anymore. There were six hours of classes the next day. I set the book aside and turned off the light. A sliver of moon sliced the dingy room because the curtains didn't cover the windows of that transformed flophouse/art studio. I thought of all the coal miners covered with coal dust who must have slept here. All the railroad men and the prostitutes who'd knocked quietly on the door to this room. Undressed. Gave favors. I touched myself for comfort.

A train was coming into town. K. C. had told me trains ran all night. A last thought drifted through my mind, though I was too tired to know the truth of anything. It was possible that no matter what anyone had tried to give me—love, caring, tenderness, a helping hand to get me over the rough spots—I hadn't believed them because I'd been stubborn about the story that was mine. Whatever evidence to the contrary, I'd been hanging on. How could anyone hug or caress me when my story was my only lover?

And this was my story: I was an invisible child no one could hear. Now and Forever. I was merely matter configured to be human, a small atom who'd assumed importance because I thought and talked, a service vehicle for that human-eating force called life that needed human procreation and carbon dioxide. That is what I was.

The room chilled quickly. There were ghosts in the walls whispering their stories about women who'd done them wrong, about men who'd skipped town. If someone listened, could the ghosts finally leave those walls and find some rest?

::

Iowa: Massena. Fontanelle. Greenfield.

Rain again. Steady rain. *Rain, rain, go away.*

To make matters worse, as soon as we started pedaling the next morning, the ligament below my left knee cramped with the same knife-blade pain I'd felt in Denver. "I'll catch up in a minute," I told C. J., jumping off my bike to stretch my calves and thighs, working the transverse ligament from my ankle to my knee as best I could. The ligament connected to my knee went from bad at times, to worse, then sometimes better, just enough to keep me going.

When we turned onto Highway 169, which would take us north toward Ankeny where my niece, Lisa, lived, we ran into Sunday afternoon traffic returning to Des Moines. A never-ending stream of cars kept at us from behind. Skinny shoulders. Close cars. Sickly yellow sky. Every sixth vehicle was some kind of truck, semi, or double tractor-trailer that preempted the road. Seventy-five thousand pounds of hurtling metal sucked up great eddies of air capable of lifting small animals, road debris, and bicyclists, and splattering them against their cold steel shells.

A dark blue tractor with a flatbed full of mashed stock cars passed too close to us. The defunct cars sported painted flames and numbers on their sides. Their chrome bumpers bounced wildly—metal against metal. The driver didn't give us more than six inches. "You jerk," I yelled to no avail. Then the road calmed for a minute. The drizzling rain swirled as if it were mist. I heard a bird's cry. I saw a black plastic horse lying in the gravel before the traffic thickened again. The hills were getting steeper.

"Get out and claim some road," C. J. yelled. "Otherwise, we'll be dead meat." I made a feeble effort to claim more of the blacktop, but then decided to ride the tightrope of the white line. A sickly yellow light radiated through the air. The road kept rising. We pumped our hearts out, shifting down, standing to power the pedals even more. Too little room to travel, too much crowding, no elbow room on the highway.

Near the crest of the hill, a thirty-two-wheeler passed, sucking both of us in as if we were scraps of paper. "We're getting our asses off this highway," C. J. yelled, her sleeves, shoes, and face drenched with filthy streaks of mud. "I almost cleaned that shithead's trailer."

"He almost cleaned your clock."

"We're off this hill," C. J. said. "This is insanity."

Adel. Grimes. A Travelers Aid motel room that functioned as a nursery school by day, a complimentary room at night.

The ligament in my knee cramped worse again the next morning. We decided to stay at Lisa's house for a few days while I saw a doctor in Des Moines. "When the muscle's worked too hard," he told me, "it pulls on the attachment point. That's probably what's happening, though you might have a case of hypoxemia where the muscle runs out of oxygen for the blood supply. You need to give it much more rest than you're giving it."

"Right," I said, knowing we had only so many days left to get to Vermont.

After a two-day rest that turned into four while we waited for thunder and lightning storms to clear, we were back on the road. Valeria. Newton. Grinnell. Hill country. Amish country, where on that particular day the air suddenly went ballistic. Fierce, scrambled, choppy wind.

"What's happening now?" I shouted across to C. J., barely able to pedal forward.

"Head for the ditch," she said into the wall of wind between us. We dragged our bikes to the closest ditch, made balls out of ourselves, and clung to our forelegs. The wind bent the few trees in sight, forced the small ones to the ground, and shook the leaves in a massive blur. Everything untethered—papers, aluminum cans, snapped branches—jetted through the air.

"An adventure means you deal with what happens," C. J. shouted, though her words were mostly carried off by the wind.

"What?" I yelled, barely able to hear myself, let alone C. J.

"Risks. Adventure." She mock grimaced, her mouth screwed to the side on the last syllable—a ventriloquist's dummy in a wind tunnel. We started laughing. Sitting in a ditch at the edge of Highway 6, being at the mercy of forces larger than ourselves, we knew we had no say in the matter. We kept laughing.

"In an adventure," C. J. shouted again between gusts, wiping tears of hysteria from her eyes. "Things are never what you ask for." Because this line seemed more hilarious than the last one, we slapped our knees, our faces turned red, and we could barely catch our breath. Then, as if someone flipped a switch, the wind stopped. The abrupt change shocked us, this suddenly calm-again day in May.

"What was that all about?" I lifted my bike out of the ditch, tightened the strap on my helmet, and flicked pieces of dead grass from the seat of my pants.

"Thank God, it's over," C. J. said. She brushed the last of her tears from her cheekbone.

We biked slowly through the debris scattered across the highway and an army of earthworms disgorged from the sodden soil. We dodged them, but pieces of worm landed on our spokes and stuck to our wet pants.

"And this is the Grand Highway of what?" I asked. "Did you see that sign? That pole holding up the weather-beaten sign that read "Grand Highway of the Great Republic" was almost buried in water." As we looped around a bend in the highway, we saw commotion: people, an oversized wrecker, a tractor-trailer on its side.

"What happened?" we asked the driver of Phil's Towing Service wrecker.

"A tornado flipped the semi. Iowa City had record winds. Trees crushed houses."

"We were at the edge of a tornado?" We looked at each other with our mouths open, stunned.

"That was a wicked twister," he said, lifting his well-worn cap and scratching his freckled scalp. "What, if it's not too rude to ask, are you two doing out here on bicycles on a day like this?"

Rain, wind, go away. Come again another day.

The next night we slept in the nursery school room of the dank basement of the United Methodist Church in Oxford. Then another day arrived. Rain poured down on our backs. The pain in my leg turned vicious as we ran into formidable, unscalable, wall-like hills. I ended up walking. I pushed my bike ahead of me.

University Heights. West Liberty. Muscatine, where we stayed another night in yet another church nursery room, the night black against the windows, which were a mirror for our reflections. Two women. Two of the billions of women on the planet. Two tiny women whom Mother Nature seemed to be using for a punching bag. Two minuscule bodies inching their way across a huge nation. Hanging clothes to dry. Exhausted. Spent.

Knowing we were only sixty miles upriver from Nauvoo, the city the Latter-day Saints had built before trekking west, déjà vu filled me when we approached the sign with a straight-ahead arrow: "Mississippi River." This wasn't far from the place my great-great-grandfather, dressed in white, had been immersed in those waters for the remission of his sins, baptized by Joseph Smith's brother, Hyrum. I imagined my ancestors singing hymns of praise and dancing in the temple, sleeping, eating, growing crops, and birthing babies—all in an attempt to build the temporal Kingdom of God. Those early Saints had been filled with unbelievable passion for the holy. When my bicycle rolled past the sign, I wondered if I'd ever have that kind of religious passion again. Passion for anything.

As our skinny bicycle tires thrummed the bridge's metal plates, I looked beyond the railing where the river ran on and on and on to the sea. We were crossing from Iowa to Illinois over the big, wide, magical Mississippi. The beautiful Mississippi. Suddenly, a surge of pure joy filled my entire body. It seemed that my pores were all singing the "Hallelujah Chorus." This was the Crossing. The Halfway Point.

We'd battled the land as my forebears had battled the land. I'd battled with what God meant to me and my life. I'd battled myself, something, I was beginning to understand, that all travelers, pilgrims, pioneers must have had to do. As we crossed over the mighty Mississippi, elation pumped through my veins. *You did it. If you don't go any farther than this, you made it to the Mississippi. Fantastic.* C. J. and I stopped in the middle of the bridge to give each other a high five. "Halfway. Yes."

Two days later in Kewanee, however, after another day with unyielding wind in the face, I had nothing left to give. No pioneer spirit. The bottom of the well. It was the Day the Knee Died. As I collapsed into the chair in our motel room we decided to rent and rubbed my leg dutifully with the Cyclatron salve the doctor had prescribed, I looked over at C. J., who looked wiped out herself. She sank onto the edge of her bed.

"I know I'm not supposed to say can't," I said, "but I'm saying I can't. This muscle is so tight it's going to split if I turn those pedals one more time."

"I've been worried about you," C. J. said, her elbows on her knees, her chin to her hands. "I think you've been pushing too hard for too many days actually, but it wasn't my call to make."

"I want legs for the rest of my life, you know?"

"For sure. But you need to know something," she said in a quiet voice.

"What's that?" I snapped, not in any mood to be patronized. Frankly, I'd been grouchy most of the way, unhappy about pushing myself to do something I didn't want to do.

"You need to know you've been amazing the way you've kept going when you were hurting so much. I know this trip's been hard. It's not the kind of thing you're used to doing. But still, you've gotten up every day and kept going. And I loved seeing you make the top of the hill every time. You thought I was impatient, but I wasn't. You need to pat yourself on the back. Big time."

"Thanks," I said, though, truth or not, all I could think was that I'd copped out.

"I want you to finish, though," I said, screwing the cap back on the salve. "You started out to do this. I don't want to keep you from finishing. We'll figure a way for you to keep going. For both of us to keep going."

The next day, one month after we'd started our journey, I rented a car in Peoria. After discarding many schemes for finishing what we'd started, we both decided I'd follow along in a car, carry the panniers stuffed full of our equipment to lighten C. J.'s load by forty pounds. We agreed I'd rendez-vous with her from time to time during the day.

But behind the steering wheel, watching C. J. get a head start the next morning, I couldn't keep from wondering if I'd created the bad leg to get out of a bad situation. I knew I hadn't "Just Done It," but I did remember the thrill of listening to my bicycle wheels cross the bridge over the Mississippi, my legs pushing them across. Whatever else happened, I'd biked a thousand miles.

::

 "I smell Jesus on you, honey," the stranger said to me. He sat across from Spinner and me in the padded vinyl booth at Roslyn's, a bar on East Colfax where Spinner invited me to hang out for the evening. He'd moved into my place the summer before when he'd needed help with his daughter. He'd stayed.

"Come again?" I asked the man with three missing teeth and three hoops in his left ear. Four minutes ago, he'd slid into our booth, uninvited, with a glass of something that looked like whiskey in one hand. "Do you mind?" he said, then sat quietly sipping his drink until those words popped out of him.

The music was too loud, there were too many Christmas lights that felt phony, too many bikers, and too much snow outside the massive front window.

"I smell Jesus on you," the man said again, louder this time, then rested his forearms on the Formica.

"What's with the Jesus stuff?" Spinner spoke loudly into my ear, and even then he was hard to hear.

"Did he say what I think he said?" I shouted back over a heavy metal strain of "White Christmas." Spinner shrugged his shoulders.

I played with the clip backs of my star earrings, the ones I always wore at Christmastime, the ones I wore when David and I used to have our neighborhood Christmas parties. I unclipped the rhinestone star to rub my too-long-pinched earlobe and felt a point of the star sharp against my palm. These were the earrings I'd worn to accompany my son Jeremy when he played Bach and Vivaldi on his violin. The same ones I'd worn when I played piano at the Heather Restaurant near the mouth of Little Cottonwood Canyon in Salt Lake City, where bagpipers piped on Friday nights. I thought of the white satin blouse with the string of rhinestones on the collar and cuffs. The crepe tuxedo I'd worn for those occasions another lifetime ago.

The stranger sipped his drink and rocked his head to the beat of the music. I scoped the big window where winter raged against the glass. I looked back at the man who held his glass up against the light and squinted at the remains.

I wanted to make a joke and say that Jesus was a fisherman and did I smell like a fish, but then Spinner wouldn't laugh. He didn't understand my sense of humor.

The man set his drink on the table, then thumped his thumb to the last of the "White Christmas" beat. "He comes like a thief in the night," he said in the space between songs.

I unclipped the other earring and propped my head on Spinner's shoulder. I felt tired, weary, hanging out in this foreign territory just before Christmas, the season of the year when I should be nestled in bed with a good man and my children safe asleep in the next room. But I was doing time for thinking I knew things, for thinking I knew what it meant to be "in the world but not of it."

Spinner twirled his glass.

Spinner, I thought. The beat-up bad boy dressed in a Harley-Davidson Reunion T-shirt. He'd probably brought me to the bar tonight to find a connection. With my empty ring finger, I felt the sticky edges of an old strip of duct tape on the vinyl seat.

As the beginnings of a quieter "Silent Night" bled through the speakers, the stranger stretched his arms toward me. "I've lost my feeling. Give me some."

Spinner pulled away from my head on his shoulder and slid back into the corner of the booth to watch.

I smiled at the stranger with my smile that fit around whatever came along and ignored his outstretched arms. I reached for Spinner's hand instead, squeezing his fingers, but his hand limped out on me as if it were a dead trout. I gave it back and clipped the stars onto my ears again, trying to keep myself busy, trying not to think of my other life in the beautiful home David and I had remodeled twice—the big step-down room with its panoramic views of Mount Olympus, our grand piano with its brass candelabra where I'd accompanied scores of musicians as well as our sons. There were so many dreams in those refinished wooden floors, the leaded glass windows, and the oversized dark blue Persian rug.

"People call me Rev," the man with mustard and brown eyes said from across the table. His faded blue baseball cap didn't hide the wrinkles in his forehead and the loose, sagging skin around his eyes.

"So, if you're a Rev," I said, "give us a sermon. We could use a good sermon."

"Pull yourself together," Spinner whispered. He was an elemental man easily embarrassed by public display. "Why did I buy you a beer? You're the cheapest drunk I ever met."

"Here is the church and here is the steeple." I played the children's game my mother had taught me: interlocked hands, raised index fingers for a steeple. "Here's a church for you," I said, holding my hands out playfully to the man who was dusky above the collar of his black T-shirt and striped vest with a torn lapel.

The Rev's eyes put a hole in me first, then Spinner. "What's with you two?" he asked, his hands pointing to each of us at the same time.

I looked over at Spinner and his ever-present cigarette. My shoulder muscles stiffened. His skin seemed colorless in the strange light of the bar. Surrounded by a cloud of smoke, he repositioned himself in the sticky red booth.

"This woman," the Rev said solemnly, pointing his slightly crooked finger at me, "is love, man." His gaze zeroed in on me, one eye squinted, his chin on his wrists on the table.

The inside of my head spun with the effects of the beer I wasn't used to drinking. The sound of the clashing glasses and the throbbing bass beat jangled my head, made it slide like a trombone. This wasn't my home or my place or my shore.

"You've got a fan," Spinner said, exercising his hands on the Formica.

"I'll take what I can get." I laughed, then reached over to pat Spinner's cheek.

"Don't," he snapped, twisting away. I could feel the way his face wasn't there, that it was gone all of a sudden. The face I thought I loved. I looked out the window again, suddenly hoping someone was watching, maybe even Jesus since we were on the subject. He might be out in the cold tonight, looking for his lost sheep, waiting to take us all back to the other ninety and nine safe in the pen. Maybe he was standing out there on the curb, his arms stretched out, his eyes beaming with the holy light of I love you/the stars love you/all the Universe loves you.

The stranger, a crabbed-up old man in eight-day-old clothes, sat across the table staring. His eyes seemed the kind that could see under every layer of a person's clothing and all the layers of their skin. Maybe he recognized something I'd lost. Maybe, even though I was dressed in Levis and a turtleneck and had buried my graying hair under a champagne dye that did no justice to my skin tones, he could really see me.

"You glow," the Rev said as the bossa nova "Silent Night" played on and he took another sip of his drink.

I wanted to say "like a round yon virgin?" but didn't. I smiled to myself at the improbable thought. I'd been a virgin once. David and I'd both been virgins when we married.

"This guy's something else," Spinner said, scratching the corner of his square jawbone with two fingers and tapping ashes into the sandbag-bottomed ashtray.

The "Silent Night" tempo cranked into a turbo beat.

"Dance with me, Spinner," I said, knowing he'd shake his head no. I wanted to capture Christmas somehow, to feel it inside and out. I wanted to sing "Holy infant, so tender and mild" as I had for so many Decembers.

The stranger slid his hand across the table. "Put your hand in the hand, woman."

I closed my eyes where water was gathering and bent over to wipe my eyes with the ribbing of my sweatshirt. Nobody knew what they were doing

when they were drunk. I hated drunk and how nobody was there for anybody else when they were.

"I need to go home," I said.

"Don't do your disappearing act," Spinner said.

"Love is everything," I said. "Right, Rev?"

The man suddenly became mute, like a neo-sphinx swaying his head
subtly from side to side.

After a community roar at the bar—the favored Denver Broncos rallying
in the fourth quarter—I turned to Spinner. I leaned in close to keep things
between us. "Do you really love me?" I asked in an as-private-as-could-be
whisper.

He leaned to the left to frisk his jacket for another cigarette, leaving me
with lots of air around myself. All the time the stranger, even though he
couldn't hear us, watched our every move as he sipped his whiskey.

"Love is a suffering thing," the man finally said. Then he sat still, as if
listening for inspiration from the PA system. "Would you like to dance with
me?" he asked, making moves to slide out of the booth.

I was speechless.

"Dance with him," Spinner said. "You were just saying you wanted to
dance."

The Rev bowed at the end of the table, one hand flat against his ribs,
the other at his back. "May I have this dance?"

"Why not?" I finally decided.

He was six inches shorter, about five foot three. His body seemed
scrawled carelessly together like illegible handwriting, a curling spine
holding a frail skeleton in place. I didn't care, though my breasts seemed
too close to his nose as I stood up and faced him.

He led me to the postage-stamp dance floor as Elvis sang "Blue Christmas." Miniature lights chased each other around the window. That man
put his hand on my back. We assumed the traditional slow-dance position.
A prefab Santa's boot stood on the bar, the patchy velour on the toe rubbed
white. A few random candy canes wrapped in cellophane, most of them
broken at the crook, were stuffed into the boot.

When he laid his head close to my neck, I didn't object. Maybe because it was Christmas and maybe because I didn't care about much anymore.

"You've got Jesus in every pore, woman," he said, his ear pressed flat against my collarbone.

We shuffled across the floor as if there were no one else in the room. Next to him I felt especially large and especially small at the moment, a raw-boned woman standing a head over the Rev, bigger and broader than he was, and yet . . .

"You can't change anybody. Look what they did to Jesus."

"But I love the man," I said. Then I felt even smaller, not unlike a bottle tossed against a curb that wouldn't break and kept on rolling.

The stranger put his hand on the bony part of my chest—a firm palm against the tops of letters stenciled on my sweatshirt. I didn't flinch because this moment felt right. I felt his life surge into mine. I put my hand on top of his and bowed my forehead against the top of his baseball cap. The song ended. It left a sudden space of quiet in the room, a sparse little comma of calm.

He escorted me back to the booth where Spinner sat against the corner with his jacket buttoned and his arms folded. "Adios, my friends," the man said as he helped me into the booth and pecked a kiss on my cheek. Then he walked to the bar, held up his finger to order another drink, and squeezed his misshapen body onto a stool. As he bent over the bar, a large gap between his T-shirt and pants appeared. The laundry-grayed elastic of his underwear stretched across the dark skin of his lower back.

"Welcome back," Spinner said, crushing his cigarette into the already full ashtray. "Did you dance your feet off?"

"Right up to the ankles."

"He was sure cutting in close. Is that a good idea to let a stranger get that familiar?"

"It's Christmas," I said.

"Don't they all want the same thing?" he said.

"Does that include you?"

He twisted the ashtray with his thumb. "So what are you trying to say?"

"Please take me home. The storm's over." I looked outside. Everything was white and still. Enough snow to make the world seem soft.

He picked up the ashtray, then let it fall back to the table, a solid thunk of deadweight sand on Formica.

::

The moment the stakes became obvious was a simple one.

"When are you coming to visit?" my mother asked every time I called her. "It's your father's eightieth birthday in a couple of weeks. Please come. We haven't seen you for a while."

"I'll be there, Mom," I said, feeling guilty that I'd been so preoccupied with Spinner that I hadn't visited my parents, who now lived in Mesa, Arizona. I'd waited much too long. I hadn't seen much of the boys lately, either. They dropped by the condo from time to time, and I went to their gigs in Summit County and to holiday dinners with the whole family, but they were busy with their music careers and I with mine.

"Dad's been peeing on my plants," my oldest sister, Elaine, said when Mother gave her the phone. "Even in his closet."

"This is too much for you," I said. "We need to do something soon."

"He's getting too hard to handle. Even for my good husband, Walt. You better come down."

Spinner had been living in my condo off and on for over six months. He'd been on relatively good behavior. Feeling pressed to get to Arizona for the birthday party, I left him in charge of the plants. When I returned five days later, I took a taxi home from Stapleton Airport, thinking he'd be at work. But his truck was parked on the street. Midday.

"Hey, anybody home? I called out after I unlocked the door and carried my bags over the threshold.

It was two in the afternoon. When he finally appeared, he was dressed in his favorite attire—green scrubs, his hair sticking out at odd scarecrow angles as it always did when he'd been sleeping. As my eyes scanned the room collecting data, it took a few moments to compute reality. My marble sculpture of a pendulous-breasted woman no longer sat in her place on the marble hearth next to the fireplace.

"What's going on here?" I asked, awakening slowly, not wanting to assimilate this information.

Spinner held his hands wide open. He started to speak. Then didn't.

As I walked from room to room, I discovered that the VCR and stereo equipment were gone. The wooden chest housing my wedding silver had disappeared.

"Where's my silver?"

"He spotted it. It wasn't my idea."

"You brought someone into my condo?" I said, my eyebrows raised to my hairline, my back straight, fists on my hips.

"I didn't want him to come inside."

"Who's this he?"

"He . . . You met his mother at rehab. The model. He picked out what he wanted," Spinner said—an empty man with no stuffing at all. "It was his idea."

"You let a dealer in this house?"

"He's slick. These young kids are ruthless. No heart."

"You don't have any heart. You don't care about anything."

Spinner sank onto the sofa. White. Strung out. No fight left.

"I don't care so much about the electronic gadgets," I ranted on, "but that silver was David's and my wedding silver. And that sculpture was made by a friend. She spent days and months on that. You better have it back to me by tomorrow. No ifs, ands, or buts. And you're going to pay me back for every missing thing, you better believe that."

"I'll paint. I'll do odd jobs. I'll pay you back."

"And don't even think of staying here tonight."

The next day he returned to my place for a meeting. He'd convinced his contact to convince her son to return the sculpture—for a small fee of five hundred dollars. The son and his friend had already fenced everything else.

When the two young boys dressed in long leather coats strolled through the door, they swaggered as only twenty-year-olds can. They walked a cock-of-the-walk walk. An I'm-the-Man walk.

"Aren't you ashamed of yourself?" one said to Spinner who sat on the sofa looking frail. "How could you do this to this nice woman? You should be ashamed."

As ticked off as I was at Spinner, I was astounded at this comeuppance from the swaggering young hotshot.

Aren't you ashamed of yourself, I wanted to yell at him when he held out his hand for my five one hundred dollar bills. *Who do you think you are, using other people's addictions for your profit, just who in the hell do you think you are?* But because he wore a long coat with pockets that might be hiding a weapon of mass destruction, I kept my tongue. I was a bit player in a bad role in a B-movie. The cowed victim. The gutless wonder.

Then they were gone. And Spinner was gone. The empty condo shouted.

I found a box of Kleenex, sat on my coral overstuffed sofa. I blew my nose. I blew my nose again. And again. Then I touched my cheek. That cheek. My cheek. This stranger's cheek. I could watch this movie again when I felt better. Someone else's movie. This was imagination, illusion, shadow pictures on the wall.

::

On the floor of yet another empty church, this one in eastern Illinois at the side of which our rental car was parked for the night, I dreamed.

I was surrounded by thunder clouds, lightning, incessant rain, plains filled with an ocean, people trapped in sunless water, arms tangling with those of others like seaweed. The scene shifted to a stark flat land made of glass. No corn, no rolling hills. The landscape was severe. A woman stood by herself, holding a bicycle upright, a bicycle shimmering like blown glass in a spotlight. She tried to release the bicycle, but it stuck to her hands. With every attempt to move away, her foot slipped on the glass, so she climbed on the bike, leg over, hands on the glittering grips. She turned the pedals fast, but the tires couldn't connect with the slippery surface. She pedaled and pedaled and went nowhere, except that the bike grew taller and she was a tiny child, all alone on a bicycle much too big for her, her legs too short to turn the pedals.

Awake, I felt perspiration on my forehead and hands. I heard the whistle of a train and could barely breathe as I turned from side to side and stomach to back. My mind clicked to "On," and I saw pictures: Geoffrey lying in a hospital bed, connected to myriads of tubing; Geoffrey, a lifeless form pumped up and down; the machines aping life; Geoffrey, chalkboard gray; a plastic child inflated like a beach toy. David standing over him, a wire-thin expression on his face. David wanting to ask for God's powers to change things, yet knowing our son was waiting at the edge of all things for a last look before he left. David taking my hand. I not wanting to give it to him, the hand that snapped, the bad hand.

"David . . . don't." Pulling it back to hide it.

Maybe, I thought as I turned onto my stomach again, *maybe I've made up this story of the bad hand. It could be that I'm in love with guilt. Geoffrey had a terrible cough that night that could have caused the hemorrhage, but maybe it gives me a thrill to wear a hair shirt. That way I don't have to be fully alive. I don't have to love David through thick and thin because I'm not worthy of having love or being in love. I don't have to love my sons because they deserve a perfect mother, not someone like me.*

But I loved my baby. Geoffrey was an angel to me. He was, he is, David's and my first child. There were times when his purity glowed from the inside as if he were translucent porcelain, the interior light clicked on, though his skin was a lampshade dulling the light, especially when there were bruises. His bones were only wires holding the shape of the shade. My angel baby lived in a body where the blood wouldn't clot and where the systems malfunctioned.

But if I truly knew how to love, I would have been more delicate, more aware of the gift of this child, especially one who bled so easily. *Wouldn't I?* But then, maybe I delivered Geoffrey from his erratic blood and allowed him to melt into the elements and the next phase of existence. He'd been in an alien bed at that hospital, a see-through boy, no longer the gross material of the flesh. The absence of true breath made him transparent. How beautiful, like a waxed lily, lying there. A lily that gradually browned at the edges and crumbled to become another element.

Is guilt the last stronghold of pride, a notion I read somewhere once upon a time? I'm not alive, living with a thumb in the dike, afraid to move for fear of another flood, getting large cramps in my thumbs, carrying on, no matter how high the price, seeking redemption from Geoffrey's death and worrying if I've served my other sons well enough. When can I stop cowering in the dark corner and move into the light that frightens me? When can I stop playing small where I don't have to serve anything except my obsession with guilt? When can I just be Jeremy, Brad, and Chris's mother? Even a good mother to myself?

"Oh, sweet Jesus, help me breathe," I whispered into the eaves of the ceiling above me, up to the walls where pictures of Jesus had been thumbtacked, colored with Crayolas by Sunday school children, Jesus with the children—"Blessed are they," Jesus who said, "Perfect love casteth out fear."

I turned over in my sleeping bag, trying my best to dampen the loud rustle of the slippery fabric. "Help me not be afraid. Help me know what love is. Help me out of myself, please."

Wedges

I found wedges for leveraging my way out of the marriage to David.

The first was Ivan the beautiful, Ivan the handsome, Ivan the tri-colored Australian shepherd. When my friend Susan asked me to dog-sit for the weekend when I still lived at the condo on Dahlia, my first home in Denver after leaving the mountains and my family behind, I fell in love. Susan had one too many dogs. Ivan needed a home. This devoted creature didn't have any theories, and, if I fed him, he wouldn't betray me.

I had to have that dog. A yard. My own front and back door. The upstairs condo where I'd been living had become an empty space marred with memories of my loneliness and Spinner's drug dealings, and if Ivan walked from room to room in the night, every paw scratch could be heard in the unit below. When the ancient radiators cranked up the heat too hot at night, making the building into a sauna with a broken temperature gauge, I knew it was time to start over. David told me he'd heard about a 1927 Victorian in Washington Park. We checked it out. It was perfect. In a show of good faith, he offered to help with the financing and the increased monthly payments.

The second wedge was Spinner's repentance after the marble statue fiasco. "I'll do anything to make amends," he'd told me. "I'll paint your new house inside and out. I'm going to do better, and I won't steal again. I promise." I wanted to believe in this surge of good works—the way he painted high eaves with a rope around his waist, the way he scoured bricks, scraped old paint from the windowsills, painted the detail on the front and back porch. He even attended AA and CA meetings. Gradually, his long days of painting turned into long nights of talking into the wee hours, of rekindling possibility.

But even as I pressed David to finalize the divorce, I ignored something essential happening inside myself, something like a black crow of caution flapping its wings in my head, its raucous voice cutting through the smoke signals. Being a Taurus and too bullheaded to listen to anyone or anything, however, I was sure I was done with David forevermore. I invited Spinner and his basset hound, Lucy, to move into the Clarkson Street house with Ivan and me. These became my wedges between me and my former life.

But on this narrow street, leaves on the tall trees sponged up all the sun in the mornings, and leaves on the backyard trees soaked up what was left in the evenings. It was a house of indistinct light, and there were Spinner's cigarettes, his eternal pot of coffee, at least three joints a day. Smoke filled the bedroom and the house, and I, the woman who had no desire for cigarettes or pot or coffee and never had, not really, didn't protest as smoke curled into the air and obscured the light in the house even more. My old Mormon ways hadn't worked, so why huff and puff over the small things? I needed a change. Something different.

Watching Spinner's favorite soap opera with him in the afternoons, I, the woman who never watched TV, fell under the spell of the twenty-one-inch screen, this salve, this placebo called *Days of Our Lives*. For a while I became a sort of zombie who forgot my belief about Divine hands scooping me up like clay from a table and shaping me into something better if only I asked with sincere heart and mind. I forgot my dignity. I pretended not to notice Spinner's relapses when he pawned my VCR and acoustic guitar, almost as if this routine were a ceremonial dance where we performed our parts—him stealing, me demanding a payback, him complying. Out the door. Back in the door.

His daughter, Maggie, now nine years old, came to live with us again for the last few weeks of her summer vacation. The three of us played house together, enjoying a sense of family, me with a daughter for the first time. We walked the dogs, bought beads for making necklaces and tools for papermaking. We screened moisture out of wet paper, rolled it out as thin as we could, and hung sheets of it on a line strung across two rooms. And, we watched *Days of Our Lives*.

Sometimes when her father disappeared and didn't come home until the next morning, Maggie and I played "Let's Pretend." She listened to my fairy tales: "He's with friends; at his cousin's; car trouble; he'll be back before you know it." I sat at the piano after she went to sleep at night—waiting, playing wistful melodies, composing blues songs while my faithful Ivan curled up next to the piano bench. I wanted to outdistance the blues and yet kept scratching the notes and lyrics on music paper. Waiting. Me finally getting ready for bed, my blurred face in the mirror, streaks, warped silvering, smoke.

::

Some lines from "Wide-eyed Blues," a song I wrote about this time, 1997:

You smell trouble, baby, You know it in your bones. (Repeat)
    You rub your hands and think about the prize / Waitin' for you.
Just around the corner, You know love's waitin' for you. (Repeat)
    Its steel-trap jaws, Will snap you up like bait, It's waitin' for you.
Love is a poacher, It wants you in its trap. (Repeat)
    But you don't care, You don't care at all, because it's love.

::

The autumn after I finished the bike trip, David drove down from the mountains to take care of business in Denver. He called to ask if I was available for the evening. "Sure," I said, no other plans.

"By the way, congratulations on what you did on your bike," he said. "I didn't think you'd actually do it, but you did. That's impressive."

"Thanks, dude," I said, calling him by the boys' nickname for him.

That night his face was lit by a candle in the Chinese-American restaurant. The gentle flame could have hinted at romance until he took my hand.

"I wanted to tell you that I still care about you," he said after we finished the Kung Pao chicken and sesame beef and had been handed an orange-lacquered tray with two fortune cookies. "But I don't want to lie about who and what I am. There will always be other women in my life. I don't have a choice."

"I know," I said, feeling my spine stiffening. I'd heard that before.

"But I still love you. There's no question about that."

The words were echo chambers. Granted, he was trying to make amends in his inimitable way as he sat across the table at the restaurant with red, gold-embossed Chinese lanterns hanging from the ceiling, but I wasn't in the mood to hear anything other than that he'd decided he couldn't live without me and would do whatever he could to win me back. Listening to the plastic wrap around my fortune cookie crackle as I ripped it open, I realized my pride needed a large amount of knee-bending and beautiful words flowing like water from mineral hot springs. That, of course, was not his style. But, the thought crossed my mind, as I opened the fortune cookie I chose from the square plastic plate colored a fiery orange, that I might be hoping for not only an apology, but for groveling. The thin strip of paper with red ink said, "You will go far in life." Hmmm. I'd been hoping for a bigger flash of inspiration.

"Fine," I told him, "but I'm hard-wired for fidelity. Though," I leaned toward him with both hands flat on the table and said very softly, "I can imagine, in a few elevated moments of nonterritorial thinking, that you're living a higher law, right? Trying to allow love to flow freely through the universe? Sometimes I get that, believe it or not. It could make sense in a different world from this one." Then cynicism flooded my best efforts at sincerity. "In a different world," I repeated myself.

He smiled. He wiped his lips with his napkin and leaned forward in his chair. "I'll always love you, no matter what you say or if there are other women in my life."

Maybe it was his English ancestry, that stiff-upper-lip sensibility, or maybe there wasn't hot enough blood revving up his veins, but the words sounded like sawdust. I wasn't in the mood to hear more words that felt like leftovers. If they weren't dead before, my feelings ran out of gas at this Chinese restaurant where Frank Sinatra's "My Way" played over the sound system. His swirling logic didn't equate with my common sense.

Back at the Clarkson Street house, he walked me to my door. I thanked him politely, took out my key, and kissed him chastely on his cheek. I didn't want this kind of romance anymore, being one among many. I'd hardened like plaster of Paris left out to dry. Brittle. Unfeeling.

"We need to file those divorce papers," I said.

"There are some tax issues I need to work out," he answered, retreating down the porch stairs before he paused. "Are you sure you want to do this?"

"I'm sure," I said with finality, closing the door.

And yet I dreamed about my boys that night, dreamed I was at one of their gigs, listening to their band called Sofa and dancing like a Gumby rapper. I missed my three sons. My battle with David had obscured the fact that I didn't seem to have them anymore either. While I brushed my teeth and washed my face and turned back covers on an empty bed, I wondered about the larger purpose of David and me being together. What had we done with the gift our son Geoffrey gave us—the gift of loss that tried to teach us to love better? Geoffrey, the angel with deep-set blue eyes, two legs, two arms, fingers, the curved banana belly of a two-year-old. Geoffrey. An angel with fire on the tips of his wings.

::

Six months later, a month after our divorce was final, an out-of-the-blue phone call came from a woman at NBC-TV. "We'd like to interview you for a possible appearance on the *Today Show* being originated in Las Vegas next month. Our staff has read *How I Got Cultured,* your Nevada memoir, and wants to interview you about growing up Mormon in Las Vegas. After all, there are 80,000 Mormons currently living and working there." She didn't mention the often-overlooked fact that a Mormon fort had been established in Las Vegas (Spanish for "the meadows") in 1855—the Mormons being the first non-native settlers in Las Vegas, rather than Bugsy Siegel as some of the Hollywood movies seemed to imply.

I called my friends and relatives and couldn't resist crowing about the coming engagement. Spinner helped me shop for the right dress. NBC had called, after all. They flew me to southern Nevada. A chauffeur in a black cap and a suit and tie picked me up in a town car. There, with the mayor,

Engelbert Humperdinck, Don Rickles, and other Sin City bigwigs scheduled for the last segment of the morning, I was interviewed by Katie Couric in front of Caesar's Palace and a gawking crowd. Nervous about the questions that might be asked about Mormonism, especially with my mother watching, I didn't want to say anything that might disgrace her on national television. I was still her daughter, whom she expected to be noble.

Katie smiled what looked to be a sweet smile on the monitor, but I saw a tightness in her face. Though I didn't begrudge the fact that she hadn't read the book and relied on notes from her staff, I concluded she must be stressed by these strange people crawling out of the woodwork for their minutes of fame on the tube. Glibly, I told her how I'd wanted to be a showgirl, even though I also wanted, at the same time, to be a good Mormon girl. Both things mattered, I told the world.

The whole thing felt like smoke and mirrors—the room at Caesars Palace, the town car with the chauffeur, the high stool where I sat in front of cameras with crowds of people hanging over the ropes protecting the set. This wasn't my Las Vegas. Even my big moment in the spotlight felt obscured by the smoke pouring from the hot cameras, not unlike the smoke in every room of my home back in Denver. It was no surprise when I returned home the next day to find that Spinner had "loaned" his truck to a drug dealer, who'd kept it and who, in turn, drove it into a wall in an alley and totaled it when Spinner and I chased him on the same afternoon I flew back from Vegas.

After a year of his trying to do better, promising to do better, me believing him and letting him move back in, and after a winter of him driving a sweeping truck in the middle of the night to clean rubbish from the parking lots of Denver and looking for crack cocaine connections at 3:00 a.m., which caused him to be fired from his job, I knew things had to change when I returned from Las Vegas and watched his truck get totaled in that alley.

The next day, I received a box of long-stemmed red roses from my mother with a note of congratulations. I was failing her. I was failing myself. I arranged the roses in a glass vase on top of the piano as a reminder. A few weeks later, after I cosigned on a used Honda Prelude on which his father made the down payment and on which Spinner promised up and down and all around to make payments, he packed his belongings in the car and drove off with Lucy—her long basset hound ears spread like wings across the passenger seat. Off to Minnesota.

::

A week later, the BBC called to ask if they could interview me for a documentary about Mormons in Las Vegas. They'd seen me on the *Today Show*. I was unreceptive. Uncommonly so.

"I don't think I'm interested," I said in a jaded voice, having seen enough of the world and none of it impressing me anymore. "I don't mean to offend you, but it's my feeling that television interviewers have an agenda and they're just looking for sound bites to fit into the script they've already written. I was a journalist for a while. I know what journalists do." The gentleman on the other end of the line assured me the BBC would never do such a thing, though I surprised myself when I said, "No, but thank you." "If you change your mind," he said, "call me back."

After hanging up, I berated myself for speaking my mind in such a point-blank fashion, probably fueled by my recently acquired cynicism and distrust of the world. A few days later, I called him back to say, "I've changed my mind. Yes, I'll come." But when I flew to Las Vegas for the second time in three months, the BBC had their own agenda, as I'd suspected—a story about a Las Vegas Mormon banker who'd loaned money to Jimmy Hoffa when no one else would. What did this say about Mormons and their ethics? Tsk-tsk. They needed filler material to sharpen the details of their flashy investigative reporting. And I was part of that filler.

I didn't cooperate when they took me to the front steps of Las Vegas High School where I'd been a student and a Las Vegas Rhythmette who danced at basketball games during halftimes and Rhythmette Reviews in the gym and during halftimes on the football field—my teenage claim to fame. I didn't say the things they wanted to hear into the sound boom they held on a long pole. My contact told me later they'd had to work hard to find a one-liner from the interview to include in the final version.

Back in Denver, I fully intended to keep true to my promise that the bike trip would have its effect on me no matter how long it took, that I'd remember how I'd stayed on that bicycle and climbed unclimbable hills in drenching rain, even if my knee did give out. I did have strength, more than I acknowledged. And now I needed to be a stronger woman not so affected by the men in my life. I was finished with David; I was finished with Spinner—his inability to rise above the shambles of his life and his ability to make shambles out of mine. We were done. And yet . . .

::

When Jeremy needed to move to Denver from the mountains in Summit County to work on a CD with his new band, Riddle House (the drummer, Kofi, being the son of Ginger Baker of Cream), I invited him to live in the basement. I needed my family. I needed my son.

We sat together for hours on the piano bench and improvised. Jeremy taught me some jazz progressions that my classically trained mind couldn't quite wrap itself around. He helped me arrange the blues songs with much more campy harmonies than those I'd been using. While working on his music degree at Whitman College, he'd become amazingly facile at the keyboard in his beginning piano classes, but then he was a genius with music, his brain able to go places mine couldn't follow. He played his avant-garde compositions for me. His conceptions were brilliant, if obscure. We laughed as if it were old times. We sat shoulder to shoulder at the grand piano that took up the majority of space in the tiny living room in Washington Park. He also played Bartok on his violin while I accompanied him, just like old times.

I consulted a therapist with a specialty: clients with strong religious backgrounds. After our first session, she crossed her legs and rested her chin on one fist. "You are an extraordinarily spiritual person," she said with care. "You're ignoring your spiritual needs. Your own needs. You're dying inside. If you'll read Carl Jung, he said that all problems past the age of forty are spiritual ones. He even suggested that people should reconsider their roots. And, since you've expressed an interest in Buddhism, you might like to know the Dalai Lama agrees with Jung. He said Buddhism could assist people but wasn't suggesting they leave their roots."

After three sessions with her, I dressed for church on Sunday mornings as I'd done for the first forty years of my life. I drove to any church that looked appealing, mostly African-American churches where I watched gospel singers rock down the aisles and reinforce my heartbeat, but also Presbyterian, Episcopal, Unity, Catholic, among others. But it was time to reconsider my own church.

One Sunday I checked the phone book for the Mormon meeting place closest to my neighborhood. My heart had been softening toward my decision never to darken Mormon church doors again. I could do that. Maybe. I'd been away a long time. Was it possible that I'd been blaming the Church rather than myself for my immature perception of the Gospel? Maybe it was time to relinquish the idea that my roots didn't matter. But I was fumbling at this point, no clear direction except a subliminal groping for Spirit.

The meeting was held in a sterile, industrial-smelling room in an old office building in downtown Denver. It was a branch rather than a ward, a branch that appeared to be struggling for its lifeline. The congregation appeared to have emerged from the old part of Denver, the tired part of the city. The people seemed equally tired and worn out. As I looked around, I saw an unusually high number of people with handicaps, people who'd probably been cashing welfare checks, people who'd been struggling to make ends meet. The sacrament meeting turned out to be a rather sad affair with weary souls like me sitting on metal folding chairs on scuffed linoleum. We sang listless hymns to the accompaniment of an out-of-tune upright piano. Admittedly, this may have been a reflection of my state of mind, but I wasn't ready to see these people as my brothers and sisters, let alone as a reflection of myself. They were the Other. Not me. Separate from me. They'd broken down somewhere along the way. I didn't want to look in that mirror.

Seeing a new face in the congregation, the president of the branch, who drove into Denver each week from the suburbs to officiate over the limp congregation, welcomed me profusely.

"We're so happy to have you here," he said. "Welcome to our branch."

Because he seemed so effusive, I sensed he might be desperate to find some help wherever it could be found. I was a new, warm body, after all, who could help bring life to this congregation in need of a major transfusion. Warm, willing-to-serve, put-your-shoulder-to-the-wheel bodies were a staple of LDS church activity. But I was still teetering on the edge of things, trying to figure out whether I belonged there or not. My response to him was uncharacteristically lukewarm. Maybe I still carried some residual anger that my family, especially David, hadn't seemed to fit into the schematics, the conventions and cultural mores that had little to do with Christ's teaching. Maybe that resentment hadn't been burned out of my heart yet. Nevertheless, I returned again for the next few weeks.

On the second Sunday, when I volunteered to play the hymns for the Relief Society meeting because the usual pianist hadn't arrived on time, the branch president's wife discovered I could play the piano.

"I hear you're quite a pianist," the president said on the following Sunday. "We'd love to have you play a solo for us sometime. Soon."

"I'd be happy to," I said. "But, truthfully, the piano's in sad shape. I couldn't make music you'd want to hear on it." I'd played on a thousand and more pianos. No exaggeration. It wasn't easy to coax beautiful music from chipped and browned keys, stuck keys, and the out-of-tune piano strings that reeked with the flavor of a barroom piano. "Maybe it could be tuned?"

He didn't have it tuned, however. Instead he found money in the branch budget to purchase a much better one. "We needed this anyway," he said when, on the very next Sunday, he showed me what he'd accomplished. To return the favor, I prepared the Grieg Nocturne for the following week's sacrament meeting. People had always told me that my piano playing spoke to their hearts as if my fingers had a voice. Appreciative of the president's efforts, I played with as much feeling as I could muster on the stiff new piano purchased with such fine intentions. I wanted to reach into some of the hearts I sensed were wanting. I wanted to give something back rather than be lost in the haze. I was looking for my soul, after all, for that thing called Spirit, even though I wasn't sure this was the right place to find it.

Because I traveled a fair amount, teaching in Vermont and at other writers' conferences, my church attendance was sporadic. I gradually found excuses to spend Sunday mornings at home when I returned to Denver. I began thinking of the branch as a depleted place, devoid of enough Spirit to move me in the way I thought I needed to be moved.

In the fall of 1997, my friend Ariel, who'd recently published her book *The Mayan Oracle*, phoned from Hawaii where she now lived and invited me to join a group of thirteen women taking a literal mythic trip to the Yucatan. "We'll be visiting Mayan temples from Tulum to Chichén Itzá to Palenque," she said, "to connect with the Goddess energy there."

Gathering at the airport in Quintana Roo with women mostly from Utah—some of them old acquaintances—we drove to Playa del Carmen to stay at a motel on an isolated beach rather than deal with the *turista* hype of Cancún—the city built for North American tourists. We sat in morning and afternoon meetings to discuss the mysteries of the Mayans, swam in the robin-egg-blue waters near Tulum, traveled deeper into the interior to Coba, climbed the pyramid temple of Kukulkan at Chichén Itzá where the narrow steps were meant for natives with a size-two foot. We hung onto chains bolted into the stairs to keep from plummeting to our deaths. The weather was hot, humid, stifling, and exotic.

One night after we'd explored Uxmal all day—the House of the Magician, the Ballcourt, the Governor's Palace with its sculptures of Chaac, the rain god, and the House of Turtles because turtles had some connection to rain—Ariel made under-the-table arrangements with a guard sympathetic to Mayan beliefs. She convinced him to allow us to conduct an after-hours ceremony in the Nunnery, a quadrangle ostensibly built for the training of healers, astrologers, shamans, and priests, but which was named so by the Spanish because it reminded them of a European nunnery. She wanted us to connect with the Mayan wisdom that had flowered in this place and, thereby, find a key to our divine nature.

Under the copious stars, each of the thirteen women, dressed in flowing dresses and capes, found separate doorways in which to stand above the vast courtyard. Ancient ceremonies must have been conducted there, even some, we hoped, for the instruction of young maidens in the art of becoming temple priestesses. Eleven of us stood beneath stone archways and watched a drama enacted by Ariel and one other woman—a call-and-response type of performance. The rest of us participated silently while literal stars filled the bowl of the courtyard—shooting stars, heat lightning, fireflies. I'd never seen such masses of starry substance. Everywhere a light show. Everywhere a swirl of illumination.

As the women enacted the process of accepting the Goddess within, the courtyard filled with more and more stars. It seemed the whole night had dropped in to join us. I dropped my cloak, which had been wrapped around my shoulders, descended the stone stairs, stepped into the middle of this living sky, and began dancing to what felt like a cosmic drumbeat, 7/4 time, changing to five, then to three, then back to seven. I stretched my arms overhead and felt the stars shooting through me. I was light and pure energy. Stars. Shooting. Into me. Through me. Transforming me into night sky and the Divine Feminine.

When Orion's belt rose over the House of the Magician, the wattage of those three particular stars amped up before my eyes. In the swirl of my imagination, they became my three sons playing in the madness of stars, their amplifiers the heavens themselves. Lead guitarist Christopher Jon Barber played as if he were Jimi Hendrix with neon wings; violinist Jeremy Scott Barber lit the sky on fire when his bow ignited his strings; Bradley Nelson Barber's drumsticks turned into lighted candlesticks at both ends. And I could hear their father and their brother, Geoffrey, singing in voices not unlike the swishing tail of a comet.

Ariel, who had transcended herself to become the embodiment of the Goddess, walked majestically, her shoulders covered in a cape of night stars, or so it seemed. She wove her way through the other women who'd also descended into the courtyard. Then she wove her way to where I stood.

"In love," she whispered to me in an intense whisper that could have made me tremble if I hadn't been listening to the default commentator in my head who insisted on remaining aloof and taking the part of the observer in all things. "Go in love. I give you the new name of Tall Deer, most graceful Felisa."

More shooting stars swirled into the courtyard as the Goddess moved on to the next woman, leaving me standing alone in the Quadrangle, repeating my new name. The sound of the two words filled me with peace and joy despite my efforts at rationality. I pulled back my shoulders and stood tall and quiet in the swirl of stars, full of a new knowledge that a hunter would be struck numb by a creature who could stand absolutely still and unafraid. "In love," I said, and the sound echoed through the canyons of stars.

When I wrote in my journal the next morning, I recorded the feeling of traveling through space with no wings or propellers, embraced by the night until there was no time, as if I'd been transported inside a huge red heart rising like a balloon. Flames poured out as the heart opened, but they weren't hot flames that burned. I felt myself rising. Rising. Rising. Spinning. Spiraling. Surrounded by flames that bathed and purified. One woman, undivided, piercing the night sky while my boys played "Stairway to Heaven."

And yet . . . I wrote.

As soon as I had written those two words, I laid my pen in the fold in the journal, suddenly aware that there would always be an "and yet" in everything I did, always hesitation—a convenient exit out of the present to consider options. Why couldn't I let the experience be what it was? Why did I have to douse everything with the cold water of "and yet . . ."?

Four days later I flew back to Denver, Washington Park, and Clarkson Street to real life. But even though I'd been truly wowed by the flourishing stars and the power of Goddess energy, truth be told, when I got on my knees to pray, I felt no desire to change allegiance and say "Our Goddess who art in Heaven." Not that anyone had asked me to do that, but I couldn't say her name when offering up a prayer even though I tried once or twice. Carefully taught about a heavenly Father, I felt as if I were playing "Let's Pretend" again when I said anything else at the beginning of my prayers. The habits. The patterns. I couldn't transfer loyalties, and yet, did loyalties need to be transferred?

Even though God had always been "my Father," some mention had been made about a Mother in Heaven in a hymn of the earliest Mormon pioneers, Eliza Snow, titled "O My Father." "In the heavens, are parents single?" she wrote. "No, the thought makes reason stare! Truth is reason, Truth eternal, Tells me I've a mother there."

Where did the male principle end and the female begin, or was it ultimately one continuum with no real separation? Why were there men and women anyway, except I guess they couldn't duplicate themselves without each other, unless they were worms or cells that could divide, and how interesting was that?

::

C. J. accomplished a century ride in Illinois. One hundred miles in one day. It happened when she missed a turnoff and rode thirty miles off course. For the next few days, she pedaled across Indiana, the tip of Ohio, until the night we camped at the Angola State Park on Lake Erie in New York. The rain, dogging us everywhere we went, fell heavily all night—a runaway train of rain, insane with rain, the bane of rain, torrential rain, then light rain, then dripping rain. Troughs of water surrounded the tent in the morning, though the rain fly had kept the tent dry inside. The circles under C. J.'s eyes were darkening. She looked exhausted as we headed east toward the Finger Lakes and the Adirondacks on Alternate Route 20, me driving ahead to see what I could see, then circling back to check on her.

"Are you sure you want to keep riding?" I asked, rolling down the car window. "It's freezing out there."

"I'm okay," she shouted, water spraying from both of her wheels. "Go ahead and do something interesting."

"Like what?"

She wasn't in the mood for banter. I knew she needed to stay on her bike until she'd ridden out of whatever she needed to ride out of.

Because I was driving the car, the camaraderie we shared had shifted. She was on her own adventure, and because I'd abandoned our mutual quest and wasn't battling my physical self anymore, I was now just an ordinary woman crisscrossing the roads in a big American car in upstate New York. My original hope that I'd metamorphose into a shining example of determination and chutzpah all seemed rather preposterous as I drove toward East Aurora. *Why the human urge for heroes and heroines? Was that the only way to matter anyway?*

"Okay. I'll wait for you in East Aurora. Meet you at one o'clock. Look for the car on the main drag."

Somehow the thought of shops and maybe even shopping seemed like such a civilized thing to do after the narrow world of secondary roads and bike wheels turning. As I drove into town, the look of the clothes in one particular store window caught my attention. I had a good eye for shops. This place looked like a winner. The thought of trying on clothes seemed exotic, even erotic, after weeks of bike pants and rain gear. I parked, locked the car, opened the shop door to hear a tiny bell ringing overhead. I told the clerk I had two hours on my hands.

"My kind of customer," she said, leading me toward the back.

"Here are some interesting linens made in Lithuania at an old Russian garment factory." She pulled one of them out of the lineup, then scraped hangers across the metal hanging rod until she found a light green cotton dress with a Chinese motif and a handkerchief hem. "This would look great on you." She added it to the others folded over her arm.

Linen and cotton hanging on a hook in a dressing room. Bicycle clothes in a heap on the floor. The sight in the mirror of a woman in bra and underpants about to slip into a dress. It had been a long time since I'd felt the nub of fabric in my hand. I held the linen one to my face, sniffed it and rubbed it against my cheek. Did this ordinary woman in this dressing room have some life pulsing inside her still, even desire and sensuality?

I slipped the dress over my body. I touched my right breast. How incredibly soft a woman could be. I'd almost forgotten. I loved this softness. This was me, the woman who hadn't cared about anything except getting out of town when she left Fort Collins. Behind the dressing room curtain, I struck a flamenco pose, smiled a mischievous smile, snapped my fingers and stamped rhythms quietly against the floor.

"I'll take both dresses," I said to the clerk, my cheeks flushing, turning red with excitement. "Your shop is wonderful."

"Always glad to hear that," she said as she totaled my bill. "By the way, you said you had time to kill. Why don't you try the Elbert Hubbard Roycroft Museum?"

"Elbert Hubbard?" I was blown away by her words. "He's my distant relative."

"Really?" she said, looking at me with new eyes. "He's a legend around here."

As I followed her directions through East Aurora, I felt dazzled. Electrified by the spectacular display of synchronicity. People and places from the past kept speaking to me, it seemed, telling me I was part of the roll call and that it was good to be alive, visiting their habitations and carrying on.

At the museum, I marveled at the awe-inspiring craftsmanship and woodworking of the Arts and Crafts period. Someone pointed me to the auditorium where Hubbard once gave weekly Sunday night lectures. Sitting in a classroom-style chair, I imagined him introducing William Morris of Morris chair fame and then holding forth in a dapper elocutionary style. The Hubbards were renowned as handsome men, someone once told me. Dashing. Creative. Noble as my mother was noble.

When I bought Roycroft mugs for my two sisters and pamphlets about EH in the gift shop, I wanted to tell someone the news: this man was a relative of mine. A distant one, but I wanted to tell someone about serendipity, that I hadn't known about Hubbard's connection to the Arts and Crafts period. I'd known him only as the author of *Elbert Hubbard's Scrapbook* and "The Message to Garcia." I hadn't heard about East Aurora, New York, or the Roycrofters. Here was a huge, artistic, expansive Elbert Hubbard I'd never known. This knowledge made me feel, for the first time in days, as if there were much more to this world than the cramped interior of my skull. And then I felt it. For the first time in ages, I felt a surge of aliveness, chi, life, bounty, energy inside.

After meeting C. J. for lunch, I bubbled with excitement as I recounted my amazing brush with yet another ancestor. "It's like I'm retracing the route my ancestors took from New England to Ohio, to Illinois, across Iowa . . ."

"You couldn't have planned this route better if you'd tried," she said, somewhat distracted.

"Probably not. It was so amazing to have the shop clerk mention the museum. I never would have known otherwise. "But C. J.," I stopped my monologue as I realized she wasn't listening. "What's the matter?"

"I think I'm ready to stop biking," she said quietly.

"What?" My fork was midway to my mouth and stopped there.

"We're on an adventure," she said. She dabbled with the cottage cheese topping on her baked potato.

"So?"

"So, I'm on an adventure. You're on an adventure. But an adventure means the outcome is part of the adventure, not something decided on beforehand. I don't have to prove anything to myself anymore. I've done what I needed to do for me, and I'm ready to stop biking. End item."

"But you're so close. I mean, what about your goal? Don't you want to go all the way to the finish line?"

"Why?" She took a first bite of potato. "I know I can do distances. I know I can do a century ride. Why do I have to keep doing either one of those?"

"I thought it was important to you."

"I'm not locked into it the way you think I am." She smiled, this stranger sitting across from me, the one I'd perceived almost as a machine who would do anything she had to do to complete her Olympian goal. "I've been working to expel as many demons as you have. Maybe I've learned something out there by myself."

"Like what?"

"Like maybe someone is just as mature and accomplished if she decides when she's had enough. When she knows what it is she wants to do, rather than what someone else decides is best for her. I'll finish out today, then it's you and me, girlfriend. In the car. Bikes in the trunk."

The next day, after a night on the floor of the Fire Department Hall

in Perry, New York, where we folded flyers and moistened stamps to earn a place to camp for the night, we stuffed bike frames in the trunk and front wheels in the backseat. We drove through the Adirondacks and the eastern edge of New York, then crossed over Lake Champlain on a toll ferry to Vermont. We turned on the radio, both of us eager to be off the road and back into the swim of our lives.

As the car hummed north on 89, a big green and white highway sign announced, "Joseph Smith's birthplace." I didn't need any more mileage out of my ancestral rerun, but C. J. surprised me. "You need to turn off here."

"I don't go to church anymore. You know that. Why do I need to see Joseph Smith's birthplace?"

"You gotta do it," she said, jabbing her finger to the right. "This trip's doing you more than you're doing it."

Sharon, Vermont. A place I'd heard about so many times in Sunday school. Green, as Vermont is green. Abundant with trees. Singing birds. A quiet shimmer of summer in the June air. The elderly missionary couple, assigned to host visitors, asked if we wanted to see a film about the beginnings of the Church of Jesus Christ of Latter-day Saints. I smiled enigmatically and wanted to say, "If you only knew." Instead, I said, "No, thank you." I didn't want to be saved by these people or by organized religion or by the shoulds of my past. I wasn't ready. I wanted to smell the trees and contemplate the man who'd been such a large part of my life and beliefs. He'd cried his first cry here. Taken his first step. Created drama in my life because he said God and angels appeared to him and I'd believed the story.

We wandered toward the stone monument commemorating the wild-eyed, mystical, creative genius of Joseph Smith, though the inscription stuck to the more rational facts. But how could a monument capture the essence of the real man who said, "No man knows my history?" How could anyone commemorate the totality of this visionary who considered such things as Egyptian hieroglyphics, golden plates, dowsing, peepstones, polygamy, communal living in a United Order, temple building, freemasonry, the kabbalah, whatever might lead to the truth? So many options; so many possibilities.

I looked up at the granite obelisk and thought of mystics guided by Spirit rather than rules. I wondered if Joseph would be interested in joining the present-day version of the church he'd founded, being that visionaries are disposed to imagining and creating, not following a set of rules. I couldn't imagine him being contained in any kind of box, receptacle, dogma, theology, or monument that comes after the visionary departs. He'd be on an adventure somewhere, searching under every stone for further clues to the Grand Mystery. "Great is the mystery of Godliness."

"Let's go," I said to C. J. "I've seen enough." As we walked toward the car, though, I looked back at the obelisk and wished I could have seen Joseph standing there.

::

The day we drove away from Sharon in the rented car and drove toward the Vermont College campus, I tried to remember the exact words of the Thirteenth Article of Faith. The year was 1842 when Joseph Smith received a letter from John Wentworth, editor of the *Chicago Democrat,* asking him to explain the tenets of Mormonism. His response, a succinct overview of his religious experience, became known as the "Articles of Faith."

I'd always been drawn to the last of these, the Thirteenth, inspired by the writings of Paul in Philippians:

"We believe in being honest, true, chaste, benevolent, virtuous, and in doing good to all men; indeed, we may say that we follow the admonition of Paul—We believe all things, we hope all things, we have endured many things, and hope to be able to endure all things. If there is anything virtuous, lovely, or of good report or praiseworthy, we seek after these things."

The line about believing and hoping all things is the one that had always spoken to me. It seemed most people wanted to find the answers in one place or in one sector in one religion, but I'd always looked for the Source, Higher Power, the Divine Mother and Father, for the Way, for God and Goddess in all things. I believed this divinity to be in all people, in all systems, sects, and styles. In the sacred and the profane. In a canary's song, in the snake's belly, in all of us.

I may not have survived without believing and hoping for the best in all things, so I said thank you to the prophet who gave me this idea in the first place. Faith in life. Faith in the truth being everywhere. Faith in a larger purpose.

As we drove up the hill to the campus, our mutual skin thin, neither of us could wait to close our separate dorm room doors behind us. Luckily, there were empty dorm rooms where we could live in quarantine and where no one else would be on campus for seven more days. Perfect. We both needed unadulterated time and space.

I unpacked the box of clothes I'd sent ahead and borrowed a rug for the sterile beige linoleum floor. Sitting cross-legged on my bed with my back  against the yellow cinder block wall and my journal in my lap, I tried to draw a bead on what this journey had meant to me. I knew I wasn't a bigger or better person, and that, maybe, I was a smaller and pettier one than I had thought. But we'd ridden across eastern Colorado, Nebraska, Iowa, and part of Illinois—a thousand miles in all—something, even in my wildest imagination, I never thought I could do. Maybe something had changed. We had endured, even if the enduring hadn't been all that pretty.

When C. J. and I gave our joint lecture at that summer residency, entitled "On the Road with Two Wild Women for a Change," we stood jauntily at the front of the Noble Lounge with the uninspired portrait of Mr. Noble hanging over a mantel at our backs. To a large crowd of students sitting at attention in plastic molded chairs, we talked about Kerouac, Don Quixote, and Sancho, and ourselves. We explored the idea of a heroic journey and why people embarked on heroic journeys, what that meant, why writers write about it, and why so many people pack their bags and head out of town, in whatever conveyance available, to seek the Great Perhaps.

Dressed in our bike clothes, we opened the lecture with a ditty we'd composed: "Spin sisters, rollin' down the highway, dodgin' all the pebbles and the big trucks, too." After the formal presentation, C. J., wearing a sky blue tank top, bike shorts, and her sunglasses hanging around her neck on a cord, hung a map of the USA and traced our route for all to see. We were cool. We were witty. We were organized. We told stories. We laughed and showed slides. I sang "Gord's Grocery Store Blues," one of the blues songs I'd written in Iowa. I was happy to be in my element. Lecturing. Teaching. Knowing I didn't have to get back on a bicycle anytime soon.

The applause was gratifying when we finished our lecture. This moment was the definitive end of our journey. *Finis. Fait accompli.* When the lecture was over and the students closed their notebooks to go to the next scheduled event, C. J. and I exchanged a few quips, folded and bagged our visual aids, and went our separate ways. We both needed time and perspective.

At the end of the twelve-day residency, as I waited for the predawn bus to the airport, C. J. came running past the line of people waiting by their suitcases. I was standing off by myself, not yet awake, and not especially interested in saying good-bye to anyone else after the hundred other good-byes to students, staff, and faculty.

"What are you doing up so early?" I said, both happy and sad to see someone who'd seen the best and worst in me, who'd shared in such a wild-eyed, half-assed endurance test.

"We did it," C. J. said with genuine enthusiasm.

"It wasn't exactly the triumphant picture we imagined with laurel wreaths, TV cameras, and crowds cheering," I said, "but you're right. We did it, didn't we?"

"We were amazing."

"We survived in spite of ourselves."

"You and your caution." C. J. held her hands out in exasperation. "Why can't you just say that you and I were fantastic? When are you going to give us and yourself some credit? When are you going to stop undercutting everything that happens?"

"When will you stop trying to make me into something other than I am?"

"It took me a while to figure things out, but," she lowered her voice and checked to make sure no one was listening, "I didn't realize how much you needed to be rage. To let things blow. You probably never got to do that in your entire life."

"There's never been much room for it."

"I was only trying to spin back into the joy of being me," she said. "Using the physical to bust the mental. We both had too much to deal with for either of us to be there for each other. And yet we were."

The bus pulled up to the curb, the pneumatic doors wheezed open, the driver descended the stairs, and began loading the suitcases into the side of the bus.

"We were just two broken carts trying to get back in traffic," I said, emotion rising up inside, the first in a long time. I looked into her eyes that couldn't be seen clearly in the dim predawn light, and, for a brief moment, we were one sensibility, a shared body of the same carbon-based material. We knew the road. We knew the rain, the wind, and the sun. For one brief moment I stopped holding her at arms' length and looked behind her mask of competence: the girl I'd seen in my own dreams—the naked one trying to bicycle on ice, the one who lived behind the fortress walls, the one who was me as I was her.

"I love you, C. J., even if I haven't liked you or me or anything much lately."

"Nothing can take this away from us," she said, her face moving away from me in the morning darkness. "The imperfection is perfect."

"It's hard for me to say thank you, being that this trip forced me to work against concrete, but there it is. Thank you."

She turned toward me again and smirked that self-satisfied smirk that made me want to take my words back. Yet I knew who was behind that expression. She put her arms around my shoulders and kissed my cheek. I kissed hers back.

As I sat on the bus in the early morning darkness, the wheels rolling to the airport, I knew the trip was something I probably shouldn't have done to my knee. It was definitely something I didn't believe I could do, something I didn't totally do, yet something I couldn't reduce to nothing. It was a hard, good thing. Slowly, I let the victory of the foolhardy, you-better-believe-we-were-on-a-brave journey together wash through my brain and my body. I allowed a certain joy to swell inside, self-effacing Scandinavian that I was. It was a journey I'd never forget—the most difficult physical challenge of my life. It was unbelievably crazy. Definitely insane. Not unlike C. J. and me.

At the moment, in the midst of a conversation with the woman next to me, I heard myself saying, "You know . . . when I was biking across America . . ."

:: The Nesting Doll ::

Brad gave up drumming for Sofa, the brothers' band, and went off to Arizona to work with premiere golf course designers at the Anthem project north of Phoenix. He'd been offered scholarships at top-notch schools, but decided to make it on his own without college. Jeremy and Chris were both living in my basement, trying to make Denver connections for their band.

I was happy to have family around me again, though I was reminded that maybe I wasn't doing such a great job as a mother if I had two sons living in my house, both in their twenties, who should be striking out on their own by now. My job had been to give them a good start but not to care for them indefinitely. Mother bird/baby bird time/enough of the nest. When the dishes in the sink began piling up again, when the boys started sleeping in and relying on my good will, when I started nagging them to keep some semblance of order in the house, I realized they'd soon have to find their own place. I told them so.

Meanwhile, up in the second-story bedroom with only Ivan at the foot of my bed, I still yearned to have a man by my side. Not just a man, but Spinner. I missed him. Something as tight as the grip of bulldog's teeth resisted my attempts at letting go and moving on. But why could I tell my sons to get on with their lives and not say the same to Spinner?

On Sundays I continued to sit on metal folding chairs at the tiny LDS branch in Denver's lower downtown. So what if they were more marginal

Mormons than the ones I'd known before? They could each be my teacher in some way, that I believed. Slowly, slowly for a few weeks as I opened up the hymnbook filled with songs I'd sung during my childhood, songs like "I Need Thee Every Hour" and "Dear to the Heart of the Shepherd," I felt my connective tissue reconnecting to something that had nurtured me as a child. I loved the familiar music and the sense of community, though I still wasn't ready to attend church more than occasionally. On Thursday nights, I attended Al-Anon for families dealing with family members' addiction. I was becoming wiser. Stronger. Prepared. Something inside me, against my reason and common sense, was formulating the idea that I was strong enough to deal with Spinner one more time.

Trouble was, even though he'd had the audacity to pawn two antique bentwood chairs and a quartersawn oak headboard and bed frame while I was on the bike trip, and even though he'd pawned my acoustic guitar and VCR at least six times since then, Spinner and I were like the insides of a rubber band. Both of us were caught in the stretch and the limp of the elastic and unable to escape the loop. We were caught, encircled, still codependent. And there was a phenomenon called love in the works.

After warming up to each other again on the telephone, little bit by little bit over the summer, he invited me to come to Minnesota to go fishing and exploring back roads in the full splash of autumn. He'd been keeping his word about making car payments. He sounded stronger than before. He sounded good. I'd always wanted to see that part of the country at that time of the year. On impulse, I decided it would be a good idea. I said yes. Where Chippewa and Ojibwa once walked and where oranges, deep oranges, deeper oranges, greens, and scarlets shimmered brilliant in the sunlight, we drove on graded roads between Bemidji and Williams Narrows. We rented a cabin for a week's vacation.

"I'm glad you could come," he said as he drove over unpaved lumber roads.

"You always bragged about Minnesota in the fall, and this is so . . . I can't think of words fine enough for how great this is. Everything seems so right when you're out of doors under the sky."

"I knew you'd like it."

Suddenly, out of the stark, clear blue of the impeccable Indian summer sky, an eagle swooped over the top of the green Ford Explorer I'd driven across eastern Colorado, Nebraska, Iowa, and Minnesota with my dog Ivan. Ivan and Lucy, together again, barked wildly as the eagle flew straight at the windshield, then lifted just in time to skim the top of the car while we watched in amazement. It was almost as if the bird had made an intentional effort to get our attention.

"Wow," I said, my favorite word when other words failed to meet the bar. "I've never been that close to a wild bird, let alone an eagle. His wingspan was wider than our car."

"Can you believe that?" he said again, then smiled his winsome smile and lit a cigarette. He rolled down the window, turned up the music on the tape player, and the smoke escaped into the autumn air. Clear. Sparkling.

Everywhere, exhibitionistic splashes of red-orange foliage danced throughout the woods, as if shouting to ask us to stop and dance with the trees and bushes right then and there. Leaves trembled in the wake of our car. Ecstasy touched their edges and my reason. Love seemed tangible. Doable. Possible on such a day as this when autumn was shouting itself silly at every curve of the road. The fact that this bird with its eight-foot wingspan had broken some kind of barrier between humans and birds filled me with a kind of reverence. Jupiter's eagle had brought Psyche water from the river Styx, after all, and the Book of Revelations had spoken of a woman being given wings of an eagle. Eagles had a big history. I made a careless pact.

If I see three eagles, I hatched the plan secretly, being a believer in God in Nature as well as God in the Mormon context, *that means Spinner and I are supposed to get back together. Seeing one at such close range is a rare gift from Nature, and three are an impossibility. I should be safe.* There was a Las Vegas gambler part of me that hoped I might see three, a gypsy part of me that kept searching the skies, a wild child that wanted to be part of the birds and the skies and the winds. Spinner was part of this wildness.

This light, the rippling shadows on the leaves, the knockout blue sky made me think all things were possible again. *Nepenthe. Oblivion.*

When the eagle flew so close to our car, it seemed that more than an eagle had entered our lives. It seemed as if the bird were a sign from the god of the woods, from an innate animism I must have harbored or from a latent Walt Whitman sensibility. But I paused. I remembered that only the foolish asked for signs. Signs were not the real thing. They only gave directions. When we were less than a mile from our cabin, I gratefully released the idea. I laid my head back on the headrest while Spinner drove and sang along with the tape in the tape deck, Leon Russell, one of Spinner's favorites. Life was beautiful on its own terms. There was no need to ask for anything more. It was best not to tempt fate. But just as I thought that thought, a young eagle flew nonchalantly ten feet above the nose of our car. I sat up. I looked up. One minute later a full-sized, actually enormous, eagle swooped across the top of our car. *Three eagles. In one afternoon? What have I asked for?*

Ten months after our "final" split in Denver on Clarkson Street, I made the move to the Land of Ten Thousand Lakes. In March of 1998, Spinner tore into the old flooring of the house I bought; he tore up the walls of one room to enlarge the space; we repainted and rejuvenated; we were happy. For a while. He paid the utilities, made his car payments, and I set aside money to reimburse him for his work if we ever broke up. He agreed to stay clean and to never pawn anything of mine again. After the remodeling was complete, however, he returned to full-time painting and gradually turned surly. He drank heavily, something I hadn't seen him do before. When the weather turned cold and he couldn't paint anymore, he took a job at a local high school as the night janitor. He hinted that I should be supporting him, that he shouldn't have to do such menial work. After all, I "had more" than he did.

One night when we were lying together in bed, he was antsy, almost jumpy. When I said something I thought was innocent enough, he twisted my words and turned them inside out. "You bitch," he said. He leapt up to stand on the bed, reached for the blades of our overhead ceiling fan, and hung like a raging gorilla, bending the blades unworkable. When I jumped out of bed and yelled at him to stop, he dropped to the floor, jammed both hands around my neck, and screamed, "I'm sick of you."

Standing inside the circumference of his hands, feeling his thumbs on my larynx, I knew with absolute clarity that I didn't give a damn what happened next. I meant it when I said, "Go ahead. Get it over with." He stared at me with glittering eyes, then slowly turned his head. "You're not worth it," he said, looking at his hands as he dropped them. "You're not worth more time in prison."

I didn't know until later that he'd just taken a hit of crystal meth.

The next day, we pretended nothing had happened. Both of us acted cheery, normal, and unusually civil for a few days, until one morning he sat at the Shaker-style dining table drinking coffee. "You don't seem very happy," I said as I pulled out a chair. "Are you happy?"

Somewhat sheepishly he said, "No," then took a drag on his cigarette with the too-long ash. We looked at each other wearily, then the ash dropped onto the table. A small, insignificant ash. The table already bore the scars of other ashes, though I'd tried not to say much about them. *Things versus people.*

"Then why don't you leave?" My eyes focused on the ash burning the finish of the table before I brushed it away angrily with the back of my hand. "In fact, why don't you leave now?"

He shrugged his shoulders. Being asked to leave by me was nothing new.

I drove to the bank to withdraw the money set aside for him. When I returned, he'd packed his car—his dog, his suitcases and boxes, his rose-colored comforter. As he pulled out of the curving driveway, I watched him from the window of this strange house that suddenly seemed frigid. I didn't ever want to see him again. And yet, three days later I suffered my usual pangs of regret. I still loved the man inside the addiction. So what if he was *my* addiction? When he called to ask if we could talk things over, I said, "Okay." But strangely, he said to meet him the next day at a downtown restaurant. *Why the next day? Why downtown at a restaurant instead of the house?*

That night, his friend called to check on me. I said I was wondering about getting back together again with Spinner. "Maybe I've been too hard on him, you know?"

"I know I shouldn't say anything," the friend who'd been drinking and was deep in his cups said, "but Spinner's been having an affair with your next-door neighbor."

I pulled the chair out from the dining table and sat down as if I were a rag doll. "I'm sick of the way he treats you," he continued. "I'm not going to keep quiet. He's with her right now." He told me the exact location.

I blurted out a good-bye and dropped the phone hard into its cradle. I paced the floor. I passed the phone. I passed it again. I stopped in front of it. I dialed information. I asked for the motel in that Mississippi River town. When Spinner answered, I told him it was me and that I knew where he was and who he was with and not to bother to meet with me the next day. Total shock on the other end of the line, then some sputtering. I hung up.

Still in denial, I drove forty miles into the dark night, down to the river, the river always rolling, rolling out to sea, my headlights cutting the night in pieces. I needed to see his car with my own eyes. As I cruised by the motel, full-sleuth, I saw my neighbor opening the passenger door to his car. I saw him at the wheel lighting a cigarette. At home I sat in the tub for hours, time after time running fresh hot water until it steamed my skin an intense red.

A few days later, after I heard via his father that Spinner had left town for Montana, I needed a lifeline, big time. I dialed David's number. He was still my best friend. "I can't pull myself together," I began. "Why have I been grasping at such flimsy straws? Why have I settled for so little?"

"Maybe there's something you need to learn."

"So what's with having to learn so much?"

"Who knows, but I'm here for you if you need me."

"But you're in Denver."

"I'll say it again. I'm here for you and I love you, even if I was unable to give you what you wanted in our marriage. I know I've done irreparable damage and wish I could have responded differently, but I'm not going away."

I didn't know what to say. These were words I'd wanted to hear from the man who had always kept to the left of the center of his emotions. An acknowledgment. No excuses. But somehow, at that moment, they seemed like a Band-Aid on a profusely bleeding elephant.

When I hung up, I was even more agitated: stranded in Minnesota; haunted by that blues refrain, "Nobody loves me, nobody cares," even if someone just said he did; me too down in the mouth to laugh at this melodramatic, bad-habit-of-a-refrain and too full of myself to look up from the grain in the wood floor.

But my legs took me to the bedroom and the drawer with my biking clothes. Some lizard-brain response said, "Water. The Mississippi." I found the car keys and opened the garage door.

::

I looked at my black cherry Cannondale, my Pegasus, that was dusty from winter disuse. It was the bike that carried me a thousand miles across the United States. It was my horse with wings that could take me out of myself, toward the source of power and imagination, toward the light. I loaded my bike into my forest-green Ford Explorer, went back in the house to rinse the old water out of the water bottles, then navigated the curving driveway and headed to Goodhue. I'd bike to the Mississippi from Goodhue.

The day was brisk, cloudy, and threatening, too reminiscent of the days on the bike trip with C. J., and too, I was out of shape. But something pulled the two wheels of my bicycle toward the water—the soft flowing, steady water. If the water could keep flowing, so could I. As I pedaled along Highway 58, each turn of the pedals seemed an effort to lift the despair that had been taking up all the room in my heart. But at the same time, I kept thinking about a Leonard Cohen song where he talked about losing your grip and slipping into the masterpiece.

After two hours of rolling through wide pastures of lush meadow grass, past fledgling cornfields and beneath hardwood trees with umbrella tops, I finally reached the river. The big, wide, beautiful Mississippi. Again. A long barge pushed cargo. A houseboat sat heavy in the water. As I watched the river, I felt a kinship, as though we were both looking for the sea, looking for open water, the place where there were no banks to contain the flow, no diversions, no constrictions of any kind.

In the company of a continuous line of passing cars, I crossed a bridge between Minnesota and Wisconsin. I found a solitary place off the highway to lean my bicycle against a tree, a grass-bent path to follow, and a railroad track to walk along. It paralleled the river. The water, except for occasional sections of marsh, last year's split cattails, and bare-branched trees where eagles had already nested for the season, was most always in sight. When I couldn't see it, I could feel it. The river. The water.

I listened for trains. They came so quickly in this part of the world. I stepped on the railroad ties, one by one, sometimes feeling the brush of tall grasses against my calves. Sometimes, I tripped on the uneven ties and wished they were spaced differently to accommodate my long legs. Yet I kept walking because the continuity of the tracks soothed me. And the way they shone soothed me. It was as if the essence of steel in this light were satin.

So absorbed was I in the rails and the ties, I didn't notice the change in the light. I'd walked into the late afternoon daydreaming that the tracks or the water might carry me to a better place. I hadn't paid attention to anything but the ties, the river, and the eddies of my mind. Not to the rest of my body. Not to the passing of the day.

When I became aware of my body, I realized I was bone-tired. I still had twenty miles of biking back to Goodhue on a country road with two lanes and blind curves. Animals. Deer, sometimes. Coyote and fox, even big cats. Cars traveled too fast to see a single bicycle, even with a blinking red taillight. But maybe I could make the most of the miles before total darkness.

If the dark overtook me, I'd be a sleuth. I'd ride in the damp grass beyond the shoulder and watch for cars. The moon would be one night short of full. I could see in the dark.

After I crossed the bridge and remembered I couldn't go faster than my two legs allowed, the heaviness in my heart returned. An ingot. Why couldn't I figure a way out of this quagmire of spirit? I was a big girl. A woman. A mature woman. But I felt locked somewhere in the faraway past. Like a young child frozen in a river that wouldn't flow, like a young child calling for someone to save her but her mouth was frozen with the request. My eyes seemed frozen inward.

The miles passed slowly, and soon the corn and bean fields took on a ghostly appearance in the approaching twilight. This was the time when people yawned and stretched and washed dishes and thought about what needed to be done before they slept. This was the time people turned for home. I was turning for home, too, but no one waited there.

A car gained on me, covering fast ground in the half dark. This was my chance: to be knocked off the road, lost in a ditch where no one would find me until my bones were bleached and animals carried those bones away. All I had to do was venture out into the lane meant for cars and stay the course. But something kept me closer to the shoulder than I wanted to be, and the oncoming driver remembered the equation: cars and dusk = headlights. The car slowed as the bulk of me and my bike pierced the sweep of its lights. It veered to the left, swinging wide over the middle line. I was safe and, unexpectedly, relieved that my plan of being tossed into a better life had been rejected.

As the car accelerated, I watched its lights highlighting slivers of cornfield and clumps of farm buildings. Pockets of ground fog swirled as I climbed out of the river valley. I tried to find clarity in this blurred night swirl, some tether to pull me back to the middle of things. Finally, I reached my car, loaded the bike, and headed for home, but a heaviness still sat square on my chest.

When I entered the town of Zumbrota, I hardly knew it was a town. No glow of bright lights, big city, only a small town, a bump in the road. But I felt excitement at the possibility of people, of a coffee shop or a gas station with cokes, ice cream, and root beer. Something besides my wheels answering to the surface of the road.

As I cruised through the heart of town, I saw a row of businesses closed for the night, parking meters standing alone on the curbside, almost everyone home except for two cars and a muddy Ford F150 in front of the bar. A pink neon light advertising "Hamm's Beer" shone in the thin rectangular window. It was backlit by a waterfall of blue neon. Most of this community had tucked themselves away—children in bed, books being read in easy chairs, the flicker of television sets, maybe the sound of the piano or guitar being practiced, or the sight of someone addressing a greeting card to someone who lived elsewhere.

I wished I could have been in an envelope, sealed safely shut. I wished I was inside that world of porch lights and houses rather than a traveler in the night, rolling along the highways, thinking she should arrive somewhere welcoming.

Then, I saw the store. The lights were on. All the lights. A man leaned into the lighted display window that overflowed with straw. POST'S, the lettering on the window glass read. Post, like mail? Like placing public notice? Post, like a station or a position? Or an outpost, a frontier settlement? I passed by, then impulsively made a U-turn, knowing full well this store had to be closed because everything else in town was locked and battened down except the bar. I parked the Explorer and walked to the door of the lighted store anyway. The man looked up, a yellow-orange fuzz-ball chick in his hands. He motioned with a jerk of his head for me to come in. "These babies are growing too fast," he said as I pushed the door half open and put my head inside the store. A dozen or more chicks scurried from edge to edge of a cardboard packing box lid sitting on the display shelf.

"We always have this window decorated for Easter, but these chicks'll be hopping all over the store before the weekend."

Coming upon light in a store in the middle of a small town late in the evening was beyond the expected, like a quiet kind of magic. "Do you mind if I look around?" I heard myself saying, surprising myself with the words that came out even though I didn't feel like words or sociability. "Why not?" the man said, setting the last chick in the cardboard lid. Then he shook his head and put two fists on his hips. "See how they've already messed this cardboard lid? They're growing between the first word and the period of your and my sentences. I wanted to keep this display for the kids until the weekend's out, but these chicks might take over the store in the meantime. I wish they weren't a tradition around here. Feel free to look around. Make yourself comfortable. My wife's in back unpacking a shipment. She has Pepsi and Sprite in the break room if you want anything to drink."

The store: a potpourri of ceramic flowers, cups and beehives, candles, teapots, cards, things I'd seen before in small gift shops. But as I approached the first of three rooms at the back of the store where the man's wife worked at a counter, I could feel something different about this place called Post's. Something deep and old. Something contrary to the usual knickknackery. The box the woman was unwrapping had the aura and smell of a faraway place. The cover paper was thick. Made of something dusky. It had postal markings from another world. Bolder inks. More intricate engraving on the stamps. I felt as though I'd walked into a wardrobe whose back wall was a door to another world.

"Your husband said it was all right if I looked around. I hope I'm not disturbing you."

"Oh no," she said. "The store's closed, but my husband had to take care of the baby chicks. I needed to unpack this shipment anyway." The woman spoke with a Russian accent.

Christmas

Master of St. Lucy Legend
National Gallery of Art

On the table next to the cash register, metallic covers for small matchboxes were spread in disarray, not priced as yet—Art Nouveau and Celtic designs. Next to them, a pile of oblong figures were wrapped in blank newsprint, a few of them open. Two Father Christmases stood in front of the pile, carved in a style I'd never seen before. And on the floor, three open but unpacked cardboard boxes crowded the aisle. Mysterious objects were wrapped in a dappled paper with cloudy blotches of color. The contents exuded a curious scent.

As I eyed the boxes on the floor, the woman bent to retrieve one of the bundles. She laid it carefully on the counter, which was already full of carved figurines. She unrolled it, cradled the contents in her hands, then next to her heart. *"Matryoshka,"* she said as if cooing over a small child. She bent again, set two more bundles on the counter, then unwrapped each one.

After clearing the top of the counter with the backs of her hands, push-ing everything else to the sides, she set three most beautifully painted *matryoshkas* in front of the cash register. The first was decorated with a winter scene, the second with a Russian fairy tale, the third with an account of the Annunciation.

"Let's see how many are inside," she said. "There will be seven or nine or eleven. If there are eleven, the smallest one will be like a comma. How anyone could ever paint it is my question. So hard not to lose. Which do you want to see first?"

"The winter one," I answered, drawn to the doll with a winter scene painted from her neck to her base: a stream tumbling between snow-covered banks. The scene was framed by a gold chain of infinity symbols. A stylized babushka, accented with gold swirls and flourishes, seemed as if it were a crown for this doll. The way s/he'd painted the green eyes, auburn hair, and a curl in the middle of her forehead, the artist surely understood the desires of this everywoman.

The woman took the first doll apart. She unscrewed the wooden pieces to split it in two. I watched the next, the next, and the next doll appear, all painted with winter scenes: a road to a house overshadowed by woods; a snow-topped barn with a picket fence; a Russian Orthodox cathedral with onion-bulb domes. The smallest of the seven dolls finally appeared. She was painted with a picture of the deep dark woods, that forbidden place where wild wolves and fanged bears lived.

Seven dolls were now lined up on the counter, each one having issued from the inside of another, except, of course, the first one—the mother who presented the prime *matryoshka* self to the world. Each birthing, each splitting, had produced another doll wearing the green-painted scarf and the gold-leaf babushka crown, yet each was a slightly different self than the one before, maybe a drooping eye or a slightly worried look. The small-est doll seemed the most mysterious, the most inscrutable of all. I won-dered if I was actually getting a glimpse of the core of something, except this doll didn't look like the be-all, end-all essence of anything or anyone. She looked more like a hard, darkened, shriveled peanut. A painted chip of wood. Something unbreakable yet not all that different from the other dolls made to break apart. Was there something profound about this last doll? The splitting of the dolls was done, but so what? What now?

Should I have made a metaphor with this smallest doll? Was it possible for humans to disassemble themselves and eventually find a pure self? What was the truth of these nesting realities? Was there a seventh, ninth, or eleventh self in each of us that was the real thing? Or were all the selves the real thing? Maybe there was only a mysterious river of divine liquid flowing through the terrain of everything. The core may not be solid after all. It may melt into the river of everywhere, everything, and everyone.

Tears started out of my eyes. I squeezed them back, though not too successfully. "These are beautiful," I told the woman still unwrapping *matryoshkas,* still unscrewing doll after doll to see how many figurines were contained in each set.

The next set of dolls had eleven. The tiniest doll resembled a comma, just as the woman had told me it would. She held it in her hand, a tiny mark in her palm. A squiggle. She watched it intently for a minute, as if it might spring to life, then closed her fingers around the minuscule doll. She looked up at me as if asking whether I thought it could be something more than a piece of wood. Then she smiled knowingly over the tops of her thick eyeglasses. A slightly curling, mischievous smile. And I felt in the middle of a fairy tale. A powerful, musky tale. The archetypal wise woman was smiling at me, having passed me something from the ancients, having handed me some kind of invisible key. In the middle of a remarkable mystery, words weren't appropriate. "Thanks for letting me look around," I finally managed to say. I realized I couldn't contain my emotions if I didn't hurry out of the store. I needed to go home. I did have a home. A warm home. A place that sheltered me, even if it wasn't full of children or a husband or a lover or anyone else. It was time to stop being sad and get on with the business of being alive. Time to forgive. Time to forget. Time to know that one can never know the whys of anything, that one has to put one foot in front of the other, and be grateful for the gift of *matryoshka,* the gift of someone changing straw for baby chicks, the gift of light in a store long past its closing hours.

:: Parting the Waters ::

My attic, my room at the top, my writer's garret—I sat at my desk on another sweltering morning in the month of August 2002. The heat was already a blanket smothering anything I might want to put on paper as well as my desire to write it.

It's hogwash to scratch ink or type words on paper and think it matters. I slammed my journal shut and ignored Mr. Peeps, my new canary, who was blissfully singing at the top of his range. *I hate writing. It's only second-hand living. Leftovers. Observation. I'm a scribe, an amanuensis to be exact. Nothing more. Even Joseph Smith said, "O Lord, deliver us in due time from the little, narrow prison, almost as it were, total darkness of paper, pen, and ink—and a crooked, broken, scattered, and imperfect language." And everyone thinks a writer's life is so exotic . . .*

And yet, last night I was reading someone else's words: *Meetings with Remarkable Men* by G. I. Gurdjieff. While wandering through primitive villages in Armenia, he came across a boy trapped inside a circle drawn in the dust. The boy gyrated as if possessed and jumped frantically up and down, but wouldn't leave the confines of the circle. He wouldn't consider crossing the line. He fell to his knees and sobbed while other children watched from a distance and laughed. Finally, Gurdjieff, observing this odd situation, approached the boy. Using his shoe, he rubbed a portion of the line from the dust. When the circle was broken, the boy ran away, ecstatic.

When I closed the book and turned out the lamp, my last thought was that maybe I, too, was the boy in the circle, crying because I couldn't get out when I could be smudging out the lines drawn around me with my own foot. It should be easy to extend one foot and erase part of the circle, erase the perimeters of my personal story. Didn't God give me two feet, not just one?

But the thought got lost during the tossing and turning and the mummification of myself in the sheets during the overheated night. Now it was the overheated tent-top of a house that morning that felt so claustrophobic. The dormer window needed washing. The venetian blinds had dust thick on the slats. When I walked to the refrigerator to find two eggs for scrambling, no oatmeal today—too hot to think of boiling water—I bumped my head on the ceiling. I slammed the door hard in response, forgetting about eggs.

It's time to end it, Phyllis. This is ridiculous. Just face it. Nobody needs you anymore. Maybe they never did. And who in the hell wants to read your writing anyway? It's too depressing and self-absorbed. People want to laugh, have a good time. Stop kidding yourself that you're writing a book anyone will want to read.

I heard footsteps. I waited to see who was here so early in the morning. It was my son, Chris, barely winded after climbing three flights of steep stairs to the attic.

"Chris," I said, tying the belt tighter on my bathrobe, trying to lighten the thickness in my voice. "Fancy seeing you."

"Hi, Mom," he said in a chipper voice. "I thought I'd drop by to see if you want to go for a bike ride." Then he stopped, as though he could feel the sensations riding the air of this room—my anger at my lot in life turning inward and raging at me in the form of despair, the presence of a roundhouse demon sitting on top of me and squashing me flat.

"Hey, Mom. What's wrong?"

I can't pretend. I don't have it in me today. I pulled open the refrigerator door, bent to stare at the carton of eggs, and wondered why I hadn't taken any out for scrambling when I was in there the first time. When I stood up, I bumped my head on the sloping ceiling. Again.

"This slanted roof is driving me nuts. I can only stand up straight in the center of the room and have to bend over everywhere else I walk. I can't take this narrow room anymore. I'm too tall. And furthermore," I said, looking at his bottom eyelashes but not his eyes, "there's no reason for me to keep on living."

"What? My gorgeous mama?"

"I know. I sound pathetic, but . . ." I started crying. "You, Jer, and Brad don't really need a mother anymore. Your dad's involved with someone else, and another marriage just blew up. What's the use of sticking around?"

"Mom," he said in his love-me-tender way, Elvis impersonator that he sometimes was, his eyebrows tenting upward the way mine sometimes did, Magic Mirror Chris. He put his hands on my shoulders and looked me dead-on in the eye. "You're having a tough time, aren't you?"

"It's like I can't get back." I sobbed at the touch of his hands, surprised at how badly I needed to be touched. "I don't even know how to talk about it anymore, but it's like I got dumped in the middle of some ocean, no terra firma in sight. I'm exhausted. I don't care about staying on top of the water. I just want to lie back and say, 'Okay, swamp me, take me, deep water.'"

As some of this perpetual ocean surged out of my eyes, he put his arms around me and gave me a most tender hug. "Oh Mama," he said, patting the back of my head as if I were his child. "I hate to see you so sad. You're my mama."

"Chris . . ." I could barely speak as the ocean filled my cavities. I rested my head against his narrow chest. "This is killing me."

"But Mom, you've always done things with style and pizzazz. If you decide to end things, you can't do it with a whimper."

"Everything feels useless. I'm dissolving."

"Jump out of an airplane if you have to. Ramp across a canyon with your car, Evel Knievel-style. But don't whimper out, Mom. That's not you."

If I could have wailed as professional wailers do at Middle Eastern funerals, I would have. Wailing. Howling. Gnashing of teeth. Raging. Trying to shout out the hurt once and for all, trying to cleanse myself of pain and its power over me. But for some reason, some totally mysterious reason, I started to laugh.

At first I didn't want to laugh. The beginning laughter came out so-so because drama queens were supposed to hang in there until the last drop of emotion squeezed out. They were supposed to swoon or faint or pound on the hero's chest with the agony they'd suffered. They were supposed to be carried off the stage in strong arms, carried to safety, but for the first time in a very long time, I laughed. And I kept laughing, as if the hand of Moses had pointed me in a new direction and I could see the parting of waters in the Sea of Funk, the Promised Land on the other side. Those lean years, those stops and starts and dead ends, felt like scattered bones on desert sand. I couldn't stop laughing, and then Chris was laughing, surprised and elated by the effect of whatever button he'd pushed.

Light flooded into the skylights of my attic room. It illuminated my too-long-somber face; it liberated my self-pity. I saw pieces of sky through the skylight—a dome, a canopy, an endless universe. How beautiful the paleness of the hot morning sky.

We both had to sit down we were laughing so hard. And crying at the same time. We slapped our knees, looked at each other, then laughed again.

There was something about beauty that I understood at that moment. Beauty was incredibly simple: leaves floating on water, the changing colors on trees, fresh snow falling, black swans floating, wildebeests running in Kenya, my only grandchild Sophia with her amazing smile, my son sitting next to me. I looked at his face that could do amazing tricks, great mimic that he was. I looked at his front tooth that had been knocked out in a neighborhood softball game when he was seven years old and an overeager adult male burned an overhand throw to first base and into Chris's mouth. The tooth we'd stuck back in his mouth until the dentist could see him still looked good, as if nothing had ever happened. I looked at his thick dark hair, so like my own not that long ago. He was laughing with joy, even as Moses might have after the last of his people crossed over between the suspended waves.

And then, after Chris hugged me one last time, I said I'd love to go for a bike ride.

"I'll be back in an hour," he said. "I have to run one errand first."

Because I had an extra hour, I finally scrambled the two eggs and mixed in some grated cheese for flavor. I toasted toast. Spread cherry jam. I gave Mr. Peeps some water, found my well-worn bike shoes, took my black cherry Cannondale out of the garage, cleaned mud off the wheels, fastened my helmet, clipped in, and pedaled to City Park to circumnavigate the geese and their droppings on the bike path. I'd warm up. Then I'd meet Chris for a good, long ride.

::

Letters mingle souls
Donne
Gainsborough
1OcUS

If I were to write a letter to David, my husband for so many years and the father of our four sons, what would I say? If I could make everything all right, what words could perform that magic? Maybe I could start with St. Paul's letter to the Philippians in chapter 4:11–12: "for I have learned, in whatsoever state I am, therewith to be content. I know both how to be abased, and I know how to abound: everywhere and in all things I am instructed both to be full and to be hungry, both to abound and to suffer need."

Maybe I'd say that I loved him the best way I could. That I was loyal. That I cared for him and still care for him more than he will ever understand. My marriage to David was and is no small thing. It matters.

I could tell him I haven't forgotten those afternoon delights when I wrapped myself in a sheer blue veil and he unwrapped me. There was the hike in a canyon near Sedona when we tossed our backpacks, T-shirts, and hiking shorts and made love on hot flat rocks and those moments when we both knew we'd conceived a child. And yet, I remember those dispassionate, dissatisfactory, even obligatory times we made love. Those times when I used lovemaking to assert my will, giving myself halfway or barely at all to let him know he couldn't be unfaithful to me. All wasn't fair in love and war.

I'd thank him for his love of Kris Kristofferson songs—"The Preacher" and "Bobbie McGee"—and the way he'd walk around the house in his underwear singing "Freedom's just another word for nothing left to lose;" for the way he played the washboard with such gusto in the family band; for the times we laughed ourselves silly with the bad country music lyrics we made up in bed while everyone else slept. I'd thank him for our sons—those amazing configurations of his nose, my hips, his hair, my ears, as well as the extras from the ancestors. I'd tell him how Brad called me one night to thank me for hanging in there, for keeping the family together until he finished high school, and how it meant everything to him. And I'd thank him for challenging my mind and helping to shape it into a much more interesting entity. I may never have been a writer had I not needed to go to the page to figure out the contradictions.

David, my husband. My lover, except he's not mine.

No one belongs to anyone, do they? But why do I want something that at least feels as though it might be mine?

All I wanted was a kept promise, something to help me feel safe in this crazy world. I tried to understand his need for other women, that indescribable frenzy of testosterone men have and the pressing need to break free from what must seem, at times, like a mountain of repression. I made an effort to understand his intellectual and real fascination with loving more than one woman and being responsible for that love, even considering the possibility that this could be the higher order of things. I tried hard not to dismiss his intricate and powerful mind that hoped against hope it could transcend the ordinary. But I just wanted that one promise kept, the one about being faithful.

I wish I could have been enough for him. I wish. I wish. And yet, maybe he never really felt safe with me. Sometimes I was madly in love with him and thought him the supremo apple of the crop. But, then there were bad-apple days, those rotten-to-the-core days. I had my mood swings: my ups when the world was brighter than the golden haze on the meadow, my downs when I knew I'd never measure up no matter how hard I tried. Sometimes I was a powder keg, so restless, so full of yearning to be someone. He must have felt it impossible to satisfy me. He did tell me he loved me. What else mattered if he loved me? he said. Maybe my disappointment oozed up out of my feeling of never being enough for anyone, even myself. Or from my belief that men would wander to other pursuits if I weren't spectacular in every way. The Scheherazade syndrome.

Wait a minute. I'm getting a flash about those one-frame pictures that finger my mind: a dead son, an emotionally absent father, an unfaithful husband . . . I've cut those wispy pieces of film from the reel, framed them, and hung them on my wall. Even though I've got tons of footage to choose from, I've got this uncanny attraction to the sad shots. I'm a bull-dog editor with an eye for despair. Toss in the guilt, and I've got pictures to prove how short life has fallen—how bad I am, how insufficient David is, how disappointing we all are.

In the end, maybe the stories I've been telling myself are only stories built around these tearful, sad, disappointing freeze-frames. That I've been wishing to tell "the whole truth and nothing but the truth" could be the biggest lie of all. In reality, I've been enamored with my sadness and my grief, with my expulsion from the Garden, and some of my friends have tried to comfort me by saying that David is ultimately selfish. But maybe there's a fact out there, floating around on the universal currents, that some humans are, by nature, polyamorous. Maybe this is the truth of who he is, and he doesn't need to be judged as selfish. The question of how he deals with his nature is the crux of the matter.

Maybe I don't have any idea who David really is, though I do know the stories I tell about him. Maybe we both wrote our stories around our disappointments and losses, which became hard wiring. Maybe we've been fixated with the holes, but we're all full of holes. Why be obsessed with only the holes? The gaps? The insufficiencies? Why not be happy for the cloth that's whole, for the part that keeps things together?

The truth is, there is such a thing as love. None of us may know how to show it well or embrace it completely, but there's enough of it to give shape to our lives and support us. I know that I love, even if I don't love as well as I might if I were grander. Or maybe even simpler. This never changes. It may be a matter of the way I give my heart, the way I open up a space for someone and that space is taken after that. It's like the men I've loved are still inside of me, as if once I've made love, the semen becomes a permanent web stretched from rib to rib. It's like the women who've been close and who've helped me carry my burdens as I've helped them carry theirs are like stones in the river, always there even if the river moves on. This business of love is not really temporary, even if it seems the most temporary and fleeting thing of all. It has always been there. It lives.

One thing I would say to David.

Dear David: You need to be commended for the way you've stepped up to the plate for me and the boys and for the way you've always been there and are still there loving us even if your timing seemed off. You were telling me the truth when you said you'd always love me. You've been amazingly loyal, all said and done. As I look back with more maturity than I once had, I can finally allow myself to feel that yes, you are speaking the truth when you say you love me. And, whatever love is and however imperfectly most of us manifest it, you should know I love you and our sons. That, my dear, is the truth.

::

December of 2002, I moved back to Salt Lake City, bought the perfect cottage near Parleys Way, and the summer in the Denver attic was a thing of the past. Knowing I needed to get back into the swim of life again and knowing I didn't want to wait around for David to have a falling-out with his girlfriend or watch hungrily from the outside, I returned to the place that felt like home. Reluctantly leaving Brad and Jeremy, my two bachelor sons, and Chris and Stacia, who were now parents to Miss Sophia Rose, I turned to a large network of friends eager to welcome me back. I was ready to start over. One week after the moving van drove away, I sent out invitations to a tea party with old friends, complete with a request to wear hats.

But I was still new in town. I'd been gone a long time.

I managed very well until one Sunday morning in October. I had no plans for the day. The hours stretched out in front of me. Books to read. Newspapers. A walk. A few telephone calls to my sons. My little house felt too quiet, however, as I sat in my rocking chair reading headlines, opinions, and feature articles. It was the Sabbath. I felt that old urge to get my Sunday-best clothes out of the back of my closet, put them on, and walk over to the chapel: the ward. Why shouldn't I partake of my Mormon community again even if I wasn't a true believer? I missed those days. I liked the sense of belonging somewhere. Maybe I should go see the bishop and submit to baptismal waters again, a second baptism, a cleansing. Some of the early Mormons were rebaptized when their souls needed a good scrub. I'd made big mistakes, I knew, but maybe I was no more a sinner than anyone else, all said and done. I had a kind heart most of the time. I tried to live the Golden Rule. I told the truth as best I could, so why make such a big deal out of this? "No man is good save God," the Good Book said.

The clock ticked. The turning pages of newspaper seemed ludicrously loud.

There were those other Sunday mornings. Southern Nevada when I was a young girl rushing to iron my dress, curl my hair, polish my shoes, all the while listening to the radio—the Mormon Tabernacle Choir and the Spoken Word from the Crossroads of the West. Mother brushing my shiny black hair she'd curled with rags and checking her three daughters' buttons and her son's necktie. One of us always had a two-and-a-half-minute talk to give, it seemed, which we usually prepared at the last minute and a half. And yes, there was that morning when I barged into the foyer of the church, my exuberance from the sunshine and the out-of-doors dispersing the flock of women talking together before the meeting. Too much me full of wind, sun, and sky. Mother pulling me to her side, squeezing my arm with her strong hand, telling me to settle down, we were in church after all.

And those other Sunday mornings.

In Salt Lake City when I was a mother. Juggling three small boys and their scuffed shoes, their unruly hair, their neckties that David knotted for them. Rushing off in the family car. Unloading. Unpacking. Hauling piano music, visual aids for my Cultural Refinement lessons, and books for David's Marriage Enrichment class. Telling our sons to be gentlemen. To behave.

Maybe what I missed was showtime. I loved a good performance. A great speaker. A great song. An inspired choir. And I loved to give a show— singing, dancing, playing the piano, zipping around like an important bee, buzzing among the saints and sinners, no distinction necessary in my mind. But, truth be known, I was never quite calm and collected enough to fit well. I was too chaotic, at times inappropriate and subtly rebellious— a Janis Joplin kind of desire knocking against the inside of my skin, *Let me out. I can't be quiet, quiet, quiet. I want to sing, sing, sing, and kick my legs high, and roar if I must. I won't be quiet, quiet, quiet. I'm a force with which to be reckoned.* But, truth be told, outside of church, I was also shy, shy, shy. Very. The ward was my refuge, the place to which I returned when I got knocked around by the vagaries of being a teenager. The people in my ward had loved me, taught me, told me I was amazing with no hesitation, and propped me up in all kinds of weather.

The sun was trying to get inside my cottage windows, but the pine tree in front kept the house in its shadow, especially in the mornings. The seasons were changing. It was too cool sitting here in this rocker. I knew I should get a sweater or turn up the thermostat, but not yet.

Sundays. The first Sunday of every month. Testimony meeting. I remembered standing, my emotions intensifying while I waited for the microphone to be passed to me so I could bear witness to the Gospel's truth. Because testimony giving had its unwritten, unacknowledged, standardized form and because I didn't feel safe with my ingenuity that sometimes jumped out and embarrassed me, I borrowed phrases I'd heard from others, things like "My brothers and sisters . . . I stand here before you today to bear witness to the truthfulness of the Gospel. I know this Church is true. I know Joseph Smith is a prophet of God." And the tears always came, even with the stock phrases. I never knew if I used them or they used me, whether or not they underscored my sincerity so everyone would look upon me as a "sweet, tender, beatific sister in the Gospel," or if they were truly a manifestation of Spirit moving in my soul.

Sunday mornings when David registered his protest as we opened the oven and took out the pot roast for Sunday dinner. "There isn't a comfortable place for me in that church." I'd start to rebut, to remind him of the value of the law of obedience, but then, standing there with a two-pronged fork stuck in the chuck roast that had been in the oven for the three hours we'd been in church, I became aware of my often petty desire to conform, to not make waves in order to be loved. I stopped. David was a brilliant man. God gave him his brain.

Sunday mornings when I hauled the children to church by myself, sat on the long bench without a husband, and watched other women and their husbands and their children. Church became a lonely place where I sat and stared at what I thought I didn't have.

Ah, Sunday mornings.

The phone rang. The only time the phone had rung this morning. It was my neighbor, Belle, who happened to be Mormon and who was also divorced. "Why don't you come to choir practice with me?" she said. "I know you don't go to church anymore. Neither do I. But singing will be good for both of us."

I was tempted. I loved to sing. I liked the vibrations in my vocal cords that resonated with the energy of the universe. I liked to shape my mouth into a long "O," find the cavity called the mask that resonates, support the tone with my abdomen. I had taken singing lessons once upon a time, after all. After considering the long day ahead of me and the emotions that could ambush me if I stayed home, I asked her if she wouldn't mind coming by for me.

Trouble was, after we got to practice, we were informed that the choir was supposed to sing for sacrament meeting. I wasn't prepared to go to sacrament meeting as I had no intention of getting involved in any major way. But I decided "what the heck," a Utah way of saying, "Why not? It's only singing. It's not a commitment to anything else."

As the singers gathered to take their seats on the speakers' stand, a man I didn't know approached me. He held out his hand to shake mine. His eyes were kind. "I'm one of your neighbors," he said. I hadn't noticed him until now. "I've heard you playing the piano when your windows are open. My wife and I walk down your street once in a while. Maybe you'll play for a meeting sometime?"

His sweetness disarmed me. His appreciation of my music touched my heart as well as stirred the performer who hadn't had applause for a while. As he made his way back to the row behind me, the emotional rain forecast that morning arrived.

While the organ played the introduction to the opening song, "There is beauty all around, when there's love at home," I did everything I could to slow the tears that had taken me by surprise. I hadn't been crying much anymore, so why then? I couldn't do that in front of everybody. I was sitting on the speakers' stand in front of the congregation. I didn't need an audience. I didn't need the sight of these people to remind me of my losses. Even if a part of me understood that the unblemished lives of these people were figments of my imagination and that they were real people who had hurt and erred the same as I had hurt and erred, I was face to face with the perfect picture I'd carried for years. These people. This picture of family unity. This setting where God was supposed to dwell. This seemed so far beyond my reach now.

But maybe, just maybe, I thought, reminding myself about being caught in one's personal narrative, I was longing for my mother's picture, the golden one she'd longed to fit into herself, the one other people hoped they'd fit as well. I dabbed my eyes with a tissue Belle handed me. She squeezed my shoulder for a brief second. She was a woman who'd known sadness herself.

Could I deal with toe-the-line children? Am I a smooth-cheeked harmonious person myself? There's something buried deep in this chaotic ocean of myself that will always swamp the dry land of me, something ancient that needs life. Big Life surging through my veins. Passion, Bedouins, and sea creatures live in my deepest heart. I love mystery and big swings at life.

Still and at the same time, I didn't want to let go of this safe shore I was experiencing: the friendly faces, the music, the families sitting together in the congregation, and the sacrament of which I would soon partake to renew my commitment to Christ. I may not have been worthy to take that sacrament, but I thought maybe I'd met Jesus again, maybe for the first time. I knew something of his sacrifice because I'd been broken. I knew about a broken heart and a contrite spirit bruised and rubbed raw, the thing Jesus spoke parables about. Because of this brokenness, cracks had appeared in my fortress walls. The Spirit was stepping through these cracks and entering my fortress, going past the iron-willed doors that had kept it at bay.

The tall windows, the two aisles, the bishop shaking hands and sometimes squeezing them before taking his place on the stand, the sconces on the walls, the sound of voices murmuring before the meeting begins, a baby crying, the rows of benches long and short. That meeting and those people worked their way into my solar plexus—that large network of sympathetic nerves and ganglia. It mixed with my regret for what might have been, with my experience of the man's sweetness, and with the knowledge that my soul was made of music and that music was large and vast and that it reflected the infinite and that Christ stood still in the middle of music with outstretched hands.

The man behind me. He'd been so kind.

Kindness was the religion taught by my father, whose tendency to care for odd ducks and displaced persons lost him points in the commercial world. He was a daydreamer, often impractical, and he sometimes bared his teeth in inappropriate anger. A performer. A clown. A mimic and a dancer. He was also a reticent man, reined in by unsurety, shyness, and a distrust of his place in the world. But he was basically a charitable man whose tender loving kindness could be kindled to even greater heights by music.

I was my father's daughter. I was also my mother's daughter. I needed to marry these two people, mother and father, inside myself—the assured, stern, stable giver of life who believed her beliefs were the law, and the generous-minded, impulsive, creative daydreamer who danced at the edge of cliffs and pretended not to. I also needed to marry the person sitting there in that chair in front of that congregation, the one who'd been slogging through the jungles with a machete, the one who'd seen many things and experienced much.

This is me. I need to own all of who and what I've been and not be ashamed anymore. There is a particular beauty in my failure. God has taught me much there and given me much. And yet, maybe nothing needs to be named success or failure. Maybe that's what eternal progression is all about—learning to accept God in the stumbling and getting back up. Maybe that's what it means to be pure in heart.

The Sunday outside the church windows was filled with treetops full of brilliant yellow leaves set against a boundless blue sky. The people in the congregation were passing babies to each other and touching one another's shoulders while they rested their arms on the backs of benches. They were full of hope about love and full of the desire to serve this collective community. They wanted to reach outside of themselves to help others. And the man who sat behind me and who'd offered his hand in simple greeting was opening his hymnbook to sing. The organ played. We all sang together.

Why had I thought I needed more?

:: Afterword ::

In 2005, David Barber read this manuscript in its entirety. I asked him to fix any dialogue or situation that was off the mark, as I wanted him to feel all right about the-book-with-his-name-in-it going out into the world.

His telephone response from his house in Denver to mine in Salt Lake City: "When I started reading this I thought maybe I should write my own book. This is your story, not especially mine. But, no one will ever fully understand my story or the way I see things. That said, you've done a good job. The book's good. In fact, it's an important story. There are people out there who've been through something similar and probably think they're the only ones. Good for you." And then, his voice cracking a little, he said, "There's love after all."

In 2007, after spending several years coming to more empathetic terms with Bill, I moved back to Denver where I could be close again to my three sons, their wives, their four children, and to my good friend, maybe for the first time, David.

:: ACKNOWLEDGMENTS ::

Because I was reticent to delve into this story, this book began as fiction about two women biking across the United States. It has seen many incarnations in the ten years of its making—a novel, a novoir (my concoction), and finally, because that is what it has become, a memoir.

I wish to thank David Barber, who, even though we are divorced, has supported me emotionally and financially as I've tried to understand the difficult terrain of love, marriage, divorce, and reconciliation. I thank him for his notes/corrections so that both he and I would feel he's been fairly represented in this text. Always, I thank the Barber boys—Chris, Jeremy, Brad, Geoffrey—whom I love and who've loved and challenged me to think in new ways. I'd like to thank Tracey Black, who suggested we undertake the cross-country bicycle trip that was the genesis of this book; my sister Kathy Gold, who has hung with me through the thick and thin of this project; "Spinner" for the love he wanted to give and for helping me see things I didn't want to see; Bill Traeger for his love after all is said and done; François Camoin, who urged me to tell the story I didn't want to tell; Carol Houck Smith for reminding me to tell my story the way I tell it; Nancy Stauffer for believing in the book; and a heartfelt thank you to Linda Newell for her uncanny ability to help me reorder things at a crucial juncture. Kudos to Joanne O'Hare, director, and the entire staff of the University of Nevada Press, for their support and assistance in bringing this story to life between covers.

I'd also like to thank Eric Gunnison, Scott Martin, and Jeremy and Chris Barber for their help in recording the blues songs that were also a genesis for this book; Gladys Swan, Douglas Glover, Chris Barber, and Jeremy Barber, early readers of the manuscript who helped steer me in new directions; to Ted Wilson for his enthusiastic appreciation and technical assistance; to Anistacia Barber for her assistance with the postage stamps; to Paul Swenson for continuing to believe in my work; and to Sue Fedenia, Penelope Duffy, K. C. Muscolino, Mary Ruefle, Ricklen Nobis, Toddy Smyth, Tracey Black, Heidi Hart, Bruce Jorgensen, Lys Chard Plotkin, Dawn Marano, Mary Domenico, and Harrison Candeleria Fletcher for assessing portions of the manuscript. Thanks to Ken Beiner of Showcase Stamps, Judith Stone, Leslie Ullman, Sandy Ellsworth, Connie Chard, Laney di Giorgio, Gil Gagnon, Charlie Marie Thompson, Jim and Virginia Pearce, Laurel Olsen, Dennis and Michelle Leonard, Susan Dudley, Shirley Smith, Marian Ingham, Marjorie McClure, Curt Bench, Stuart Hinckley, and unnamed others who helped along the way.

Last, but not least, a thanks to Mr. Peeps, my yellow canary, whose song soared above everything else while I finished this manuscript.